A Various Language

A Various Language

by
Bob Lonsberry

CFI
Springville, Utah

© 2007 Bob Lonsberry

All rights reserved.

No part of this book may be reproduced in any form whatsoever, whether by graphic, visual, electronic, film, microfilm, tape recording, or any other means, without prior written permission of the publisher, except in the case of brief passages embodied in critical reviews and articles.

ISBN 13: 978-1-59955-007-7

Published by CFI, an imprint of Cedar Fort, Inc., 2373 W. 700 S., Springville, UT, 84663
Distributed by Cedar Fort, Inc. www.cedarfort.com

LIBRARY OF CONGRESS CATALOGING-IN-PUBLICATION DATA

Lonsberry, Bob.
  A various language / Bob Lonsberry.
    p. cm.
  Collected columns.
  ISBN 978-1-59955-007-7 (acid-free paper)
  I. Title.

PN4874.L62A25 2007
070.4'42--dc22

                              2006039832

Cover design by Nicole Williams
Edited and typeset by Kimiko M. Hammari
Cover design © 2007 by Lyle Mortimer

Printed in the United States of America

10 9 8 7 6 5 4 3 2 1

Printed on acid-free paper

Dedication

To my family.

Gratitude

To Mike Ramsager, who has expertly and faithfully hosted my website from the first day.

To Tolga Soyata, who handed me a piece of paper with a dream written on it—www.Lonsberry.com.

Table of Contents

Introduction XIII

One

Welfare is a cancer and a sin 1
Is there true poverty in America? 3
Welfare check has made men unnecessary 5
Cut spending—and taxes 8
Self-esteem programs destroy young lives 9
Diversity is an idol they worship 12
Thirty years of lives unlived 14
Six billionth baby is cause for celebration 16
Global warming is a crock 18
What does Columbine say about us? 21
It is possible for civilization to fail 23
There's nothing wrong with a political fight 25
Illegals must acculturate and assimilate 28
Seatbelt laws save lives, kill liberties 31
It's not really about homosexuality 33
We should know our history 35
There is no liberty without morality 38

Two

I hear he was putting his life back together 39
The story of a man who heard God 41
What they found yesterday in the mountains 44
See no evil 46
Something that happened in the country this week 49
About a mother, a father and a daughter 51
Good guys 2, Bad guys 0 53
The story of Trevor Wagner, first-grader 56

What a couple of guys did the other night 58
The saga of Fluffy Pillows 59
It was bright in Batavia yesterday, and warm 62
An idiot, a crook and a saint 64

Three

I pledge allegiance 67
A day that will live in infamy 69
Maybe it's a holy war 71
To our nation's defenders 74
Something that didn't make the news 76
A note to a Coast Guardsman's little boy 78
A story from down by where I grew up 81
One morning at Parma Union Cemetery 83
A note to World War II veterans 85

Four

The only Christmas I remember 89
Out on Willow Bend Road 92
From the house on Third Street 93
I tried to kill myself once 95
What I would give my mother 98
To the guy who stole my wife's car 100
A day in the life of an American family 102
It's a family tradition 105
It's not parenting 107
The decay begins 109
On paths and the straying therefrom 111
On the subject of having a very bad day 113
When your strength is your weakness 116
Good-bye, Ike, I love you 118
Godspeed, David 120
What I did on Christmas 123
What do you do when you crash your plane? 125
To move in, you must first move out 128
It was the prettiest cake you ever saw 129
I walked through a blizzard once 131

Five

At least I have my health	135
Does Triple-A do plumbing?	137
The day I became a man	139
I hear they make good fertilizer	141
Reefer madness	143
Maybe I'll just get a litter box	145
Facts for fogeys	148
Last night in the park with the kids	150
Living in harmony with nature	152
Abandoned husband bemoans woes of single life	155
The saga of Dave and Lamar	157
My son is full of crap	160

Six

"I did my best" is only an excuse	163
A girl on the radio	165
Optimism, gratitude and courage	168
Of deserts and mirages and the world of cyber dreams	170
Why can't we reproduce ourselves?	172
I am my children's friend	174
Delaying family is usually unwise	177
Love and forgive, or lose	179
Come here, it's time we had a talk	181
Guilt destroys happiness	184
A word about adultery	187
Something I learned while running	189
Addictions are not diseases	191
Whose fault is it when children stray?	193
Shoot the close ones first	195

Seven

Good tidings of great joy	199
On the subject of speech	200
Why does God let us suffer?	202
The shortest verse in the Bible	204
Judgmentalism can blind us to God's hand	206
How about tolerance for all?	209

The story of Cain and Abel 211
When it seems the Lord isn't listening 213
Faith is the first principle 216
A letter to a friend 218
As we forgive those who trespass against us 221
Blind obedience isn't so blind after all 223
Whom say ye that I am? 225
It happened while they slept 228
Holy Week with Jesus 230

EIGHT

It's hard when your kid turns 9 237
A father, a son and a dog 239
What my daughter taught me 241
A Thanksgiving weekend at home 244
Christmas in America 247
Happy Birthday, Lee 249
A story about a friend of mine 251
Godspeed, Elder Lonsberry 253
Our trip to Mexico 256

ABOUT THE AUTHOR 259

Introduction

When I was a boy, my hero was the man who wrote the shelf of books in my grandmother's bedroom. He was a newspaperman, a friend of her father's, a columnist named Arch Merrill. I think he was dead by then, but his books were still around, and I read them all. And I was attracted to his ability to put little bits of life down on paper.

Later, I would discover others like him, newspaper writers with a space of their own and a voice of their own that sang the American song. The greatest of them was Ernie Pyle. They did what John Steinbeck said every writer should do—explain people to one another.

I was 30 when I became a columnist in Arch Merrill's town. A couple of years later I had Arch Merrill's job. Except what he did once a week I did five times a week. It was the greatest job on earth. But I came along too late for newspapering. The columnists aren't writers anymore; they are activists, stamped out with a cookie cutter in the politically correct mold. And I don't fit that mold. I'm white, straight, male, conservative and Christian. I believe we have the right to carry guns, keep what we earn, say what we want and love our country. And that doesn't play in American newspapers anymore.

Which is why I'm grateful for the Internet. Freedom of the press presumes that you have a press, that you are a publisher, that you have a way to take what you write and communicate it to people. In the age of the World Wide Web, anyone can be a publisher, anyone can type away and put their work out for all the world to see. It is a wonderful, American and democratic thing.

This book owes its title to William Cullen Bryant.

These columns were first written for the Internet, though many of them have been printed in newspapers and elsewhere. They set out to be what a daily column should be—a little bit of everything. Life is sacred and profane, sweet and sour, light and dark. So is a good column. Today we laugh, tomorrow we cry. These columns hope to do that. Sometimes they try to make a point, other times they just try to make a joke. Hopefully at least some of them will be useful to you.

Hopefully this is a volume that would have been worthy to put next to Arch's stuff on my grandmother's bookshelf.

Bob Lonsberry
Mount Morris, New York
December 27, 2006

ONE

Welfare is a cancer and a sin

Like a fool, I went back and forth for most of three minutes, from the apple bin to the scale and to the apple bin again. I had two dollars and I wanted two apples and two pears, for lunch yesterday, and if I could find an apple small enough I could just afford it.

The right fruit finally found, I went to the registers and took my place in line.

The woman in front of me was in her 20s, healthy and young, with a fancy fruit drink and a gourmet salad. The salad looked pretty good. She had a leather coat and several pieces of garish gold jewelry.

And then I had one of those American moments.

One of those commonalities that bind us together and drive us crazy and are the foundation of folklore.

While I stood there with my miser lunch, the leather-coated, jewelry-wearing, designer-beverage-drinking, foo-foo-salad-eating healthy young woman opened her money-stuffed purse—and paid with food stamps.

Years ago, it would have made me angry. Now I take it in stride, as just another testament of a curse upon our society.

And welfare is exactly that, a curse which steals money from taxpayers and initiative from recipients. A scourge which damages and divides by promoting resentment and debasing responsibility.

Welfare, in its various forms, is a social cancer quickly metastasizing across our land. Its consequences, now spread over a third and fourth generation, include a savaging of the family unit, a dissolution of social connection, permanent poverty and a culture of criminality. And tragically, it is so broadly and automatically accepted as to be above criticism or reproach.

Welfare is seen as a right. Its recipients are seen as fully functional.

And that must end.

For the benefit of society, for the salvation of recipients, for the preservation of the Republic.

The first step is to return to welfare the stigma it once held. The sense of embarrassment and shame. Not for the truly deserving—the handicapped, elderly or infirm—but for all others. For all who have a mind and a body capable of gainful employment.

Being on welfare should be something which tugs at the pride of recipients, which doesn't sit right, which prompts them to do what is necessary to provide for themselves.

That sounds harsh, but it is best. And it is right. Because the fundamental responsibility of life is to provide for yourself and for your family.

When that fact is overlooked—when it is actively attacked by government—the damage is far larger than financial. Granted, tax slaves fret at the burden of entitlements, grand schemes to take money from those who produce and give it to those who do not.

But that effect is temporary.

A wage earner can typically make more money, and even the most heavily taxed worker can usually eke out a pleasant and worthwhile life. The people who pay for welfare are robbed, but they can replace that which was taken from them.

The people who receive welfare, however, cannot. Because taken from them and their children is their initiative, their self-respect, their sense of responsibility and commitment. Their chance for ever earning a life which takes them above the lowest economic rungs of this society.

See, when you give someone a welfare check, you usually guarantee that person will always be poor. You steal from them economic mobility—the American Dream.

Welfare is a sin of government. And its great irony is that it fosters resentment between its two groups of victims. Class division, which is not part of the American character, is enflamed by a government program which cuts the belly out of both sides.

And it most particularly attacks families.

Among those who pay the taxes which support welfare, the burden of taxation requires two incomes to satisfy—pushing mothers wholesale into the workplace since the dawn of the Great Society.

Among those who receive welfare, there is no need for the wage-earning male—radically cutting marriage rates and raising illegitimacy rates during the same period of time.

On one end, families lose mothers. On the other end, they lose fathers. And all together are held down economically. It is a servitude and bondage which affects both groups profoundly.

Welfare reform has begun.

But welfare doesn't need reformation, it needs extermination.

The push to reduce benefits and rolls must continue. Not as an act of selfishness or stinginess, but as a conscious choice of a better way. The truly needy should never be abandoned, but the reality of what constitutes true need should be acknowledged.

The fall of America, like the fall of Rome, will not be driven by attack from without, but by decay from within.

And welfare is the seed of a fair portion of America's moral decay.

Is there true poverty in America?

Poverty rose 4 percent in America last year.

That's what the government says.

Common sense, however, says something different.

Common sense says that, compared to the standard of history and the rest of the world, there is no poverty in America.

Don't shoot me yet.

I'm not saying people don't have it hard. I'm not saying people don't have financial catastrophes. I'm not saying there isn't an economic underclass. I'm not saying people don't go to bed wondering where they're going to find the money they need.

I know about financial hard times.

And I know about doing without.

But I don't think there is poverty in America.

Not true poverty.

Face it, most of our poor people are fat. And have cable TV.

And a cell phone, with customized rings. And a bed and a roof and inside plumbing and a benefits card to keep the refrigerator filled.

Poor people in America can afford cigarettes and beer, or marijuana. Poor people in America get the best health care in the world.

That all may sound like an unfair indictment of the poor, or like some insensitive screed, but the simple fact is that, no matter how hard things get, nobody in America needs to go to bed hungry or go to bed outdoors.

Many do, but mostly it is because of their own choices or incompetence or because of the neglect of their parents. Services and benefits are available to all, from the government and from charities, and those who end up going without are usually those who have squandered their opportunities or allotments.

Compared to what our ancestors knew, or what the rest of the world faces, American poverty is a walk in the park. Poor people in America live better than hundreds of millions of people in nations around the globe. They have not only the necessities, but many of the luxuries of life.

And yet there is great discontent, as entitlement has replaced gratitude and extravagance has become a right. We see suffering where there truly is none and identify poverty where it doesn't truly exist.

The question is: Why?

The answer is that poverty, as we define it, has become a powerful tool for social engineers and politicians. Specifically, it is the lever being used to push our country into socialism.

By broadly and incorrectly declaring poverty, activists attack our economic system from the top and from the bottom. By creating the perception of poverty, they give themselves an argument for more social welfare programs. By pointing at the supposedly impoverished, they make the argument for expanded government compassion.

That increases the load on taxpayers and hastens the transfer of wealth from those who produce to those who don't produce. It creates the social expectation—contrary to our national tradition—that the poor have claim on the resources of the non-poor.

By doing this, the concept of individual property rights is eroded. If money is the means of acquiring property, and increased amounts of money can be taxed to support the poor, then the possession of property is substantially jeopardized. And a fundamental American freedom is endangered.

Broadly defining poverty also creates class envy and division, which is the engine of socialism. Increasing the number of people who see themselves as poor increases the constituency for more entitlement programs or policies. It also fosters anger on the part of the supposedly impoverished, which creates social instability.

As poverty grows, so does the government. As taxation rises, freedom falls.

Both dangerous trends are encouraged by our mistaken concept of poverty. It seems like a minor matter, just one more government statistic, but it is a major thread in the spider's web that entangles our national liberties.

Certainly, times can be hard. Money can be exasperating. Bankruptcy and economic failure are real. Many families struggle throughout their lives with money issues.

But nobody said life would be free of struggle.

And nobody should think that the difficulties faced by the poorest of Americans are anything like the daily reality of millions around the globe.

Millions who would be offended if you told them that they were poor.

Welfare check has made men unnecessary

The premise is simple. Families go better with a man around and married life is better than single life.

And as soon as you say that they wheel out their stories about abusive men and broken homes and this and that and the other thing.

Which mostly misses the point.

Because nobody is saying women and children should be in abusive situations, or that money is sufficient cause to get married, but rather that the welfare check should stop being used as a club against the traditional family and the institution of marriage.

In the welfare family, there is no husband. Not usually. Because there doesn't need to be. The husband has been replaced by the welfare check. He simply isn't needed.

And so, wherever welfare has sunk its roots sociologically—mostly among urban blacks and rural whites—marriage has declined and illegitimacy has soared.

Which, in turn, has been used as an argument to increase welfare spending and availability. And it's been a vicious cycle. Welfare causes what it is supposed to cure.

If you have a husband, you don't get welfare. If you don't have a husband, you do get welfare. If you don't have a husband, and you do have a baby, you get more welfare. If you don't have a husband and you have five babies, you get a lot of welfare.

Tell me, what kind of social incentive is that?

Welfare has single-handedly killed the black family. It has spread black poverty, it has brought out the worst in black men and it has put an incredible number of them in jail.

And the same is true of any community of people caught up in welfare.

Here's why.

A variety of factors bring people together into marriage. Love is one of them, so is the desire to have children, and to establish a household of one's own, and to create your own life.

And to pay the bills.

People associate in families in part because if they don't, they go broke. In a more primitive time, failure to form a marriage-based family would have resulted in death from starvation or marauding.

Does that mean women are property bought with the man's paycheck? Does that mean men are nothing but a source of income? Is it merely an economic relationship and convenience?

No.

But it is still important. Women have an innate need to be provided for, in general, and men have an innate need to provide.

I know. That sounds Neanderthal. But it's true.

And when the natural fact of self-reliance is shorn away from people and couples by the welfare check, that incentive to form couples and marry is gone. And in the mixed motivations of marriage, that increasingly leaves people just short of what it takes to marry.

Add to that the permissiveness that allows sex outside of marriage and it takes a whole lot of romance for people to take upon themselves the vows of matrimony.

Much more, to be honest, than many people have.

So marriage declines. Precipitously.

And that leads to illegitimacy. Which leads to more poverty, less social stability, less educational achievement, more juvenile criminal activity and more reliance on welfare.

And that's just among the women and children.

Among the men its poison is also deadly.

Because when men aren't needed to be men, when they cannot do what nature and God equip them to do—provide for a family—their energies and vitalities are directed elsewhere, in damaging directions. Because a man's got to be a man.

And when he can't be the kind of man he's intended to be—a husband and father, providing for and protecting his family—he often becomes the kind of man society doesn't need. Instead of being a protector, he becomes a predator.

And boys raised without fathers, in a welfare culture where the option and expectation of marriage is marginalized, are boys who disproportionately end up in prison or dead.

That's a fact.

Whether they're black boys in the city or white boys in the country. Men need to be men, and men need to be needed. And with the welfare check, they are not.

For more than a generation, welfare policies have torn apart American families. That destruction has been sped along its way by tax policy.

For more than a generation, the government has—on purpose or accidentally—had policies which have profoundly discouraged marriage. We have reaped the bitter harvest of those policies.

It is time now to change them.

The family—based on the marriage of a man and a woman—is the basic unit of society. Government must stop attacking marriage and family.

Government must stop doing the work of evil.

We tried 40 years of tearing down marriage at taxpayer expense. Now it's time to try building it up.

Cut spending—and taxes

Taxation, essentially, is theft by democracy.

Not in its best form, when government prudently funds its essential functions, but in its corrupted and perverted form, when greedy constituencies clamor for an ever-increasing share of other people's money.

That's where we are today.

People demand services and benefits as rights, angrily protesting and attacking when their gravy train is threatened. Their anger is directed toward one set of politicians and championed by another set of politicians and amidst it all is forgotten the fact that they're talking about money that's currently in someone else's paycheck.

Your paycheck.

Government has become part of the consumer society with all thought going to what people want and not what they can afford. And people are so accustomed to getting a free ride that they can't imagine or care that their lust for money is pushing countless of their fellow citizens into tax slavery.

As layoffs blanket the land and the recession lingers in uncertainty, the only growth industry is government services. And efforts to cut budgets—because of gaping deficits—is met with howling anger and indignation. The various consumers who glut themselves at the public trough are expert at holding press conferences demanding that their particular piece of the pie be spared from economic reality.

Libraries and day cares and schools and senior citizens' shuttles, environmental funds and food pantries and museums and symphonies and humane societies each shout that their mission is essential. That they can't take a cut. That somehow society will be irreparably damaged—that its "essential character will be lost"—if they don't get their entire allotment of taxpayer money.

People who get the goods or services, or the people who get paid to administer them, are certain that their interests are absolutely paramount.

When, in fact, they are not.

When, in fact, they are most typically not even a legitimate function of government.

The government in America was once primarily a defender of liberty. Now it is primarily an enforcer of socialism. Those who produce are ever more burdened with tax in order to support those who do not. Even those who believe they "earn" their money in taxpayer-supported agencies or programs are really dead weight on the backs of people whose employment funds the entire scheme.

We are a society whose greed has combined with its spinelessness to run roughshod over the quaint notion of private property. We used to believe that what you earned was yours, that you had a right to it. That it belonged to you. But that is not true anymore. The real taxation rate for those in the middle and upper classes is above 50 percent. Those people are not the prime beneficiaries of their labors. The government is.

They are sharecroppers, serfs and slaves.

They are you.

And those who howl for funding for their programs are your enemies.

Because the money they want is yours. Earned by you, potentially to benefit you. But instead it will be collected in ever-increasing tax to meet their selfish interests.

It is theft by democracy.

And you are the victim.

And you will remain the victim until the greed of the dependent and the spinelessness of the government are overcome by the angry will of the people.

It's time to throw the tea in the harbor.

It's time to take the hand of government out of your pocket.

Self-esteem programs destroy young lives

I was talking to a woman the other day and she told me that the most important thing parents could give their children was self-esteem.

I didn't say anything.

I didn't want to be impolite.

But she was, of course, wrong.

Dangerously, completely, horribly wrong.

The most important thing parents can give their children is religious faith, the ability and desire to live a life in harmony with the divine. A life that will carry them into the eternities. A life with God at its center.

That's the most important thing parents can give their children.

But I don't want to talk about that. I want to talk about self-esteem. The poison of self-esteem. This crazy fixation that occupies American educators and child psychologists, the psychobabble that has become unquestioned policy.

A policy that has crippled untold young people's lives, and which will continue to do so, just as long as we foolishly focus on self-esteem building.

First off, self-esteem is a consequence, not an objective. Self-esteem is not something you should pursue. Rather, you should pursue the traits and habits that produce self-esteem. Self-esteem is an innate self-regulatory mechanism. We have it when we are useful and good; we don't when we aren't.

Self-esteem is first cousin to our conscience, and we cannot have self-esteem if we do not have the approval of our conscience.

But we'll come back to that.

Let's first look at the current ruinous policy of "self-esteem building." In schools across the country self-esteem agendas, particularly among minority and disadvantaged students, are creating nothing but a generation of arrogant, self-absorbed narcissists. We are raising a generation of young people with wildly inflated views of themselves and absolutely nothing to back it up.

We teach them to talk the talk, but not walk the walk. Self-esteem building is teaching them how to do a dance in the end zone, but not how to score a touchdown. Ironically, self-esteem building—which the theorists say is so "empowering"—is making incredible numbers of young people useless to themselves and society.

In the name of self-esteem we inflate grades, we give smiley faces and gold stars and certificates when they have not truly been earned. And by so doing we cheapen achievement, and we deny young people the opportunity to learn from their failures. And by doing that we make it impossible for them to succeed. For, without the possibility of failure, there is no possibility of success.

If praise comes automatically, regardless of our effort, then we will demand it as an entitlement. And we will be taught that effort and outcome are meaningless.

Which is tragic.

Because the only true self-esteem comes from achievement. And achievement comes from work, from what you produce and earn. You feel good about a test not because of the dishonestly high grade, but because you know you worked, studied and learned.

Praise too freely given weakens. It produces spoiled brats. People who are permanently handicapped in life by virtue of their distorted sense of self-importance and worth. A child told over and over that it is beautiful—or smart or strong—will come to believe it. Those words will become fact in that person's mind. And how unfortunate that it is if those words are not true, or if those words weaken the impulse to strive and improve.

In life, it doesn't matter what you think, it matters what is. And it is far better to teach a child to work and strive, to give it expectations and standards, than to smother it in ridiculous self-esteem schemes.

The person who does what he knows is right will feel good about himself. The person who does his best will feel good about himself. The person who knows how to work and take a task to completion will feel good about himself.

Guilt and disappointment—the opposites of self-esteem—are the consequence of bad choices and personal failures. They can't be chased away with pep talks and meaningless honors; they can only be replaced by making better choices and by replacing failure with success. The key to self-esteem, therefore, is making right choices and achieving.

So the key to helping young people have happy, balanced lives is teaching them to make right choices and to achieve.

That is the road to true self-esteem.

Tell your children that you love them. When they have done something which shows true effort, integrity and persistence, tell them that you are proud of them. Teach them that they are children of God. Help them learn that when they do what's right and when they do their best they will feel good and be happy, but when they don't, they won't. Let them know that they have the power to decide whether they will have happy or unhappy lives.

And forget this self-esteem nonsense.

It is a misguided philosophy with catastrophic consequences.

Diversity is an idol they worship

Few words have been more popular in recent years than "diversity."

And few concepts have been more destructive.

Destructive of our social fabric, destructive of our moral well-being, destructive of our ability to make judgments.

In schools, non-profits and government programs across the nation, diversity has been held up as a great and noble prize. Some objective to be fought for and given prominence. It has become the top priority in institutions from colleges to corporations.

And it has become a philosophy handed down like the word of God from the pulpits of education, business and government.

And yet it is a bunch of crap.

It is not a panacea, it is a poison.

It is the latest ax wielded to bring down American heritage and values. In the name of brotherhood, justice and tolerance, it fosters enmity, inequity and chauvinism.

And that's not the worst part.

The worst part is the moral relativism which is inherent in it. A moral relativism that poses a great danger to our individual and social health and stability.

The foundation of the diversity movement is an almost shamanistic belief that it is good in and of itself. That diversity must be sought and advanced and that's that. It's like a magical thing. College presidents in their exit interviews with reporters boast of increased diversity while ignoring educational outcome. Businesses brag about having a diverse workforce at the same time they lose money.

Diversity has become an end in itself, instead of a means to another end.

And that's no good.

Because diversity for diversity's sake is a recipe for disaster.

The goal is not to be diverse; the goal is to be one. The goal is not to be rewarded for differences, but to be enabled by commonalities. At church, in school, on the job, people become better and more successful when they identify as a team instead of as individuals.

Particularly individuals who are highlighted by their contrasts.

Our society is drawn together when we see ourselves as Americans, not as various splintered racial, linguistic, religious and lifestyle groups.

People work best together—as employees or neighbors—when they work toward a common interest, not from a disparate background.

People with a chip on their shoulder cannot shoulder the burden of citizenship.

The diversity movement actively sows the seeds of division and conflict. It will result not in a tolerant society, but in a civil war. People do not grow closer under its tutelage; they grow further apart. People don't become sensitive to one another's interests; they become hypersensitive to one another's offenses, typically seeing them where they do not in fact exist.

Whereas Martin Luther King Jr. hoped his children would be judged by the content of their character, the diversity movement identifies and values them by the color of their skin.

Which is racist and wrong.

The harshest blow dealt by the diversity movement, however, is not to social relations, but to moral fiber. It fosters a life view which tears down values and morality. It attacks the notion of absolute truth and leads to a moral anarchy or chaos, a state where all rules are thrown out.

Diversity teaches that the mores of the majority must not be given ascendancy. That the views of one group must not be given any more respect than the views of any other group.

In fact, diversity actively promotes minority and divergent views and values. It ignores the normal to exalt the aberrant. It purposely avoids the mainstream.

It insists on a parity that does not in fact exist. And it often achieves that parity by debasing all value systems. In making sure that no morals are treated any better than any other morals, the practical impact of diversity is to abandon morals altogether.

Instead of it being a disagreement about what truth is, it leaves its followers believing that there is no truth. That there isn't right and wrong, just difference. And difference is good.

And there are no answers.

Which is false.

There are answers. There is right and wrong. Truth is absolute.

And absolute truth should be sought. Sadly, the society raised to worship diversity will never know to search for it.

Thirty years of lives unlived

I don't talk about abortion.

On the radio show, in the column. In life.

I just ignore it.

Because there is no talk. There is merely shouting. Catch phrases spit out over and over. Two groups of fools ranting at one another, each disgracing the decent people who might otherwise agree with them.

So this isn't about abortion.

It's about a sadness.

A strange sadness I thought of yesterday in the quiet of the predawn.

Yesterday was 30 years.

Thirty years since the Republican-controlled New York State Assembly passed, by one vote, what would become the nation's first law permitting abortion.

Until then, it was illegal across the country.

For two years the Republican governor, Nelson Rockefeller, had pushed the legislation. For two years Catholic Democrats in the Assembly stopped him.

Then a Jewish guy from upstate got a pang of remorse. If you can use that word. He rose emotionally before the Assembly, after having voted against the bill, and reversed himself.

And his was the winning vote.

He stood there, almost in tears, talking about his faith and his family and how he promised his son he wouldn't defeat this bill. Then he said that his vote would probably end his political career, but that it was more important for him to sit with his family at Passover and have a clear conscience.

So legalized abortion came to America.

And for two years, until *Roe v. Wade*, New York was an abortion magnet. Women came from all over to get abortions in New York.

For 30 years in America unwanted pregnancy has ended in abortion.

But I'm not talking about that.

I'm talking about them.

The tens of millions who today are not.

The oldest of them would be young adults now. Not quite 30, making a way in life, in the flower of youth and health.

They would have college out of the way and have started careers and maybe families or put on the uniform of their country.

They would be our co-workers and our friends, our neighbors and our spouses. The couple two pews over in church, your child's second-grade teacher. The cop who patrols your street at night.

Olympic athletes and valedictorians and Eagle Scouts. Volunteers in hospitals and medical students and the crew chief on your neighborhood ambulance.

The flower of youth and health.

But they are not.

They never were.

Not the way they were supposed to be.

Because life is not only what is, but what might have been. And we'll never know what might have been, because we'll never know who might have been.

People are the defining characteristic of this planet, the great and magical variable, the reason and the fruit, the conduit through which God acts and blesses us all.

And tens of millions of tasks were never taken up. And tens of millions of futures were never begun.

I hold both sides in contempt. The obnoxious shemales boasting of a womb they never use. The freakish lifers with disgusting placards, chaining themselves to clinics.

They are both wrong.

They are both arrogant and hateful. And the truth of either side is lost in the self-absorption of the fight.

All I know is what is lost.

The people I suspect we would have loved.

People are odd, and unique, and given to quirks. Each trods a path unlike any other. Yet in the peculiarity often lies the value and worth. The broad and variegated range of humankind is the spice that makes life rich.

That little touch of genius that graces us all, that sets us apart from the anonymous masses which surround us.

That is lost.

Disrupted in a place and time of vulnerability. Sucked and flushed and forgotten.

While marchers march and screamers scream, and the status quo grinds inexorably forward.

Thirty years. By legislation and by litigation but never by consensus. America never agreed to this. We went along, we kept our mouths shut, but we never agreed.

It was one guy in Albany and five guys in Washington and after that it was tens of millions, here and there and everywhere. And nowhere.

At least not here.

And that's what I thought about when I heard.

Thirty years ago in New York the flood gate opened. Thirty years ago in New York the flood gate closed. More abortions, fewer people.

And that makes me sad.

Because I never loved an abortion.

And I never called one friend.

This isn't about abortion.

It's about people.

The oldest of whom would be young adults by now.

In the flower of youth and health.

Six billionth baby is cause for celebration

Yesterday, just as scripted, a refugee baby was born and the world's population rose to six billion.

But don't send a cigar.

This is bad news.

It has to be. Kofi Anan said it was.

In fact, a massive United Nations PR campaign blanketed the country with slick press kits decrying the number of humans crowding the Earth.

We're supposed to think deeply on this subject, reflecting on the world's resources and our stewardship of them. We're supposed to look at a graph climbing sharply and see human beings as bad.

Which is odd.

Because they are not.

In fact, people are good. And the birth of a baby is not a bad thing. It is a miracle. Something to celebrate and rejoice over. The great glory of our world, a new soul, plopped down from heaven to delight us and inspire us and replace us.

That's what a new life means.

But instead, the smart people see vermin.

Rats on two legs, subhmans who need to be managed and pared back and prevented from breeding.

If there were just fewer of you, the smart people are actually saying, the world would be better off. And they are eagerly out and about making sure that fewer and fewer people reproduce.

Often funded with United Nations money or Western foreign aid, various agencies and non-governmental organizations crisscross the world, preaching condoms and Norplants and IUDs and abortions. Anything to stop up the fruit of the womb.

Which is how liberals practice racism.

They go to parts of the world that don't meet their arrogant do-gooder standards and keep brown people from being born. Apparently one-world liberals don't think average folks around the globe are capable of deciding for themselves how many children they'll have.

They need a Friend of Bill around to tell them.

And they saw yesterday as proof.

These damn fools have made six billion of themselves—we better "educate" them about the dangers of over-population. But elitist propaganda by any other name still smells like horse crap.

And their position is flawed in one fundamental way: It sees people as a problem for the planet, instead of as the purpose of the planet.

They see people as the problem, instead of as the solution.

And the loudest crowing yesterday came from Communist China, which said it was responsible in large part for delaying the arrival of the six billionth living human.

China said that its 20-year policy of forbidding couples to have more than one child had suppressed the population by some 300 million people.

Quick math: Isn't that something like 50 times bigger than the Holocaust?

And isn't denying existence to 300 million people a crime against humanity? Isn't there something deeply chilling about a government dictate which has denied life to more people than currently live in the United States?

Isn't there something vastly immoral about a government policy that strips people of the right to reproduce?

And yet isn't that exactly what the population control people are advocating—depriving life to those who otherwise would receive it?

And family relations.

What kind of society must China now be, a nation without brothers and sisters, uncles and aunts and cousins, the binding ties of extended family.

And what kind of world will it become when a bunch of elitists in a skyscraper in New York City determines "reproductive policy" for the world?

Yesterday was a day to celebrate, not to mourn. A day to congratulate, not chastise.

Our family is larger, and we are all better for it—simply because we are all better for the advancement of our kind.

Schools, musicians and politicians all conspire to advance the cause of "zero population growth." And all err in so doing.

Because just as your birth was a glorious and useful thing—as were the births of your children—so, too, is the birth of the little Third World child, no matter what his economic straits.

God or nature has always worked through humans, little babies which grow with talents and abilities that advance the rest of us. They improve our technology and invent our medicines and solve our problems, the great renewable resource of humanity.

And it is a bitter wrong-headedness that tells you that their birth is a bad thing.

Global warming is a crock

I don't believe it.

I'm not sure why. But it just doesn't ring true.

This whole global warming thing.

I don't believe it is real, I don't believe it is a threat, I don't believe it is manmade.

I believe we live in a large world where man is the creature, not the creator. I think this world was shaped for us, not by us, and that we are no more capable of destroying it than we were of making it.

I bring this up because of a big United Nations report that is coming out. A bunch of U.N. scientists has put together a study that claims the world's temperatures will be 10 degrees warmer at the end of this century than they are at the beginning.

That's 40 percent warmer than their projections from just five years ago.

So they think we're going to heck in a handbag.

And I think they're wrong.

I think their report is much more about politics than it is science. I think it's about the economy, not the environment. I think they're more interested in dollars than they are in climate change.

Actually, I think the entire global warming thing is a con intended to tear down the technological and economic advantage of the United States. It is a weapon being used against us, to get us to handicap our industry, prosperity and lifestyle.

And I'm not buying it.

Because the climate is not static. It is constantly in a state of change. I thought we learned that in ninth-grade Earth Science class. That's why we have glacier striations in New York and seashells in the Rockies. What's up was once down and what's down was once up. The dry places were wet and the wet places were dry and where it snows now there used to be jungles.

And back and forth for thousands of years the ice sheets have expanded and contracted as the environment warmed and cooled, driven by forces we cannot begin to understand. Driven by forces we cannot begin to influence.

Here's an example.

Last week in one of the big city newspapers there was an interesting story about this glacier in Scandanavia somewhere. A massive glacier. And it's breaking apart. It's retreated three miles in the last several decades and this scientist guy says that sometime in the future it will just go away. It will disintegrate.

Which gets your attention. When the glaciers start melting you figure things are in bad shape.

But there's more to this story. The glacier in question is only 300 years old. Which is pretty old for a human or guinea pig or a ham sandwich, but in the terms of earth things, it's pretty young.

In fact, in a valley through which the glacier passes, humans used to carry on advanced agriculture. It was a farm region. There were villages and barns and homes.

Within historic time it was habitable and temperate. But the climate changed. And the glacier came, clearly as a result of natural processes and weather fluctuations.

So why should its disappearance be any different? Why should a return to the historically normal condition for the valley—no glacier—be cause for alarm?

And why should temperature variations—up or down, if they in fact exist—should be considered proof of human harm? Why would these not simply be meteorological phenomenon we are observing? What evidence points to human fault for something which may be nothing more than the natural decline of a minor ice age?

The oceans have risen and fallen more times than we have the ability to detect. Why is it that this prediction of ocean rise—which has not yet even begun to occur—be cause for either alarm or the restructuring of the economic order?

Well, there is no logical reason.

And I reject the premise. I don't believe there is man-made global warming.

In part because of the clear political agenda of its proponents.

It is clear that global warming—and its reputed remedies—are in the bailiwick of the socialist left, promoted with the same vigor and by the same people as women's rights and gay rights and trade unionism and animal rights.

And, coincidentally, the solutions they offer—fewer personal automobiles, higher energy taxes, a debasement of industry, restrictions on electricity generation, centralized government planning, collective farming, mandatory mass transit, and restrictions on land usage, development and sprawl—are exactly the things the people of the left have advocated for years.

I think it's a con.

I think nature or nature's God controls the weather. Daily and climatically.

I think we are little ants on a big blue marble. I think the global warming people are trying to slick us.

I think we ought to tell them to drop dead.

What does Columbine say about us?

The president said that the tragedy at Columbine should make us look critically at ourselves as a society and as a nation.

That we should search out our obvious weaknesses and failings as a people and as a culture.

The president saw Columbine as a day of national shame.

I don't see it that way at all.

I look at Columbine and I am proud to be an American. I am touched and inspired by the goodness and courage of average people, and the extent to which decency and faith spring from the American breast.

I mean no disrespect, and I am not overlooking the great pain that carnage wrought on so many lives and families, but as I look at what happened in Littleton, I see proof not that things are going wrong in America, but that things are going right.

Countless people, from Joe and Betty America to their politicians and commentators, have waxed gravely about what the Columbine murders "say about us." A Utah state legislator said it all started when "they took prayer out of schools." Rosie O'Donnell ranted angrily that we must "stand up to the NRA." A minister at a Denver memorial service said "gun manufacturers must be held accountable for this tragedy."

For two days on my radio show I have heard from people who blame abortion, poor parenting, a lack of personal responsibility, Bill Clinton, liberals in general and a growing lack of spirituality in our society. Each of them has seen some great flaw in the American heart that gave rise to the butchers of Columbine.

And each of them has been wrong.

Because to see the two murderers and the evil they did as a product of our national soul, and then to simultaneously ignore the hundreds of heroes and the goodness they did is to misrepresent the truth. If the tiny evil minority is a product of this society, so too is the overwhelming good majority.

If you look at our failures, you must also look at our successes.

I'm humbled to belong to a society which produced a hero teacher who, shot through the chest, his lifeblood glugging away, led a group of students to the barricaded safety of a classroom. For three and a half hours, as he knew he was dying, he calmed the students, and gave them direction.

I am proud to know that my country raised the youngsters who clustered around that teacher, tending his wounds as best they could, keeping him conscious, using a cellular phone to call paramedics for advice. I am honored to share citizenship with the boy who thought to pull out the teacher's wallet so that he might look upon pictures of his family as he fought to stay alive.

It was this culture which produced another teacher, his charges hiding in a room, brave enough to stand with nothing more than a fire extinguisher to drive away a threat to his students' safety.

The teenagers who knelt to shield and comfort their wounded classmates grew up in this society. As they carried the injured to safety and stopped to pray with the frightened, they were acting out of a set of values they learned as Americans.

One boy in the library threw himself on top of a fellow student, whispering to her to be calm, saying he would protect her body with his own. That boy, that hero, grew up in a world with legal guns, violent video games, hateful rock'n'roll, no prayer in schools, countless abortions, grizzly movies, Bill Clinton in the White House and record divorce rates.

Yet he, and hundreds of others, acted with the purest of human virtues and in a noble and selfless fashion.

What does that "say about us"?

It says we are a good people. And while we have weaknesses and challenges, we are fundamentally strong. Our heart is essentially good; our children are raised with natural decency.

Lunch ladies shouted directions for students to flee, ninth-graders organized into groups for protection, children's cell phones told cops where the shooting was and when it had died down.

And in the wake of it all, children with shattered lives stood before cameras and politely and clearly told a nation what they had seen.

Strong enough to care, strong enough to endure, strong enough to witness.

As the tears are wiped away and the shock and grief begin to fade, Columbine will leave me with pride. Pride in the students and teachers of that suburban school, one little community that represents us all.

With dignity, compassion and courage.

The America those kids grew up in helped them to be some of the best and strongest people in the world. They are not the product of a failed society, they are the offspring of the greatest culture and nation on earth.

The president who saw no flaw in himself is too quick to see a flaw in us. Those who hate our way of life, or who seek to use tragedy to advance their political causes, will see deep trouble in the American soul. But their perception is not true. It doesn't reflect us, it reflects them.

This is a good land. We are a good people.

The children we raise are overwhelmingly decent and pure.

For us to mistakenly assert otherwise is to deny them and their virtue. It is to deny the testament of the heroes of Columbine.

It is possible for civilization to fail

Civilization is not automatic.

In fact, it is fragile, and can wither easily, and even die.

As our times show.

There is a decay among us, a failure of civilization, a breakdown of the social structure essential to what we most consider our humanity.

It is not widespread, but neither is it rare. And like a disease it spreads through the social body, infecting and sickening and moving on to taint the healthy.

Civilization can be different things, depending on time and place and people. Some eras and some cultures have manifest it one way, some another and others yet a third.

But any civilization must include certain traits to propagate and protect itself. If it lacks them, it fails.

These traits are easily identifiable.

They are:

- The ability to bear and rear children in a stable family environment.
- The ability of individuals to support themselves.
- The social ability to establish and sustain order.
- The recognition of personal property.
- The tendency to promote the general good.

Those things define civilization and are its essential components. And for a growing number of Americans, in pockets of micro-culture, they do not exist.

For a growing number of Americans, in pockets of micro-culture, civilization does not exist.

And if we don't stop the spread of the social pathogen they represent, we will collapse as other great societies have collapsed. Rome stopped being Rome primarily because its civilization frayed and tore, giving way to an anti-civilization, a backward savagery that brought it to its knees.

American anti-civilization is most common in our inner-cities and in our rural communities. From both places it is spreading into the vast American middle-class, happily snoozing in suburbia.

What are the symptoms?

The failure of marriage. Not in individual divorce, but as a social institution of choice. Forty percent of children born in the United States today are born outside of marriage. They never have the opportunity to truly belong to a family.

And that wildly handicaps them. Most of their situations are flawed and even failed. They are not reared successfully, giving rise to further social pathology and destruction.

Increasingly, a class of people is flourishing which, under other circumstances, would starve to death. The dependant class, unable or unwilling to support itself materially, would naturally be self-limiting. But empowered by responsibility-deadening welfare checks, it is exploding.

The danger of that to civilization cannot be overstated. People disconnected from their own sustenance are people whose lives are built upon a fundamentally false premise. They are, in effect, raiders—a cultural lifestyle which has always tended toward tribalism, not civilization.

Civilization is the subjugation of the individual or group to the interest of the civil entity or imperative. Not as slavery, but as an elemental compact of society. Civilized people belong to a whole, the interests of which they see as somehow both essential to themselves and yet greater than themselves.

We are breeding people in America who see the civil as their enemy, and whose lifestyles are predicated upon putting something over on the larger society and its structures.

Many of those same people have an infantile view of the possession of property. Whatever they can put their hands on becomes theirs. Thievery is one manifestation, so too is callous disregard for the property of others. Rented apartments are trashed ruthlessly and unthinkingly, public places and structures are vandalized and defaced, things are broken just for the thrill of breaking them.

And finally, the general good—the thing which will benefit the most—is not considered. The personal good or desire is paramount in all circumstances.

These conditions exist in America.

Civilization, in those regards, truly is decaying. And we are reaping the whirlwind.

And like all diseases, the infection in our civilization will grow geometrically. It must be fought and stopped now, while it can be, instead of later when it probably cannot be.

How?

Through the children and through an almost missionary like preaching of a better way.

The specific weaknesses of the growing discivilization must be listed and explained. People must be graciously and respectfully shown the weakness of their lifestyles. Those weaknesses must not be accepted in the mistaken cause of tolerance.

Additionally, society must move quicker to take children out of situations which will ruin them. The first months and years of life often determine the totality of life, and children reared in chaos will face near insurmountable obstacles to escape it.

Our civilization is weakening primarily because families are dissolving or never truly forming.

Children must be spared that.

There. That was easy to say and easy to understand. But will we as a society do anything about the decay beginning to engulf us?

Probably not.

And our very civilization is in great jeopardy as a result.

There's nothing wrong with a political fight

I believe the Constitution is inspired.

Literally.

I believe that God whispered to the Founding Fathers during the constitutional convention, and after, and that the Constitution and the

Bill of Rights contain his will and wisdom. I believe they were divinely calculated to give form and foundation to our great Republic.

I don't question that.

I believe it is literally true.

And when you apply that belief to the history of the matter, certain lessons appear. Lessons about how God and greatness work among a group of people to achieve a worthy end.

I think those lessons are useful and comforting today because of the light they can shed on modern politics.

First, it is essential to know how the Constitution did not come about. It did not issue forth in some great revelation chiseled in stone and brought down from Sinai by a prophet. It did not appear as a whole wrapped up in a bow.

It was fought over and compromised about and its various tenets were plucked from several plans and personalities. One person would have brilliant ideas that are preserved in the Constitution and also have horrendous ideas that would have doomed the Constitution. What one person thought was essential another thought was pointless.

It was in the dogfight and conciliation of competing interests and philosophies that this document was forged. It was not really a meet-in-the-middle affair, but rather a case of hardball politics blending with persistence and a commitment to getting something done.

It wasn't a bunch of guys holding hands and singing campfire songs. There was precious little consensus. It was a bare-knuckle parliamentary brawl in which some participants were openly hostile and contemptuous of others.

And yet it worked.

Those pieces of brilliance were collected together, the dross was washed away, and the greatest political document of all time remained. God worked through those men, and through their disagreements. And though few of them probably realized the totality and magnitude of what they were creating, they were all part of the miracle.

Even those who disagreed with the document, and opposed its ratification, were essential to making it better. The federalists tried to build public opinion in support of ratifying the Constitution, and the anti-federalists argued for its rejection. But in so doing, they demanded and listed a Bill of Rights which was shortly added to the Constitution, completing and perfecting it.

It all seemed like a barroom brawl, but look at what came of it.

I think there is comfort in that as, in our day, we look at politicians and the struggles between them. Sometimes they seem to do nothing but fight, and seem to be driven exclusively by a desire for partisan advantage.

The experience of the writing of our Constitution shows that even from such political chaos great things can emerge.

And the same thing applies to the sharp differences between our two political parties.

Some of the disagreements of the Constitution grew, over a few years' time, into two competing political parties. These parties were at one another's throats. They could not stand one another and fought vigorously.

Just like they do today.

And yet, even that is a gift and an inspiration.

In the arguments of our two parties there is another check and balance on power. Though not listed in the Constitution, our party system grew out of the Constitution and is a firm defender of the Constitution. Government officially has a series of mechanisms to limit power. The two-party system is another unofficial way.

When one party gets too big for its britches, the other party cuts it down to size. There is a back and forth of both philosophy and power which, our history shows, seems to serve the Republic quite well.

In fact, the greatest service seems to be during the times of greatest contention. At least that's the lesson of history. People of very strong conviction, on both sides of the issues, battle it out in the public marketplace, hoping to advance their view and bring public support to their side.

It can be a bloody mess.

But it also seems to be the cauldron of freedom.

And I point it out because often we are told that the disagreements of our parties today are somehow damaging to the country, or a fruitless course to follow. But our history doesn't teach us that. Our history teaches us just the opposite. We seem to do our best as a nation when true believers on both sides fight vigorously for their principles.

Somehow, the cream does tend to rise to the top, and the best ideas of both sides most typically advance.

So I'm not bothered by disagreements and contests—within a party or between the parties. I have strong ideas and I am passionate about them, and I want to see them implemented. But I understand that my opponent is also my partner, and that from the ashes of our struggle something great can arise. My ideas need his opposition and his ideas need mine, and we each should have faith that ultimately the right will prevail—often in bits and pieces from each of us.

So I don't mind fighting for principle.

I don't think it hurts anything.

Rather, I think it is essential. It is the way things have always been in our country. It has, time after time, been the means of great and momentous progress.

And there's no reason that can't be true today.

Illegals must acculturate and assimilate

If they're going to migrate, they have to assimilate.

The marching illegals.

If they want to be Americans, then they have to be Americans. Speak the language, learn the culture, live the life. Get the chip off their shoulder, forget this "la raza" crap and do what generations of immigrants before them have done.

Become Americans.

That's the challenge, the requirement and the objective. And the future of the country might depend on it.

Illegal immigrants and their liberal friends have shown an unmatched ability to put people in the streets. They have turned out more marchers in a month than the civil rights movement and Vietnam-war protesters did in years. It has been an impressive and sobering display.

It has shown that 15 years of neglect by the president and Congress have allowed a literal invasion of many American cities. The number of illegals in the United States has passed the tipping point. We have imported a Quebec. And in recent days it has taken to the streets.

And the future will be determined not by what Congress decides, but by what the illegals decide. Namely, whether they decide to become part of the American mainstream, or whether they choose to be an external and antagonistic subgroup. Will they take the minority model, or the mainstream model?

Will they demographically and sociologically end up more like Italians and Poles, or African-Americans?

If they follow the one course, America will be strengthened and invigorated. If they follow the other, America will be further Balkanized and divided. One path leads to a better America, the other leads to an endangered America facing generations of civil discord and eventually civil war.

The best choice for the illegals is also the best choice for this country—acculturation and assimilation. It is the course followed by every previous generation of immigrants. It is the key to America's successful pluralistic society. It involves embracing American culture and abandoning the dysfunctional cultures of their homelands. Though no longer politically correct, the melting-pot metaphor is still true. Immigration has worked for America because immigrants have left their homelands and their home languages behind.

The grudges and arrogances of the old country have stayed in the old country and a love for and pride in the new country have redefined and redirected the newcomers.

Illegal Latino immigrants have to look no further than to legal Latino immigrants—and native-born Americans of Latino heritage—to see the path to success. Hard work, an embracing of American culture, English fluency, American patriotism, obedience to law. Those things have brought prosperity and acceptance to countless immigrants, and they still work.

If the illegals are in fact hard-working people who are merely looking for a better life, then they should personally and collectively set the goal of rapid acculturation. And the various agencies which seek to support them should facilitate their assimilation. Non-profits should teach English classes instead of welfare classes. They should teach American heritage instead of Latino heritage. They should offer programs that encourage illegals to self-identify as Americans.

The Roman Catholic Church—which stands to benefit tremendously by the much-needed infusion of believing and observant Catholics—should lead in this effort. It should do what it did to help great numbers of German, Italian and Polish immigrants over the last 100 years. It should assist them in becoming Americans in their hearts.

All people working with illegals should take that as a goal.

But it's unlikely they will.

Rather, it's more likely that liberal activists, liberation theologians and the Democratic Party will try to push the illegals and their children into the minority mold imposed on African-Americans. These newcomers will be told that they are an oppressed minority, that they are being denied their due and that they have a right to the possessions and privileges of others. They will be taught Marxist class envy and an unreasonably arrogant pride in their own group identity. They will be encouraged to see themselves as Latinos first and as Americans second.

After enough heritage months and multicultural fairs the simmering anger of a chip on the shoulder will come to define their relationship with the larger society the same way it does for many African-Americans.

And the liberal activists and the Democratic party will win, and newcomers and America will lose.

The illegals came to America the wrong way. They have broken the pattern of immigration. They have nothing in common with those who passed through Ellis Island.

But they are here. In great numbers. The masses in the street prove that. It is unlikely any of those people will be forced from the country. It is likely they will live out their days in this country and that their children and grandchildren will increase geometrically.

And the future of the country depends on what kind of citizens they choose to be. Will they become America's newest minority, or will they become America's new backbone?

The question is simple and the stakes are high. Did the illegals come to assimilate or to colonize?

One will lead to American greatness, the other will lead to American destruction.

Seatbelt laws save lives, kill liberties

What do you think of seatbelt laws?

Are they a good idea, or a bad idea?

You know the ones I mean. They vary from state to state, but they're basically alike. If you're driving a car, and you don't have a seat belt on, you can get a ticket.

Sometimes it's just the driver; sometimes it's everyone in the car.

You've heard the sob stories. They roll out some state trooper, or a paramedic, and have him tell you a heartbreaking story about how many accident scenes he's been to, and how it breaks his heart to see the carnage, and how seatbelts are the only hope we have.

And we see how much the state loves us, passing laws to protect us, shielding us from our own stupidity.

And we're grateful.

We see seatbelt laws as a sign of social progress, as proof we're an enlightened society.

But are we right?

Are seatbelt laws a good idea?

The answer to that, surprisingly, has nothing to do with seatbelts.

Because there's no question about that. If you don't use a seatbelt, you are an idiot. The benefit and protection that come from seatbelts cannot be denied.

Buckle your seatbelt. Don't start the car until you have, and until everyone else has as well.

But that's not the point.

Seatbelt laws aren't about seatbelts, they are about freedom. And the role of government.

The question isn't, "Should you wear a seatbelt?" It is, "Can government force you to wear a seatbelt?'

And, in spite of what the state legislatures have done, the answer to the second question, in America, is clear. The answer is, "No."

We are a free people. Our government, as envisioned in our founding documents, is small and weak. It is not meant to make every decision or to legislate in every area. It is not meant to run our lives.

And yet we have come to let it.

Piece by piece, inch by inch, American freedom has dwindled and dwindled.

We are the victims of tyranny in the name of compassion. Slavery in the guise of protection. Each benefit of government has come at the cost of a corresponding liberty.

We are safer, but we are less free.

And we have been robbed.

Because freedom is better than safety. Liberty more important than life, and self-reliance of greater worth than governmental paternalism.

We are a nation built on the belief that all power resides with the people. Government can only exercise the power it has been granted by the people. In America, the power of government was meant to be severely limited. In America, the government is to be the servant, not the master. In America, people are believed to be the best off when they are the most free, when they run their own lives and make their own decisions.

But our government treats us like children. It takes our liberty from us with hardly a second thought. It expands its power over us without restraint. It mandates by force of law in matters that are and should be entirely personal and private.

Like seatbelts.

Sure, the government says it is acting for our best good. But, shouldn't we decide as free individuals what is in our best good? Doesn't government's desire to protect us from harm unavoidably separate us from God-given liberty?

Of course it does.

And yet we have taken it like sheep.

We have thanked and re-elected those legislators who have orchestrated our bondage. We have cooperated with the squandering of our national birthright. What others fought and died for, we have flushed down the toilet.

Because we haven't been smart enough to remember what this country is all about.

Freedom.

And every policy or decision of the government must pass a simple test: Does it diminish our individual liberty?

If it does, it must not be allowed. If it does, it is inherently unconstitutional. If it does, it is dangerously and unacceptably un-American.

We must be able to distinguish between what counts and what does not. We must not be confused by irrelevance.

Like those sob stories the cops and insurance people tell about seatbelts.

They are beside the point.

Seatbelt laws aren't about seatbelts.

They are about law, and the proper role of law.

And whether or not you wear a seatbelt is your business. It is not the government's business. You are free to be stupid, and the government has no right to outlaw stupidity.

Seatbelt laws are velvet chains. We're told they are for our own good, but they are nothing more than government oppression. They are Big Brother pretending to be our mommy.

And one more example of how we have come to accept what earlier generations of Americans would have fought to the death to resist.

It's not really about homosexuality

On the radio show yesterday I couldn't make the guy understand.

And I've felt bad about it all night.

He was a Christian guy, like the woman before him, and he was talking about homosexuals. And he had chapter and verse. Sodom and Gommorah, the crowd outside Lot's house, on and on and on.

And he wasn't wrong.

But he wasn't right either.

In fact, he made the same mistake the woman did, the same mistake many of us make. He had lost the forest for the trees. He was so intent on showing that homosexuality was morally wrong that he lost sight of the obligation to proclaim what is morally right.

He got so caught up in a minor detail of Christianity that he forgot the essence of Christianity.

Don't get me wrong. The practice of homosexuality is a sin. If left uncleansed, it is a permanent obstacle between man and God.

But a lot of things are. A lot of things many of us do. There is sin all around us, and if we are lucky and wise we avoid it. But not all of us are lucky or wise, and some of us take a while to get that way, maybe our whole lives.

So, it's true that doing gay stuff is morally wrong. But most of the time it is also irrelevant. Most of the time it is also none of our business.

And almost all of the time it is the wrong way to begin a religious discussion.

That's the part I couldn't get the man or the woman on the radio to understand.

I asked them both why they were Christians. Neither of them had the right answer; neither of them seemed to grasp the essence of their professed faith.

So here's the answer, the only reason to be a Christian: because you have a personal faith that Jesus Christ was the Son of God, that he lived and died and was resurrected, that he atoned for our sins and that through faith in him and obedience to his commandments we may go to heaven.

It's that simple.

Without that, there is no particular value or unique doctrine to most Christianity.

So, if you are proclaiming Christianity, it only makes sense that that is what you should proclaim. When you try to take people the essence of your belief, you should take them the core of your belief. The first and fundamental principle.

And that's why I think Christians—and other conservative religious people—make a mistake when they approach homosexuals and homosexuality initially and primarily from a standpoint of condemnation. It is better to speak to people of hope than of doom. It is better to tell people the good news you have for them than the bad news—especially when the good news can heal and wash away the bad.

I told the man on the radio that he had wasted an opportunity. He had an audience of thousands, he was talking religion, and he had spoken only of darkness and damnation. He had wasted the opportunity to give cause for the hope that presumably enlightened his life.

Translation: Maybe Christians should talk about Jesus instead of sin.

Maybe you do more good for someone in homosexuality—or anyone else doing what you believe to be a sin—if you talk to them about the Savior. Christianity is fundamentally an evangelical religion. It's not enough to believe you are saved; you must do what you can to help others be saved as well. It is not enough to know Christ; you must introduce others to him as well.

And the presumption is that such an introduction, if it leads the other person to faith, will also lead the other person to obedience.

Before you construct a building, you must lay the foundation—and the foundation of the Christian lifestyle must be a profound and enduring belief in the divinity of Jesus Christ.

You can't put the cart before the horse.

And you can't assert that homosexuality—or anything else—is a sin until you establish the concept that sin exists, and that it is constituted by disobedience to the Savior of the world, in whom you believe with all your heart.

The first principle of the gospel is faith in the Lord Jesus Christ. The second principle is repentance.

You cannot successfully declare repentance if you have not first declared faith.

And that's where we go wrong, worrying too much about our brothers' sin. We demand they repent, and be like us, without first giving them a reason to.

So forget homosexuality. Your neighbor's life is none of your business. There is a time to call people to repentance, but for most of us, that time is not now. This is the time, however, to declare faith in Christ.

And that's what I was trying to tell the guy on the radio show yesterday, but I couldn't find the words.

The issue isn't homosexuality, the issue is faith in Christ.

Forget about the former and focus on the latter. If you do that, the one will take care of the other.

If you want someone to put his life in order, lead him to faith. If he chooses to accept it, he will put his own life in order.

I think that's why Jesus commanded us not to judge. I think that's why Jesus commanded us to teach people about him.

I think Jesus has this whole thing figured out, and that we only get in his way when we spend our energy condemning his children.

We should know our history

Who'd have thought a day would come in America when George Washington would be nothing more than a caricature in a television commercial.

And that Abraham Lincoln would be his foil.

We used to honor these great men. Now we mock them. And worse, we ignore them.

Our understanding of American history has become so weak and distorted that we fail to comprehend and appreciate our heritage. Names and events sacred to us mean nothing.

And instead of grateful we are indifferent.

It's hard to see this development as an accident. Instead, it is the result of a steady revision and repudiation of our history. Heroes have become villains, ancestors have become enemies, truth has become falsehood.

Our teachers have become liars.

Not just the teachers in the classrooms, but all the institutions and people of society whose role it would be to repeat and reinforce the stories and goodness of our country and birthright.

Heritage is transmitted from generation to generation in a methodical form. But somehow into American society has crept a hateful and anarchist spirit which seems intent on severing our ties with the past. Specifically our reverence and admiration for the past.

Instead of teaching what was good with America and its origins, we are bombarded with what was bad. Columbus was not an inspired explorer, he was a racist conqueror. Washington was not the father of his country, he was a slave owner. Lincoln was not the preserver of the Constitution and Union, he was a manipulating politician. We did not settle America, we genocided the Indians. We did not create a prosperity unequaled in the world, we oppressed the developing nations. We were not the seedbed of the purest liberties history has known, we were the land of Jim Crow.

It goes on and on.

The history which should inspire and unite us is mocked and belittled—precisely because it would inspire and unite us. There is an effort afoot to attack us by attacking our past, to weaken us by tarnishing the glory of our beginnings.

But we don't have to take it.

We don't have to surrender the history of the building of America to those who are intent on tearing America down.

We stood up in patriotic response to the attack of September 11, and we should stand up just the same to this more insidious attack against us and our past. We should reject the so-called historians and intellectuals whose dishonest arrogance so detests the goodness of America.

We can do it by learning the truth, by speaking of it often, and by teaching our children and families of the greatness of this country. Your children should learn American history in your home, to compensate for the bias and inadequacies they may encounter in the classroom and in the curriculum.

History is heritage, and you must never surrender the teaching of heritage, particularly to the government. That is your job. Teach your children—or discover for yourself—the glory of America and the blessing of being an American.

Here are some beginning principles.

First, the discovery of this continent and the founding of this country were directed by God and carried out by heroic and principled men, some of the greatest who have ever lived.

Columbus was a tool in the hand of God in opening up North and South America to civilization and development. George Washington was essential to the establishment of the United States. His service as the general of our Army and as the first president created and defined American liberty.

The Declaration of Independence and the Constitution of the United States are inspired by God and the best political documents and philosophies in the history of humankind.

The conquest of the American continent—including the unfortunate displacement of Native Americans—was one of the most useful events ever. A raw expanse of waste was transformed by two or three generations of pioneers into a prosperous and vital nation which has benefited and fed the world as no other before or since.

The history of the United States—from 1776 to the present—is one of non-stop progress. No other nation has been freer or more prosperous. No other nation has done so much to help and inspire the rest of the world. No other nation has had a political or economic system as pure and free.

And no other nation has been home to so many great and good people. Some of them have been famous, but most of them have not. They have been the quiet, hard-working people whose names are in our family Bibles.

The people we should draw inspiration from, the ones we should try to live like.

The ones we must teach our children about.

Including Washington and Lincoln.

They weren't comical figures to be exploited to sell cars and linens, they were men to whom we owe our freedom and admiration.

They were some of the greatest men ever to live. And today we're supposed to remember them.

But we don't.

There is no liberty without morality

A free society can only survive if it is moral.

Without the restraint of conscience, the freedoms which liberate a people can turn around and cut their throats.

Too often people believe that to be free means to operate without restraint, to do whatever one wants whenever one wants.

But that's not exactly it.

To be free—in our society and our economy—means to be free of government restraint. To operate without government meddling and control. That is what it means to be a free American. In the Constitution the goal is, clearly, to hold back the government, and to keep it out of our lives.

But it was not the intent of the Founders to create a nation driven to chaos by the worship of individual self-interest. They did not see a land where freedom turned people against one another in the exercise of their personal desire.

That's because of conscience. Because of a generally assumed sense of right and wrong. Because a common morality, and the structure of values and ethics, would provide personal guidance in matters where the government had no right sticking its nose. It would be the grease that kept society free of the friction of exploitation.

A free society and a free market can only survive if they are moral.

And the basest acts of egocentrism are kept in check by the individual sense of propriety. A sense of propriety which may be no more complex than, "Do unto others as you would have others do unto you."

If we would be free, we must first be moral. And if we cease to be moral, we cannot long expect to be free.

Two

I hear he was putting his life back together

If you believed what you saw on TV, you'd think Ricardo Torres was a victim.

But you're too smart for that.

You don't believe what you see on TV.

Instead, you know that Ricardo Torres is a piece of trash who's lucky to be alive. One more street hood who combined stupidity and evil in a potentially deadly proportion.

It was Saturday night on Clifford Avenue and Ricardo decided to play bang-bang with Officer Friendly. A whole lot of gunpowder later, Ricardo is laid-up at the hospital and his posse is on the TV cussing the cops.

Baby-mama says it ain't right. Ricardo's parents say the cops went too far. A city councilwoman said the city has "to do more." The hand wringing has begun.

Don't forget, in urban America there is just one response: Blame the cop, blame the cop, blame the cop.

Anyway, about 11:30 Saturday night, Ricardo Torres was driving down the street in a car that looked amazingly like one police were looking for in connection with a robbery and which, my oh my, had the exact same license plate number as the car cops were seeking.

So a cruiser with a couple of Rochester's finest came up behind Ricardo and turned on the light bar and over he pulled.

According to the bull crap his family told the newspaper, 18-year-old Ricardo was running to the store to buy milk for his mother.

Apparently he takes a gun shopping with him because as the officers walked toward his car Ricardo threw open the door and from a distance of 10 feet fired a .357 Magnum directly at Officers Andrew MacKenzie and Chris Renz.

Should I mention that it was a stolen gun? And that there were drugs in the car? And that Ricardo has a criminal record a mile long?

Or that the cops had families?

The officers fired back. They both opened up.

Renz—a SWAT man and former Marine—fired 13 times. MacKenzie shot six times.

Ricardo was hit seven times.

It took that many rounds to get him to stop shooting. After the police began firing back, Ricardo shot his gun two more times.

Which brought out the math majors. Various idiots who see 19 bullets on one side and three on the other and start smelling racism and police brutality.

Reminder: Blame the cop, blame the cop, blame the cop.

"I don't know why there had to be so many shots," Ricardo's father angrily told reporters.

Hopefully he'll get a chance to read this, because I know the answer. I know why cops shot so many times.

Because his teenage dropout son, with the out-of-wedlock baby and the stolen gun, driving a car used in a robbery and containing illegal drugs, pulled out a big-caliber revolver in the dark of the night and without the slightest word of warning started blasting away at police officers.

They fired because he fired, and they stopped firing when he stopped firing.

It's that simple.

Police keep shooting until you stop trying to kill them. As soon as you stop being a threat to them, they stop being a threat to you. When Ricardo dropped his gun, the cops stopped firing theirs. That's the way it's done. That's the only way it makes sense to do it.

And yet the same idiot reporters went out to gather the same idiot quotes and those of us who sat down to watch the so-called "news" heard all about a poor boy out on a milk run who got victimized by the police.

They even got a couple of city council people to cough up daffy quotes.

For example: Councilman Ben Douglas said, "I'm just wondering whether some of these young guys with a gun just don't have the maturity to know what to do when."

I, personally, lack the maturity to know if Douglas was talking about street hoods or cops. Was he offering an excuse for Ricardo Torres, or a criticism for Officers Renz and MacKenzie?

I don't know, and neither do the cops and cops' wives I've heard from.

Councilwoman Gladys Santiago said she may try to contact and comfort the Torres family, and whined to a reporter, "We have to come together with the community."

She's right. City leaders should come together with the community to condemn scum like Ricardo Torres. City leaders should come together with the community to say that anybody who shoots at the police deserves a round of taxpayer-funded ammo right between the eyes. City leaders should come together with the community to take a side in the daily battle of good-versus-evil that plays out on the streets of Rochester.

But they won't.

Instead they'll do what they always do: Blame the cop, blame the cop, blame the cop.

On Sunday afternoon the police chief stood up to defend his officers. Unfortunately, he had to stand up by himself.

The mayor wasn't there. No one from city council was there. Nobody from the community groups was there. The ministers weren't there. The Catholic bishop wasn't there. The activists weren't there.

It was the cop standing all alone.

Just like it always is.

The story of a man who heard God

I believe in a God who whispers.

And I believe he whispered to James Wilkes in the howling dark of the Utah wilderness. I believe he sent James Wilkes to do a job and I believe James Wilkes did it.

You've heard the story.

A little boy, in footy pajamas, left alone in a truck in the heights of the mountains. Two years old. Asleep in the child seat while his dad went off to hunt.

And he woke up and got out and toddled away, looking for Daddy.

At least that's what we think. That's what we conclude. That's what his body seems to say.

James Wilkes found him.

It was an odd thing, really. There were the official searchers and there were the family searchers and then there was James Wilkes. Some guy from down in Salt Lake. Some guy living his life, doing his thing, not involved in the least.

But apparently he heard something. Something that called him to the mountains.

So he drove up the canyon and he set out and he just walked. He just walked. And the oddest thing happened.

He got lost.

He lost his bearings and the mountain wasn't familiar anymore and he had a stupor of thought. And he was a man alone, lost in the cruel vastness of the American west.

And he stumbled on and he shivered through the night and he pushed on at daybreak some more.

And then he saw him. In the fetal position, the snow beginning to collect on his little body. The soles of his footy pajamas tattered away. His face scratched from pushing through the tight brush of the mountainside.

A little boy dead.

Two years of blonde hair and blue eyes and going to the woods with Daddy. And he died wanting his Daddy in an outdoors that doesn't forgive.

And James Wilkes picked him up.

Hungry and spent and chilled to the bone, the man who didn't belong there, the man who came on his own. The man, himself weakened by the elements, with the dead boy cradled in his arms.

And on they went that way, in deepening snow and over barely passable terrain, the man and the boy.

And James Wilkes started crying.

He started crying because he couldn't go on. And he explained that to the dead boy in his arms. He explained it and he apologized and sometimes he ranted inconsolably, staggering under his burden, feeling a sense of failure and grief.

And after two hours he had to stop.

And under a tree near a fence he put the youngster tenderly down, heartbroken, with tears streaming from his face.

When a woman and her dog found him later she thought he was incoherent. Incoherent and insistent about a tree and a fence and somebody has to be sent back now. He was rambling and emotional and she thought it was the exposure and the terror of the wild.

But the searchers went back anyway and along the fence under the tree there he was. Just like James Wilkes had said.

And at 2 o'clock in the morning there was a notification. Prayers had been answered.

Not the first prayers, but the second. Not the prayers of deliverance, but the prayers of recovery.

First they wanted their baby home alive. But as the snow fell and the days passed they just wanted their baby home. The aunt who cried on the TV and the cousins and grandparents.

And their prayer was answered, and the boy will rest in a family plot, and there will be no more wondering about what happened. He came home to them, in the arms of James Wilkes.

There were a hundred searchers at first, trained people, and helicopters with infrared and trackers with dogs. And they worked a grid pattern and they coordinated their efforts and they searched like he was one of their own.

But it didn't work and the sheriff called it off and the best they could the family continued on.

But it was James Wilkes who heard the whisper. It was James Wilkes who was led.

And I don't know why.

And maybe it was luck and maybe it was God. But Monday when he went to the mountains it was impossible, and Tuesday when he came back it was done. And I can't explain that.

And neither can you.

But I believe in a God who whispers.

And I don't know why he didn't whisper to the searchers, or to the father with the gun, or to any of the others who sacrificed and hunted and criss-crossed the mountain.

I don't know why he called that little boy home.
And I don't know why he called James Wilkes up there.
But I believe he did.
Maybe it was for the family. Maybe it was for James Wilkes. Maybe it was for us.
But I believe in a God who whispers.
And I suspect James Wilkes can hear him now.
"Well done, my good and faithful servant."

What they found yesterday in the mountains

Must be he went up there in his suit after court and climbed into the mountains and looked down at where his toddler had frozen to death and steadied the muzzle against his head.

It's hard to do with a deer rifle, but it can be done.

And he looked out through teary eyes over the peaks he loved and said goodbye.

And they found him there a day later when his lawyer worried that he was late to turn himself in.

Paul Wayment, 38.

It was no contest. Some kind of misdemeanor homicide thing. He had been hunting, he loved to hunt, and he had his little boy with him. A real little boy. Gage Wayment. Age 2.

Anyway, Gage was asleep in the truck in the mountains and Dave thought he could get in some hunting while the little boy dozed and he did a fundamentally stupid thing. The worst thing. He slipped out of the pick-up and took his rifle and went into the scrub looking for deer.

Miles and miles from anywhere, in the mountains east of Coalville, in Summit County, Utah.

That was five days before what would have been Gage's third Halloween, the first one, probably, to register, when he would have gone out dressed as some cute monster to smile and gather candy at doorsteps.

And run giggling back to the sidewalk and on to the next house and the next treat.

But he woke up. He woke up and his nightmare began.

A little boy alone in the mountains. And he went looking for Daddy. He opened the door and climbed out of the cab and scampered into the bush and the woods and the rocks. And five days later they found him a mile away half covered by the snow.

The soles of his footy pajamas were tattered away and the brush through which he walked had torn at his face.

They thought for a long time before they charged Paul with anything. Some said that his loss was punishment enough, others said that his negligence had killed the boy. It was a big hullabaloo.

But they decided to bring this misdemeanor homicide against him and the lawyer got him to take a no contest and on Tuesday the prosecution and the defense each told the judge that they didn't think he ought to go to jail.

But the judge thought otherwise and gave him 30 days, with the sentence to start yesterday.

And the reporters said he looked kind of different as he left the courtroom. Kind of disconnected or something. Like he wasn't really there.

It was 30 days meant to help him heal and help him make amends. The judge thought some punishment was appropriate, for the best interests of justice, and for the best interests of Paul. So he said 30 and brought down the gavel and gave him a day to put his things in order.

And after a manner of speaking, he did.

He balanced the books. An eye for an eye, a tooth for a tooth, a life for a life.

And when it broke on the radio people across the Wasatch and the country got a sick feeling in their stomachs. An "Oh my God" kind of revulsion that is part incomprehension and part sorrow.

What has he done?

My gosh, why did he do it?

Poor man, what must he have thought?

He killed the first time accidentally, he killed the second time purposefully. But if the first was out of stupidity, so was the second, and for a time confusion and chaos reigned and the only thing that made sense was the thing that made the least sense.

Because you can't atone for one tragedy with another.

You can't wash away blood with blood. Not this way. Not at your own hand. Not in your suit in the cool air of the summer mountains when all you think you have left is the power of a gun in your hands and in your mouth.

If a rifle cracks in the alpine air and there is no one to hear it, does it really make a sound?

Of course it does. A sound that reverberates through the eternities for Paul Wayment and through a lifetime for the people who loved him. People who buried first a nephew and now a brother.

What a sickening and wretched mess. A hold your head in your hands and sob kind of mess.

Born out of shortsightedness.

The shortsightedness of a decision then and the shortsightedness of a decision now. The poor miserable man.

He failed his son in this life by not protecting him. And he failed his son in the next life by proving unworthy to join him.

But that could be wrong.

There may be understanding beyond that Paul did not find here. Perhaps beyond there is a God who knows something about the pain of losing a son. A God who can embrace and hold the disconnected man who left the courthouse and drove to the spot where he had parked once before. The disconnected man who wandered into the wilderness as his little boy had done before him.

The disconnected man who would lie dead in the night with only the stars and the angels as witnesses, as his little boy had done before him.

Paul Wayment was the last person Gage saw in this life. I suspect Gage Wayment was the first person Paul saw in the next.

And I suspect that is what Paul wanted. What he sought. What drove him to this. Some horrid amalgam of sorrow and guilt and loneliness.

God bless him. God bless us all.

See no evil

There was a time when this would have shocked us. When we would have been up in arms. When we would have given a damn.

But that time is long past.

The savagery has gotten so out of hand, the cultural decay is so advanced, the violence is so much the norm, that it's become water off a duck's back. Nothing more than the background noise of Rochester's rot.

I'm talking about the 2-year-old.

I'm talking about the 2-year-old and everybody else. The pile of dead and dying and decaying who are fodder for the evening news and proof of the city's slide into barbarism.

Like the 2-year-old.

Half past 11 on a Monday night and there's a little 2-year-old playing in an abandoned lot off Clinton Avenue. Everybody's in the streets and there's a lot of noise and then it sounds like somebody blows off some fireworks.

At least that's what they told the cops.

It sounded like fireworks.

That's a lie, of course. Everybody up in that neighborhood knows what gunfire sounds like. They've heard it countless times, they've probably seen its effects, sometimes they've been the source of it.

But there were some loud noises, something like fireworks, and the 2-year-old was bleeding.

Out playing in an abandoned lot in the worst neighborhood in the northeastern United States at half past 11 on Monday night.

It was about 22 hours earlier that Lisa Baker got hers. She was 35 and it was the wee hours of the morning and she came out of a bar at Thurston and Brooks and some guy came up behind her and plugged her and she was dead before dawn.

It was a couple of hours before she was shot that a bunch of teenage boys—we're not allowed to call them "gang members"—were beating the living hell out of one another with baseball bats when somebody decided to spare the lumber and pulled out a gun.

A 15-year-old took a round in the head.

Just like the 21-year-old guy that morning. At first light Saturday Raymond Nevares came out of a house party—Tupperware?—and there was some "mother f'ing" and some general disagreement and then there was some gun play and he'd joined the shot-in-the-head club.

A brief rundown of the city police blotter for last week shows another guy shot in the head, three guys shot during a fight, a woman half dressed and half decayed, some 15-year-old shot in the ass and a would-be car thief who lost his femoral artery and his life when an angry car owner tried to castrate him.

If I were feeling snide, I'd point out that in response to all this the mayor went to Toronto to cut some ribbon having to do with his fast ferry.

But I'm not snide. I'm cynical.

And I'm not the only one.

Which brings us back to our victims.

First, Mr. Tupperware.

After exiting the house party at 5:30 in the morning, the recently alive and tragically unarmed Raymond Nevares was mercilessly gunned down in front of a crowd of people.

In response to this, in time-honored fashion, officers of the Rochester Police Department inquired of the hangers-around if they'd seen anything or could identify the gunman.

Not surprisingly, nobody seen nothin'.

Which was also exactly the case outside that bar at Thurston and Brooks. A large crowd of people, Lisa Clark gets shot to death, and nobody seen nothin'.

Zero witnesses.

Which brings us to the 2-year-old.

He's apparently a pretty tough little kid because he lived. He might walk crooked, but he's probably going to live.

That's surprising because typically toddlers can't take a gunshot for crap.

What's not surprising is that nobody seen nothin'.

When the 2-year-old—his name is DeTavious Wynn—was shot, nobody saw anything, according to his cousin—LaQueena Mitchell. Everybody just zipped their lips. In fact, his mother—Candiance Wynn—isn't cooperating with the police investigation.

There seems to be a lot of that going around.

Two people murdered in cold blood, in front of crowds of people, and nobody will tell the police anything. A 2-year-old boy is shot in front of a crowd of people, and nobody—not even his mother—will tell the police anything.

"We have information that there were many people around at the time of the shootings and we really challenge the community to come forward and do the right thing," police Sgt. Mark Mariano told a TV reporter. "And the right thing is to provide us with the information that we know that they have."

My advice: Don't hold your breath.

It didn't used to be this way. There was a time when if a teenager got shot, the ministers came out and people prayed for the cameras and politicians promised that something would be done. There would be marches and folks would go on TV saying they were going to take back the streets. There would be all of that. It was all meaningless nonsense, of course, just posturing for publicity, mostly.

But at least it happened.

Now nothing happens.

Nobody cares. Nobody talks. Nobody notices.

The savagery has gotten so out of hand, the cultural decay is so advanced, the violence is so much the norm, that it's become water off a duck's back. Nothing more than the background noise of Rochester's rot.

Something that happened in the country this week

Really, the whole thing didn't take but a moment.

It just happened and that was that.

Then Mr. Fritts got back in his truck with his grandson and drove the dog to the vet.

That was Monday morning, before the state police helicopters got there, after he saved Mr. May's life.

Canaseraga is a little place, down between Swain and Arkport, past the Garwoods swamp. A couple weeks back on a Sunday they had the annual ham and leek dinner at the Legion hall. That's about the biggest thing that happens down there, except sometimes when they have the demolition derby and the homecoming dance.

My great-grandfather's second wife was from there. Grama Ruth. She got him into playing cards. His first wife, Grama Pearl, was a Baptist, and Baptists didn't play cards back in those days.

Anyway, Canaseraga is a long ways from most places, and so it was kind of odd on Monday that those two young guys were down there. They weren't from there or from anywhere near there. They said they got lost, but they might have been lying.

One was 19 and the other was 22 and about 5 o'clock in the morning they started breaking into places. There are a lot of deer camps down there, and summer cabins, and they were breaking in and taking what they could.

Chuck May wasn't home then. He was downtown at the diner where his wife works, having breakfast. When he got done he went by the Legion to sign the book and then he swung by the house.

And saw the doors were open when they shouldn't be.

Mr. May is 73.

So he watched for a moment and then his wife came along and he sent her back into town to get help. Then he parked his truck to block the long driveway and began walking to his house.

That's when Taylor Fritts and his 4-year-old grandson came through town on the way to the vet's. The dog needed a visit and the boy needed a babysitter and Grampa got the job.

Mr. Fritts is 64.

And Mrs. May flagged him down in front of the Corner Cafe and said her husband needed help and could he go up and check on him. So while she ran into the diner to call the troopers and the deputies, Mr. Fritts and the boy and the dog drove quick-like the half a mile to the Mays' house.

From the road he could see the truck blocking the drive, and the open doors, and then he saw trouble. It was like they were grappling, he said. Mr. May and these two young strangers.

So he pulled over quick and told the boy to stay put and locked the truck.

After he got the gun.

The 9 millimeter pistol he keeps in his glove box. He got that gun and he locked the truck and he started running up the drive.

They were stomping him by then. This 19-year-old and this 22-year-old and they had Mr. May on the ground, one of them laying on top of him punching him and the other kicking the 73-year-old for all he was worth.

They were about a dozen feet away, a couple of body lengths, and Mr. Fritts pulled up the gun and told them to get off. And they got off. Not that they seemed very afraid, and not that they got docile, but they did get off. Then they said all sorts of crude things, threatening things, and Mr. Fritts kept the gun on them as they walked to their car.

He told them to stop but they wouldn't, to lay down on the ground, but they wouldn't, and they got in their car and tried to get away. But Mr. May's truck was in the drive and when they tried to get passed they slid into the ditch.

Then they got out and walked into the woods.

Which, down by Canaseraga, means they disappeared.

It was another 24 hours before a guy in a highway truck spotted them and called the troopers.

It's all the talk down there. And they tease Mr. Fritts about being "Barney Fife." But he's taking it OK.

And one thing is certain.

It's a damn good thing he had that gun.

About a mother, a father and a daughter

He promised.

On his deathbed he promised.

Leroy Autry, riddled with cancer, having fought the good fight, through the delirium of pain and decline, promised his wife.

That was two weeks ago.

They had a good life together. A good life, but hard. Especially the last year. Harder than a mother and father ought to be asked to bear. She was the youngest of their five babies. A girl grown up to young womanhood, 15 years old, with pretty red hair and a full-face smile.

That was her.

That was her the last time they saw her.

Which was the twenty-third of June, last year, at their home in Hyrum, Utah. Way back up in the mountains, in southeast Cache Valley, where things are different. Where a Mormon temple stands watch on a hill and there is a certain innocent wholesomeness. The old families came here in the 1860s, sent by Brigham Young, and the new families came here in the 1990s, sent by fears of crime and immorality in the outside world.

All come to Cache Valley in search of peace.

Which used to reign in the Autry home. As it did early in the morning of the twenty-fourth, at something like 4:30 in the morning, when mother JoAnn Autry heard Trisha in the bathroom.

But 90 minutes later, when the family roused for the new day, there was no Trisha.

She had vanished.

Nothing else was gone. Not her money, not her purse, not her personal belongings.

She was just gone.

That's when they began searching. They scattered in the family cars, searching the country roads and village streets. And they found nothing. They found nothing. And when they went to the police for help they were blown off. And days passed and the cops said she was a runaway and there was nothing they could do.

Leroy had the cancer pretty bad, even then, and it was a great trial for the family.

But they sold the house anyway. They sacrificed it to get Trisha back. They got the church people in to help them spiff it up and then they sold it.

To pay for the private detective.

If the police weren't going to search, the Autry family was.

It got real hard after that, with so much work and so little to show for it. Nothing to show for it, really, just some posters and some pictures on the Internet and people saying prayers all up and down the valley. And 11 months of fear and uncertainty.

And then Leroy started slipping away, his baby child unaccounted for. And he made his promise.

He looked up at his wife in a moment of clarity and he told her that if he met Trisha on the other side he would get a message back to her.

If after he died he met their daughter there, dead, he would let his wife know.

That was two weeks ago. And then he passed.

Now, Leroy was a faithful man, the Mormons would say that he "honored his priesthood." Just like the two investigators. A couple of guys who had been in stake presidencies, the lay leaders of something analogous to a Roman Catholic diocese.

It was two God-fearing men out of the sheriff's department, empty handed after almost a year's work, and two weeks ago another God-fearing man met his daughter.

And in Cache Valley they say that sometimes the veil between this world and the next is thin. So thin that messages can be passed. Whisperings. Impressions or words, moments of clarity and understanding, voices from the air or providential happenings. Sometimes a hand from beyond can guide the actions or thoughts of those who are here.

And two weeks after her husband promised, JoAnn Autry has her message. She has her answer. And she has her daughter.

Back off on some federal land, where they study coyotes, under almost 12 feet of mountain till, they found Trisha. In a hole that must have been dug with a backhoe. On land that isn't open to the public. Where no one would ever look, so deep they would never find, back off from the valley in a place most people didn't know existed.

They found her.

The sheriff's department hasn't said how yet, but they found her.

It was a simple promise.

When I get to the other side, if I meet our daughter, I will let you know.

And now she knows.

And before the television cameras JoAnn Autry stood beneath the weight of the world. A new widow, bereft of a child, her life and her future all in the wind.

And she testified of the power of prayer.

She said it was prayer that brought her through, and prayer that brought her peace, and prayer that brought her daughter home.

She thanked people for the prayers that had been said, and for the prayers that were still needed.

And she had her peace.

Wrapped up in pain and loss, but she had her peace.

And her husband had kept his promise.

Good guys 2, Bad guys 0

Thank goodness.

Somebody killed a bad guy.

Better yet, it was a twofer.

Monday night, in the city of Rochester, the sun set on a burglar and a home invader. Literally. By morning they were dead. They each came down with a terminal case of courageous homeowner.

Bang, bang. You're dead and my home is my castle.

It started about 8:30 at night, on Ravine Avenue. Some guy is standing outside his house when another guy comes up and pulls a gun on him. Then he stong-armed him into his home—the victim's home—and started to steal his VCR.

Must be somebody was having a sale on crack.

So the bad guy is there trying to get the VCR under one arm while holding the gun in the other hand and the man who figures he's about a minute away from being permanently removed from the witness list lunged at the gun. I guess he reasoned that if he was going to go out he might as well go out with a fight.

So they're grappling over the gun, and the homeowner gets it away. Maybe the bad guy squeezes off a round before he does; the details aren't that clear.

Anyway, then the bad guy goes to his belt and pulls out another gun. A big ugly handgun. And he aims it at the homeowner and pulls the trigger. And it grazes the guy's face. So the homeowner raises the gun he wrestled away from the bad guy, and aims it at him, and pulls the trigger. And hits him right square in the head.

Dead bad guy Number One.

He had a bad case of stupid and it killed him. First off, he picked the wrong motor scooter to rob. Second, he had a pellet gun as his backup. And when his gun went "ffft," the other guy's gun went "ka-freaking-boom!"

Repeating with glee: Dead bad guy Number One.

You'll be happy to know the VCR was not injured in the fracas.

Then, about six hours later, in the wee hours of the morning, there's an 89-year-old guy on North Street who is awakened by a banging, like the neighbor's storm door flipping open and closed in the wind. So he goes out to look.

But on his way he hears the glass break out of his back door. So he goes back to his bedroom and fetches the .22 Beretta he keeps under his pillow. By the time he gets back to his kitchen the bad guy is through two and maybe three more doors — in the house — and grandpa pops off a couple of rounds in his general direction.

Now, he's old but he's not dumb, so he figures there's going to be paperwork over this. And he calls 911 to have them send somebody out so he can report the burglary and the broken glass. It was after the cops got there that they said something along the lines of, "Excuse me, sir, but did you know you've got a dead guy out here?"

Which made it an even bigger paperwork job than he had expected.

Dead bad guy Number Two.

By yesterday morning all the reporters in town had come to pay court and ask the old man if he was going to move out of the neighborhood. He allowed as how, having lived there for 60 years, that he wasn't about to go anywhere.

And he shouldn't have to.

Because he should be safe in his own home. And the city government having failed to make sure that he could be, he took matters into his own hands.

Just like Mr. VCR.

A man's home is his castle, and crime comes at a risk, and you get what you deserve.

And this should be repeated over and over. It should dominate the news and be on the front page of the paper. The word should spread. If you rob someone's home, you could die.

I suspect if more potential bad guys were aware of that we'd have fewer burglaries and home invasions.

The good guys won and the bad guys lost. Way cool.

But not enough.

It isn't enough to applaud the other guy's courage. It is better to show some courage of your own. Nobody should hanker for a fight, but neither should anyone surrender the right to fight back.

Maybe there ought to be more Berettas under pillows and shotguns in the corners. Maybe we should remember that we are Americans, with a right and obligation to defend ourselves with force of arms.

Maybe we should remember that the police can't and don't guarantee our safety, that it is typically impossible for them to respond quickly enough to protect our homes and our families. Maybe we should remember that someday whether or not we live will depend on our ability and willingness to defend ourselves.

Maybe the best way to stop the bad guys is for the good guys to fight back.

We got two of them Monday night, and that's a good start.

The story of Trevor Wagner, first-grader

Trevor Wagner should be in school today.

In the first grade.

A brand-new six-year-old in fresh clothes tottering off on a great adventure, three days into the new school year, the prospect of learning to read rising before him.

But he's not.

He's not in school.

He's dead.

His back is broken in two places and his head is caved in and when his mother came back from work he was naked in the other room with a bag of ice on his chest. His brain was swollen by then and the doctors tried taking off part of his skull to relieve the pressure but it was too late and he was dead.

And the boyfriend is in jail.

Just like always. Mama's boyfriend did it. Allegedly. Just like always.

Only this one is worse. The cops had been out there, and the social services people, and she took Trevor and his baby brother at the beginning of the month and went off to a shelter. A shelter where the boyfriend couldn't get them and she stayed there. Safe.

But she went back.

Back to her place, where Bobby San Juan was waiting. Yeah, that's his name. Bobby San Juan. What a prize. Thirty-five years old and in the house while the paramedics worked on the little boy he told mama that he really blew it this time.

The bastard. The big stinking bastard.

Allegedly.

Maybe Trevor Wagner did trip and hurt himself. Maybe it was an accident. And maybe his mother doesn't have blood on her hands for taking him back into that hellhole.

But then again, maybe she does.

Maybe she is responsible for exposing her son to the likes of Bobby San

Juan. Maybe she is responsible for leaving her son alone with a man who had allegedly chased the entire family into a domestic-violence shelter.

Maybe the whole string of mamas who exposed their children to mama's boyfriend needs to be held accountable for the evil they brought into the lives of innocent children. If a woman wants to stay and be beaten that's one thing, but when she leaves her children in that situation, she's wrong.

And it's time society started saying so.

Because this weeping-sister routine is getting old. The pain and terror of domestic abuse — physical or sexual — is real and hellacious and repugnant. But women must first help themselves. As hard as that sounds, as much courage and daring as it requires, it is essential.

She must take the first step.

And have the strength to keep taking them. To walk out and to keep on walking. To pick up the phone and dial 911 or to go to a minister or to sneak out in the night or to jump in the car and flee or to simply say no. And mean it.

And I know how hard it can be. Or, better put, I know as well as a man can know. Because I am not a woman. I am not being beaten. I am not dependent on someone else for my livelihood. I am not left with a child or two or three to provide for on my own. I am none of those things which a domestic-abuse victim typically is.

But I have been beaten. I have been beaten pretty good.

I know a little bit about being Trevor Wagner.

And I can picture the agony of his mother and the wrestling in her mind. But I cannot forgive her. I cannot forget the fact that on August 6 that little boy was safe in a shelter and that by August 19 she had taken him back to the room where he would be killed.

There is some powerful force which pushes women back into situations where they are beaten and misused, where they are treated like beasts by weak and hateful men. Whether it's love or habit or low self-esteem, it is powerful and deadly. But it must be resisted.

If not for themselves, then for their children.

Trevor Wagner had his back broken over the weekend, in two places, and his head caved in. One more dead kid, victim—allegedly—of mama's boyfriend.

I think it's time we started holding mama accountable.

What a couple of guys did the other night

You don't work the ambulance because you want to get rich.

You do it because it interests you, maybe, or because you like the uniforms and the sirens and the adrenaline. More likely you do it because you want to help.

Because there's no glamour in puking kids and choking grandparents. It's not like on TV. In the real world it stinks and hurts and turns your stomach.

So if you're sitting in a rig in the middle of the night waiting to be dispatched, it's because you're a Florence Nightingale. Under the crust, and the foul language and off-color jokes, there's a softy. Somebody who cares. And somebody who can use his smarts and his hands to do some good when somebody else is really up against it.

Like the other night.

A couple of young guys doing overnight on a Monday, sitting in their rig across from an adult book store waiting for the radio to crackle and the next run to come in.

When all of a sudden the whole place just went to crap.

Ka-freaking-boom.

Fireball city, baby. Twelve thousand gallons of high test and a sideways tanker and the whole mess sparked on Main Street, USA. More specifically, on West Ridge Road, Rochester, along a line of houses. At 1 o'clock in the morning, while everybody was asleep and two young medics are half dozing in their rig a block away waiting for their shift to end.

Paramedic Shannon Holley and Emergency Medical Technician Kenneth Stavalone. The one guy was 30 and the other guy was 22. And they are eyewitnesses to the biggest fire in years. A couple of no-names from Monroe Ambulance. The kind of guys that turn out to be heroes.

It sounds like a little bit of hell. Rivers of fire, volcanoes of burning fuel, everything going up in smoke and down in flames. Fireballs rising maybe a hundred feet into the air.

And that's where these two guys went. Right at the fire. They spun the rig and got on the radio and flipped on the siren. One of those big van ambulances, and they got it yelping and they blew the air horn and drove right for the fire.

Because that's where the people were. All along there, sleeping in those houses, while fire rained down on their roofs and lives.

They hoped the siren would wake the neighborhood and they lept from their rig to give it a hand. Pounding on doors and hurrying families, one guy with a kid under his arm as he led its mom to the safety of the ambulance, something like a dozen people — including the gasoline-truck driver — as they hauled the first batch out of harm's way to the police command post down the street.

It was a heck of a deal. A five-alarm fire and hundreds of emergency workers and two medics leading the charge.

And when it was over there was just one lady dead. The poor lady whose yard the truck landed in. She never had a chance. And neither did the other ones. Except for the two medics and a cop who joined them and the army of neighbors who responded to the pounding on the door.

In the dark of the night as a tanker lost it on a curve.

When regular people did irregular things. When a couple of schlumps in an ambulance became heroes. When the instinct to serve overcame the instinct to escape, when it was others before self and life saving over life itself.

Shannon Holley and Kenneth Stavalone and a dog cop named Dan Nowack. Heroes. Life savers. People like you and me.

Who responded when they were needed.

Setting an example we each must resolve to follow. Who knows how or even if we will be needed. But if we are, we must respond. We must be as good as these brave men and the others who flocked to save this neighborhood from an inferno.

It doesn't matter what you are called to do, only how you answer.

These men answered without hesitation. And they saved lives.

And enriched ours.

The saga of Fluffy Pillows

It's funny how life puts things together.

How one place can be more than one thing, and how those things taken together can be ironic or sad.

Like the other night.

I sat next to the lectern as Matthew Clark, the Catholic bishop of Rochester, stood to speak to some of his most faithful.

He has been sick, but mending, and he stood there a humble tall man, standing not quite at full height as humble tall men will do. He looked down mostly, at a piece of paper with nothing written on it.

No notes, no script. Just a comfortable rolling of thoughts and words, rising sometimes with a hand in the air, as if to literally grasp a point from the ether, his eyes rising to meet and pass his fingers as he bore witness to the crowd.

"Christ's love," he said, "is bigger than my faults and my failings."

And what was true for him was true for us all. That was his point. And he was right. He was right about a faith which can consume life's woes and disasters, and sublimate their evil to good, in the great reformation of the personal struggle which defines our lives.

The personal struggle that vindicates some people and consumes others.

Like Fluffy Pillows.

That's the part about how life puts things together.

The bishop was speaking at a banquet center across the parking lot from a motel where one dark night a stripper named Fluffy Pillows brought an end to her career and her life by placing a 9 millimeter against her head and pulling the trigger.

She had been dancing up the avenue, at The Cordial, and she was the headliner. Headliner, freak, whatever you want to call it.

She did five shows a day in a filthy and depressing little pit in the rotting underbelly of a cold Eastern city. A week in this town and a week in the next town and it went on that way for years.

Until one night she finally had enough.

And in a strange room in a strange city she ended it. Or it ended her.

And in the building out her window a few years later the man in the Roman collar would stand up and talk about Christ's love.

She had started out just one more stripper. Some 20-something easy-money chick caught up in a lie that benefits nobody but the guy raiding the till. She danced and she liked the money and she got past the drunks pawing her and kissing her and sticking their dollar bills in her panties.

She got past it all but to help it some she took up cocaine. And that was it really, she was had. And she needed the cash and the dollars went from one exploitative man to the next, twirling stoned around a pole in the filthiest bars in America.

She wasn't Fluffy Pillows then.

I don't remember her name. Nobody does. And that's the point. She was a body. Everything else had been whittled away and eventually the road took its toll and even the body wasn't cutting it.

That's when she had the first surgery.

Not to enlarge, but to tuck. To rejuvenate.

And that bought her a little more time on the circuit and it fed the cocaine hunger but it didn't last and then she was in trouble. Because when a woman starts looking like a woman those places won't have her.

At that stage a lot of them become prostitutes.

They will settle out in a town, usually in some kind of arrangement with a drug dealer, and they will turn tricks until they die.

But Fluffy Pillows decided to be a freak instead.

She got a surgeon and she began a series of operations. And her b-cup breasts became something else, something gargantuan, and they became her ticket.

It was ugly really, in the light of day. The ridges of scar on the underside welted up, crossing each breast two or three times. Visible in the filthy magazines too cheap to hire an air brush but lost in the darkness and colored lights of the bars she hit, week after week.

Fluffy Pillows.

And it was so much to watch and so much to feel and she rode that as long as she could bear it, dank smoky hell-holes with fat broken men hunched over beers gripping dollar bills.

And up in that motel next to where the bishop spoke one night she just couldn't take any more. And the hair and the face so many men had mistaken for beautiful were splattered across the wall by the broken jerk of a trigger.

And there was no one to claim her and she lay up there in the medical examiner's refrigerator for months, this week's headliner at The Cordial, replaced by another freak trucked in on the circuit.

"Christ's love," the bishop would later say, "is bigger than my faults and my failings."

He knows that. And you know that.

It's just too bad Fluffy Pillows never knew that.

It was bright in Batavia yesterday, and warm

He was 8 but looked 6.

A little scrawny kid with a tail of hair at the base of his skull and a Bart Simpson T-shirt.

He told me to go "f" myself.

Three or four times. And he made another reference, to a homosexual act, as he yelled at me.

I told him to go away, to go back to the home across the street, where the woman with the rotten teeth lived. I told him he didn't want to be on TV. That it wasn't the right thing.

I had been on the apartment steps, by the peeling and flimsy door, talking into a microphone and staring at the camera.

And he was mad.

Because I said his home stunk.

There was the rotting food and the soiled diapers strewn around and the urine-soaked mattresses where the six children slept. The urine-soaked mattresses in the crumbling tenement where last the police say his mother walked out the door to go to the city on a crack binge.

Leaving the kids.

Alone. All six of them. The 1-year-old and the 12-year-old and all the ones in between.

"She pretty much abandoned them to go to Rochester to use [crack]," said Detective Randy Baker. "There was no food for the children."

And I said all that for the 10 o'clock news and what the little boy couldn't take was that I said his home stunk. And he came around the corner of the house, swearing and glaring. And I tried to send him away.

But the woman from across the street, with the rotten teeth, came and said he could talk if he wanted to. So I appeased him and lowered the microphone and asked him what had happened.

Eight years old.

"I'm not going back to my mother," he said.
"Why not?" I asked.
"I'm going to make [a neighbor] adopt me."
"Why, buddy?"
"Because I don't love my mom anymore."
"Why's that, son?"

And then he glowered and leaned in. There was a cold and almost homicidal tone in his voice.

"Don't call me, 'son.'"

Around him the other neighborhood kids laughed, entertained by his rage. He didn't shift his gaze. He looked at me with hate.

"Why don't you love your mom anymore?"

That was all he could take. He waved his arms, he shouted.

"Well, take one guess," he spit. "She does crack. She does weed. She does all this other junk."

Police said she went to Rochester on Thursday morning, from crack house to crack house, while back home her children were alone. By late Friday they were hungry and had called relatives for food. And a friend of hers, another addict from Batavia, had come to the city looking for her, telling her she needed to look after her kids.

"The kids were hungry," said neighbor Emily Smith. "They were dirty, they were filthy. Absolutely filthy."

"A bunch of times she's gone off and left 'em."

"She left the little baby sitting on the couch while she went and got high," said neighbor Virginia Bates.

Batavia is a pretty little city, famous a century and a half ago as a hot port on the Erie Canal. It doesn't have a slum, really, but it does have bad parts. And this happened in one of those parts. The woman and her rottweiler and the children and they're all crammed in the first apartment of a long block building crumbling and dank. Door after door of squalid hovel, overweight women sitting in some of them, little children scampering at their feet.

A little boy in a bicycle helmet pedals up and talks about the Department of Social Services caseworker who had been there earlier in the day. He is a handsome kid, from down the block, and his sister stays by his side, a beautiful little girl, clean and combed.

"I know her, she's pretty nice," the boy said. "She handled my case, too."

"They took us away once, and put us in a foster home. But we're back now."

Just one of the kids thronging the sidewalk, curious to see a TV camera and to wave at its lens.

"She's really trying," said a friend of the crack mother police charged. "She's giving it all she's got to get everything she's got to do right for her kids to come home."

But not everybody thinks that.

With her kids away, the mother came back to the apartment, neighbors said. They said she carried in a 24-pack of beer.

"She had a party going on," Gerry Smith said. "Music blaring, smoking weed. You know, drinking."

I asked the little boy if he could forgive his mother. He said maybe.

"I'm giving her one chance," he said. "She does it one more time, hmph, she ain't going to see me no more."

It was bright in Batavia yesterday, and warm.

And hopeless.

And that's what it's like behind the news.

An idiot, a crook and a saint

This is the story of an idiot, a crook and a saint.

And the little baby who brought them together.

Elizabeth Kate Whitney. Six weeks old.

And one night, a little after 7, her mother ran her out to the car. It was cold, probably in the mid teens, and mom was leaving the nursing home where she is the night manager and had just wrapped a present and needed to go somewhere and forgot the present inside so she put Elizabeth Kate in her car seat in the back and remembered the present and slammed the car door and ran back into the nursing home.

The mom's name is Katie Whitney.

She's the idiot.

I'm sorry to say it that way. But that's the way it is.

She left her baby in the car and she ran inside and she also left the diaper bag in the car and it had her purse in it and her keys were in the purse and so there they were, the car and the keys and the baby, unattended, unlocked and open and available to all the world.

That was about 7:15.

The police put the Amber alert on the TV a moment or two after 8.

Mom came out of the nursing home with her present in her hand and the car was gone and she laughed and was a little irritated and thought that this was an odd practical joke to play on the boss. But it wasn't any joke and nobody knew anything about it and there she stood, outside in the cold, with no car and no keys and no baby.

Elizabeth Kate was gone. Six weeks and maybe no more.

It happens as regular as clockwork.

A ditz with a baby in the backseat takes a powder and leaves the car unlocked, usually with the keys in the ignition, often still running. You've read about it in the paper and seen it in your life. Out in front of the convenience store, in the neighbor's driveway, in the parking lot at the mall.

A car and a kid and an opportunity.

Which must be how the crook saw it. Some guy whose name we don't yet know. Some one of the myriad of predators in our society, on the prowl for a target of opportunity.

Like Elizabeth Kate on a silver platter.

Car thieves who realize they're kidnappers when they squeal away and turn to look and see what's in the back seat. Car thieves who mostly are just car thieves, and don't want anything to do with other people's kids. Thankfully. But someday the molesters will learn that mommy's car is as good a place to troll as the Internet or the playground.

The cops were on it hard and fast and the balloon went up and the signs on the Interstate started running the alert and the TV broke into its programming. While somewhere a crook panicked and ditched the car and the baby and ran.

And Elizabeth Kate sat there, six weeks old, in her car seat, and the deadly chill of a Utah winter's night crept into the car to take her in its arms.

While several miles way, in the quiet warmth of his home, a man settled down to relax and watch his TV. That's when the alert went out. And he felt the darndest thing. Some nobody on the couch. A voice almost, but not a voice probably. Just an impulse, a whispering, a command.

"Go save that baby."

A stranger. At least to the people involved. But not to God. And apparently not to God's voice. Some things can be heard with good ears, but other things require a pure heart, a spirit worthy to receive, a life practiced in hearing and obeying the divine.

"Go save that baby."

And he was up and after his coat, and he stopped just long enough to pray, just long enough to ask God to lead him to that baby.

We don't know how it went after that. The man wants his privacy and the police aren't saying, but over the next 10 or 15 minutes he apparently turned this way and that, led by the Spirit, out of his neighborhood and down the road a few miles into the next city to the big mall and an upper parking terrace on the south side.

To Elizabeth Kate.

Hundreds of cars, thousands of possibilities, in a metropolitan area of a million.

And he drove right to the spot.

He said he was led.

And he got her in time. He won the race with cold and death. He did what he was told to do.

Sometimes we are dumb, and sometimes we are evil, and sometimes God saves us from ourselves.

Like he saved Elizabeth Kate.

This is the story of an idiot, a crook and a saint.

And of the God who is father of them all.

Three

I pledge allegiance

I pledge allegiance to the flag of the United States of America.
And to the Republic for which it stands.
One nation under God.
Indivisible.
With liberty and justice for all.

And I pledge allegiance to a lot more than that. I pledge allegiance to my country and to my countrymen. I pledge allegiance to the soldiers, sailors, airmen and Marines who right now are standing between us and evil.

I pledge allegiance to the notion that we are all free and equal, that whether you came here on the *Mayflower* or a slave ship, as a refugee or a reject, a great hero or a nameless nobody, you are an American. And you are my brother or sister. And we are family. And nobody crosses us.

I pledge allegiance to the cab drivers and the waitresses, the firemen and the cops, the nurses and the teachers. The withered old people clinging to life and the squawking babies still pasty from their mothers' wombs. The people at computers and standing at assembly lines. The moms and dads, sons and daughters, the families who are the backbone of this land.

I pledge allegiance to the farmers in their fields, and amidst their herds and great orchards. The men and women who feed the world and turn nature's bounty and raw materials into the fullest supermarkets and bellies on the planet. Who produce in such abundance that the poorest of the poor eat well and the starving of the globe open relief boxes stamped with the American flag.

I pledge allegiance to two hundred and some years of doing it our way. Of conquering a continent and wrestling it into productivity and kneeling in gratitude to the God who made it all possible. I pledge allegiance to the faith of our fathers, spoken in different ways but offered up with like sincerity. To the churches and synagogues and mosques. Wherever good people learn love at the Creator's hand.

I pledge allegiance to the Founding Fathers and to their vision. To the Constitution they wrote and the nation they forged. To Washington and Adams, Jefferson and Madison, Lincoln and Roosevelt, Truman and Reagan. To Clara Barton and Frederick Douglass, Luther Burbank and Meriwether Lewis, Thomas A. Edison and John M. Browning, Dwight David Eisenhower and Harriet Beecher Stowe. To all who have gone before and done so with greatness, known to the world or consigned to obscurity. Who have contributed to the nation I love.

I pledge allegiance to the Congress of the United States, and the presidency, and the various legislatures and executives of the sundry states and municipalities. To the notion that our voices together select our leaders and laws, that through accountable intermediaries we govern ourselves, from the school down the street to the Capitol in Washington. I pledge allegiance to the courts, where justice is blind and the standing is equal, where the murderer and his victim find justice and representation before the might of the people. Where a nation of laws serves a nation of rulers.

I pledge allegiance to the future, and to the nation we will give our children. We will work to leave it as prosperous, free and strong as we received it. To give as good as we got, to bequeath our descendents a land as great as the one delivered to us by our ancestors.

I pledge allegiance to the force of arms against our enemies and attackers. I will fight in any and every way to protect my nation, its interests and people, be that in the arena of opinion and public attitude, or on the field of battle. I pledge allegiance to the notion that American victory must be unequivocal and absolute, that no weapon or means should be spared to protect this nation and that no consideration should be allowed to temper the fury of our defense. Those who attack us must surrender unconditionally, or be annihilated.

I pledge allegiance to the flag of the United States of America.

And to the Republic for which it stands.
One nation under God.
Indivisible.
With liberty and justice for all.
And I pledge allegiance to a lot more than that.

A day that will live in infamy

So many people spoke of Pearl Harbor and the day that will live in infamy. Of how that historical hell was surpassed in a morning in similar fashion.

With kamikaze pilots against the symbols of our land.

Of death dealt to the innocent by the darkest of the dark. By the killers of the young and weak and pure. A brilliant and simple plan from the chambers of evil's heart.

And we watched on live television.

An accident, for a moment we believed, like that Army bomber at the Empire State Building, with flame and smoke and, "Oh, my God!" And the silhouette of a plane, banking hard, and then a fireball and a sick feeling and a shock that most people never know, shared instantly, by tens of millions in front of their TVs.

They blew it up, live on the satellite.

Oh, my God indeed.

A day that will live in infamy.

The Pearl Harbor of our generation, only 10 or 50 times as bad, a new "Arizona" hit and burned and sunk. And a pall hangs over Gotham and the home of the free and the brave. A great white cloud of fire and destruction, ignited by hate and fueled by trust. We lived like men and the savages have gone for our throats.

A day that will live in infamy.

December 7, 1941. That's what it made us think of. Of the last sneak attack. Of the last time some no-nut bastards were too cowardly to take us on man-to-man. Of the last time vile infidels spat in our face. The last time some deranged subhmans prayed to their pagan gods and went thirsting for American blood.

And this time it may be in the tens of thousands. A small city of Americans killed. A year of the Vietnam War crammed into an hour and a half. Depending on how many got out and got away before the great monument of the 1970s came sloughing to the ground, a thundercloud of evil spreading from Manhattan across the globe.

The most casualties sustained in combat in one day in American history. More than Guadalcanal and Iwo Jima and D-Day and Gettysburg and Antietam Creek.

A day that will live in infamy.

The first enemy assault on the American homeland since the War of 1812. A new page in our history.

A day that will live in infamy.

December 7, 1941. That's what they all said. It was just like then.

Except that then wasn't just then. Then was the beginning. And it was inextricably tied to the end.

To August 6, 1945. To the day America returned the favor. The day the world learned you don't mess with the red, white and blue. The day the sneak attack came home to roost. The day America might buy American security.

That is the date we look forward to now. The new day of payback. The day of justice and accounting. The day we blow them to hell.

In a flash of light with munitions from a plane, or in the heavy bombardment of offshore guns, or in the nasty bite of a .45 through the head. They have tried to beard the lion in its den, and it will now rise up and devour them.

Cause somebody's going to burn for this.

Not some trial in three years with polite arguments at the Hague, not with blustering press conferences, not with hollow rantings at the United Nations, but with cold steel and hot lead. This was an act of war. It must be responded to with an act of war, ruthless and savage war.

Somebody's got to pay for this, just on principle. Somebody's got to be pounded good. Not a surgical strike, not a commando raid, but blood for blood, life for life. Not as an act of vengeance exclusively, but as an act of prevention and protection, because the failure to retaliate and demonstrate national rage and power will do nothing but invite further violence and attack. We must declare war on terrorism, on all terrorism and all terrorists; they are all our enemies. And we must physically destroy them and the nations and interests who support them.

If you do not repay the defiler of your home, if you do not recompense him fivefold for his violation, you have surrendered. You have empowered and enticed him and those who would emulate him. You have shown yourself weak.

And it is only the strong who are safe.

A day that will life in infamy. September 11, 2001. Nine-one-one. They called, and we're going to answer. We will bury our dead and nurse our wounded and soon we will visit our enemies, and the jackals will pick their bones.

Because Pearl Harbor was not an end; it was a beginning. A beginning of the end of our enemies' might. Because the American spirit is not slain or wounded. It is only pricked, pricked and awakened and enraged.

We will pray and mourn and comfort, and then we will gird up our loins. And heaven help the bastards who did this.

Because their days are numbered. We didn't start this, but we're going to finish it.

And 50 years from now we will remember our dead, and piss on our enemies' graves.

Maybe it's a holy war

Perhaps in the rubble there is promise, the promise of a better nation and a better people.

Because we have been different. In our hearts, in our words, in our deeds.

We have fled to God and country, clutching each to our breast, seeking comfort there, and purpose. We have wrapped ourselves in the flag and defined ourselves by our faith.

We have been humbled and scared.

Or emboldened and heartened.

But either way it has been around the same themes. God and country.

In the shock and uncertainty, the best in us came out, the nobility of citizenship became evident, the goodness of America was on display.

Unsuspected qualities came to define us.

So we bought up all the flags and we filled up all the churches and old divisions faded away. The issues and partisanships of our former lives evaporated in the face of the new national brotherhood. Hillary Clinton walked arm-in-arm with Rudy Giuliani and Dick Gephardt made as much sense as John McCain, and the nation rallied behind an honest man named George W. Bush.

We are America in a new and unimagined way. We are a free people and children of God and those things seem suddenly to trump, to be all that matters and all that we cherish.

And we have to see where it goes from here.

Whether it fades and retreats in the growing comfort of a new normalcy, or if it expands and hardens into the new national definition.

And the choice is ours. As individuals and as a society. Do we embrace the new or return to the old?

This is a hope that we use current sentiment as a foundation, not a benchmark. That we build from here, not measure up to here. That this be the foot of the mountain, not the peak.

So let us hold sacred our patriotism.

Let us remember the zeal and the love. The brotherhood and bond. May the symbols of the last week, the flags and the signs and the songs, stay with us and stay fresh. May we rally behind them and continue to cherish them.

May we choke up at certain thoughts and hold true to certain virtues. May we stay American and may we stay true in the days and years that follow.

May we be forever changed for the better.

And may we be forever closer to God.

We have relied on prayer and faith in the last week as we seldom have previously. People who have held their faith private have worn it on their sleeves, and it has been a glue, a commonality, a bond between us.

Faced with the impossible, we have turned to the eternal. When nothing could protect us, we asked God to. When there was no earthly comfort, we sought the divine. And we were blessed.

And we have learned what our forefathers knew, that to be truly American is to hold close with deity, to be agents and servants and children of God. We have discovered what the founders wrote, that we are endowed by our Creator with the liberties we love.

And we have learned that true freedom comes only with fidelity to God and oneness with his will. We have learned that this is God's country and we are God's people.

Conrad Hilton said, an even 50 years ago, that "in this struggle for freedom, at home and abroad, our greatest weapon, both a sword and a shield, will be our love of and faith in God."

That was never truer than now, when the battle in which we find ourselves is so starkly and truly defined in terms of good versus evil. This is not a conflict of policies and perspectives, a matter of national interest or pride. It is about the senseless slaughter of innocents and the natural pursuit of murderers.

This is right versus wrong, good versus evil, God versus Satan. And it is our great privilege to be on the side of right, to be given by God and fate the responsibility of removing a scourge from the earth.

Our enemies have, in the name of their god, taken up the work of evil and hatred. Driven by racial and religious prejudice, and the sinister whisperings of evil, they have attacked us.

And we will fight back and win. Total victory is potentially ours.

And that victory is assured if we stay true to the God who has called us. If our turn to him in recent days is made permanent and sure.

If our lives and our motives are righteous and pure.

Like they have been the past week.

See, patriotism and faith, in this matter, are not different things. They are an equal commitment to what is right. We love America not because we are jingoistic or arrogant, but because it is God's gift to us, a gift of liberty and plenty and love. A gift for which we are grateful.

A gift he has called upon us to defend.

As a beacon to the world, and as a birthright to our children.

We have changed in all this.

And it has been for the better. We have rallied around our flag, and we have rallied around our God.

To our nation's defenders

Dear Troop,

It's time to pack up and go. Time to leave crying babies and dazed children and spouses keeping a stiff upper lip.

Yesterday you were a citizen, today you are a soldier.

Or a sailor or an airman or a Marine.

Yesterday was peace and today is war.

And you have been activated. Mobilized. Called to arms. And it's not about drill anymore, or two weeks of annual training. It's not a part-time job; it is a commitment. And it's time to pay up.

In a way your fellow citizens can't begin to understand and can only partially appreciate. You will put on the boots and load up the duffle bag and they will see the story in the paper and not quite comprehend it.

Not like you will.

And not like your loved ones will.

This is where the rubber meets the road. And you're picking up the tab. This is the price of freedom. Bought with tears and uncertainty and maybe blood.

Your relationships will suffer, your bank account will suffer, your career and education will suffer. It's all on hold and you're not in control anymore. You've got orders. You belong to Uncle Sam. You are a G.I.

And you are all that stands between home and hell.

Because this is not a drill. You're not going on an exercise. You're making a stand at Concord Bridge. You're taking the hill at Gettysburg. You're going ashore at Normandy. You're drawing the line in the sand.

And nobody gets past you.

No more nine-eleven. Not on your watch. Not while you wear the uniform. Not while you've got breath and two strong hands.

The giant is awakened and he's got your name embroidered on his uniform.

So go. And Godspeed.

Know that we will keep faith with you and with what you are doing. Know that, though the politicians my ramble and rage, and play games with sacred things, the people of the United States—the United States itself—will never desert you or forget you.

You will always be in our hearts and in our prayers. In the darkest night and bleakest circumstance. You are never alone, and what wounds you wounds us all. The scars of battle and the scars of separation.

You are never alone.

And you should not fret. Your fears are natural, but you are their master. You are an American.

And Americans go to war with a jaunty air. With their heads held high and their chests thrust out and with a confidence that is born not of arrogance, but of certainty that our cause is just, that our victory is certain and that our destiny is great.

You are leaving your home and all its joys and responsibilities. The world you have created for yourself has been put aside and will have to make do without you. America is your family now, and its heart your home.

And your country says, "Thank you."

Think about that. Let it sink in. The land of your birth. The land of your people. The land which has made you one of the freest citizens the world has ever known. The land which has given you an education and a dazzling prosperity and the benefit of a society of peace and decency.

That country, which has given you so much, wants to express its gratitude—to you.

Thank you.

For preserving its promise. For renewing its meaning. For paying the tab on the next generation's blessings. For guaranteeing that the holy experiment began more than two centuries ago continues a success.

George Washington answered when he was called, and so have you. You have accepted the title of defender of the free and vanquisher of the evil. Babies will sleep safely at night and family homes will be undisturbed because of the effort into which you are now inducted.

Ancient and modern evils will be held at bay and the American homeland will be preserved because of you and the cause which now claims you.

You have embarked on an errand of history and someday classrooms and grandchildren may well speak of your exploits. Your service will be sacred. To the family you love, the nation you serve and the God you obey.

It's time to pack up and go. Time to leave crying babies and dazed children and spouses keeping a stiff upper lip.

Yesterday you were a citizen, today you are a soldier.
Or a sailor or an airman or a Marine.
Yesterday was peace and today is war.
And you have been activated. Mobilized. Called to arms.
To be your nation's defender.
Godspeed, America.

Something that didn't make the news

Maybe you'd like to hear about something other than idiot prison guards and naked Iraqis.

Maybe you'd like to hear about a real American, somebody who honored the uniform he wears.

Meet Brian Chontosh.

Churchville-Chili Central School class of 1991. Proud graduate of the Rochester Institute of Technology. Husband and about-to-be father. First lieutenant in the United States Marine Corps.

And a genuine hero.

The secretary of the Navy said so.

At 29 Palms in California Brian Chontosh was presented with the Navy Cross, one of the highest awards for combat bravery the United States can bestow.

That's a big deal.

But you won't see it on the network news, and all you read in Brian's hometown newspaper was two paragraphs of nothing. Instead, it was more blather about some mental defective MPs who acted like animals.

The odd fact about the American media in this war is that it's not covering the American military. The most plugged-in nation in the world is receiving virtually no true information about what its warriors are doing.

Oh, sure, there's a body count. We know how many Americans have fallen. And we see those same casket pictures day in and day out. And we're almost on a first-name basis with the pukes who abused the Iraqi prisoners. And we know all about improvised explosive devices and how we lost Fallujah and what Arab public-opinion polls say about us and how the world hates us.

We get a non-stop feed of gloom and doom.

But we don't hear about the heroes.

The incredibly brave GIs who honorably do their duty. The ones our grandparents would have carried on their shoulders down Fifth Avenue.

The ones we completely ignore.

Like Brian Chontosh.

It was a year ago on the march into Baghdad. Brian Chontosh was a platoon leader rolling up Highway 1 in a Humvee.

When all hell broke loose.

Ambush city.

The young Marines were being cut to ribbons. Mortars, machine guns, rocket propelled grenades. And the kid out of Churchville was in charge. It was do or die and it was up to him.

So he moved to the side of his column, looking for a way to lead his men to safety. As he tried to poke a hole through the Iraqi line his Humvee came under direct enemy machine gun fire.

It was fish in a barrel and the Marines were the fish.

And Brian Chontosh gave the order to attack. He told his driver to floor the Humvee directly at the machine gun emplacement that was firing at them. And he had the guy on top with the .50 cal unload on them.

Within moments there were Iraqis slumped across the machine gun and Chontosh was still advancing, ordering his driver now to take the Humvee directly into the Iraqi trench that was attacking his Marines. Over into the battlement the Humvee went and out the door Brian Chontosh bailed, carrying an M16 and a Beretta and 228 years of Marine Corps pride.

And he ran down the trench.

With its mortars and riflemen, machine guns and grenadiers.

And he killed them all.

He fought with the M16 until it was out of ammo. Then he fought with the Beretta until it was out of ammo. Then he picked up a dead man's AK47 and fought with that until it was out of ammo. Then he picked up another dead man's AK47 and fought with that until it was out of ammo.

At one point he even fired a discarded Iraqi RPG into an enemy cluster, sending attackers flying with its grenade explosion.

When he was done Brian Chontosh had cleared 200 yards of entrenched Iraqis from his platoon's flank. He had killed more than 20 and wounded at least as many more.

But that's probably not how he would tell it.

He would probably merely say that his Marines were in trouble, and he got them out of trouble. Hoo-rah, and drive on.

"By his outstanding display of decisive leadership, unlimited courage in the face of heavy enemy fire, and utmost devotion to duty, 1st Lt. Chontosh reflected great credit upon himself and upheld the highest traditions of the Marine Corps and the United States Naval Service."

That's what the citation says.

And that's what nobody will hear.

That's what doesn't seem to be making the evening news. Accounts of American valor are dismissed by the press as propaganda, yet accounts of American difficulties are heralded as objectivity. It makes you wonder if the role of the media is to inform, or to depress—to report or to deride. To tell the truth, or to feed us lies.

But I guess it doesn't matter.

We're going to turn out all right.

As long as men like Brian Chontosh wear our uniform.

A note to a Coast Guardsman's little boy

Dear Tyler,

This column was written on your father's 24th birthday. On his 24th birthday, two days before his funeral.

As this is written you are a baby, an infant, just seven months old. Your mother is a new widow and the two of you are alone in the world.

As you read this you are older and you both have gone on. Life has taken you each in new and unexpected directions. Your father is a name and a photograph to you, but he is not a memory, not a memory of your own recollection.

So this is meant to tell you how it was. How it was when your father died and what people thought about it and what people thought about him.

The last part is easy.

They thought he was a hero.

They thought he died for his country, in the service of his nation and flag, on a mission to protect America's borders and patrol her waters.

His last act was one of bravery and compassion.

Bravery in that he and his shipmates were on patrol, set out in the dark to enforce the laws of the land. And compassion in that the four of them put into the mighty Niagara to be ready to help those in trouble.

He died in the service of his country and in the service of his fellow man.

And you should be as proud of him as his country was.

And do not doubt that at the time of his passing he and the other fallen Coast Guardsman were the center of the country's attention, pride and gratitude.

The day after your father and his friend died, national radio broadcasts began with the story of their overturned boat, the long night in the icy waters and the miraculous survival of their two shipmates.

The accident which claimed your father's life made the network television news and a nation responded with grief. People felt for your dad and your mom and for you. Your dad and your family were in the nation's thoughts and prayers.

The president of the United States himself stopped at the beginning of a speech to bow his head in silence and remember your father.

Your father was a great man.

Not for how he died, but for how he lived. Because he lived decently, and he lived right. In his short life he impressed people, and served them, and made something of himself.

He went to college and he went to the Coast Guard and through his own hard work he earned the right to wear the uniform of his country. And he earned the right to have draped across his casket two days after his 24th birthday the flag of the United States of America.

Your dad didn't live long, but he lived well. And he made his mark.

He married your lovely mother and the two of them brought you into the world. And you survive him and carry on his name, and hopefully you feel the call to carry on his goodness and decency.

Your dad was a man. A good man.

And you should be one as well. You should remember his example of service and sacrifice and courage. You should remember that you have been in the prayers of the nation, that your father's friends and strangers from across America have worried for you and hoped for you.

So take strength and courage from him and them.

And maintain a connection to him. Always treasure his name and legacy in your thoughts and dreams. Listen for him and his influence in your conscience and impulse, expect him to be a part of your life.

And know that if nowhere else you will have communion with him when you yourself are a young father, and you hold his grandchild in your arms. You may be assured that as you look down at your own baby, the love you feel, the wonder and the gratitude and joy, will be an exact mirror of what he felt as he held you.

That is another thing you should know.

That he loved you. He loved you with all his heart. He was living the American dream and you and your mother were the crowning jewels.

The Coast Guard gave him a purpose and a paycheck and a way to provide for you. And he took up his duty cheerfully. The duty to country and the duty to family.

Your father was a hero.

And so are you.

Because you have sacrificed for your country as well. He lost his life, you lost your father. He paid in the night in a cold winter river. You paid over years of growing up without a dad.

You have known your nights of suffering and borne your burdens, and it has all been in the name of duty.

And your country is grateful. Grateful for your sacrifice when you were a little baby, and grateful for your sacrifice all the years since.

Your father served under a motto: *Semper paratus.* Always ready.

You may want to take a motto for yourself: *Semper recordor.* Always remember.

Always remember, young Tyler, that your daddy was a hero, that he loved you, and that he died for his country. And that he all these years has missed you as much as you have missed him.

Thank you, and God bless you.

Signed,

America

A story from down by where I grew up

SCIO, NY—This is a small town outside of a small town, in the hills of Western New York, where most people work with their hands and their backs.

Where the men chew tobacco and drive pick-ups, where the women make pies and babies and look after husbands who live large and loud.

It's a place so rural most Americans can't imagine it, but a place so pure most Americans can't forget it. It's the place where we all grew up, or at least the place where we all dreamed of growing up, watching Mayberry or reading Huckleberry, skipping school to splash in the creek and run barefoot through the fields.

It's that kind of place. The land of the free and the home of the brave.

And they had a funeral here.

Up at the gym where the Tigers play. At least a thousand came, to hear the talks and see the casket rest underneath the basketball hoop. Then most of them walked the couple hundred yards up to the cemetery to see the Marines fire the guns and fold the flag.

It was the biggest thing ever to happen around here.

From all accounts, he was a great kid. Nice to people, not stuck up about his good looks or athletic ability. He was popular in school, where his mother teaches, and knew most of the younger kids in town because he'd babysat them one time or another. And in a place like Scio—pronounced sigh-oh, with the accent on the first syllable—it seems everybody knows everybody.

He wanted to go to college, but he didn't have the grades for it. So he went in the Marine Corps.

That's an easy thing to say—"He went in the Marine Corps"—but people who've never done it can't begin to understand what it means. To lie in bed at the position of attention and sing the Marines Hymn every night at boot camp, to wear arguably the most honored uniform in the world, to be part of something larger and more noble than yourself. It gets into you.

And it got into him.

At least that's what you figure from what happened.

It was in Karbala on check-point duty. There had been an attack on a convoy and things were a little tense and the 22-year-old from Scio was large and in charge, a squad leader with some cars to stop and some Marines to protect and, out of nowhere, one of these Iraqi guys starts running. Out of a car and away like crazy and the Scio kid was on him. The big farm boy fighting for somebody else's freedom and from what the report said the Iraqi turned and let loose with a grenade.

In a movie, things would go into slow motion at a time like that. The rolling grenade, no pin, the Iraqi, your two buddies, all kind of slow on the screen. But life is never slow motion, there's never time to think or calculate, there's only time to act. You do what you do.

The cemetery in Scio stretches back from the main street up a side hill. The oldest graves are near the road and the newest graves are higher up, in the rear, above the level of the town. From the back of the cemetery, near where the mound of daisies and asters, roses and carnations, lies fresh and alone, you can look back down the hill and across the road to a house with two flags—one for the country and one for the corps.

It was a split-second, really, one of those split-seconds we remember for an eternity, when something so singular and sacred is done that the world stops and notices. Or maybe it doesn't. Maybe there are just a few, and the angels in heaven.

It was the grenade and the Iraqi and the buddies and he threw himself on it.

They were his men and he was the corporal and he was a Marine and he was an American and he grew up in Scio and he threw himself on it.

And he was so strong it took him eight days to die.

That was at Bethesda Naval Hospital with his parents at his side. He never regained consciousness.

Somebody posted this on a website about what happened:

"There is only one word for a man who would throw himself on a grenade to save his squad—

"Marine."

His two buddies made it through. Because he used his body to shield them.

Because that's what a man does.

That's what an American fighting man does.

From a place like Scio.

Where this weekend there were yellow ribbons on the trees around the school, and on the utility poles, leading up to the cemetery with the mound of fresh flowers.

And the little metal marker from the funeral home.

Cpl Jason L. Dunham, 1982—2004.

One morning at Parma Union Cemetery

The baby was in the tent, next to the grave, and the bugler was by the honor guard, behind the rows of firemen in their dress uniforms.

Two lines of paratroopers had lifted the flag from the casket and folded it into a triangle and ceremoniously handed it to the general.

There was silence. The slightest rustle of a January breeze and the distant passing of cars on country roads, but essentially there was silence.

Two and a half hours after the funeral began, some 300 were gathered there at the cemetery, bundled against the cold, most with tears on their faces.

And from the quiet of their grief there arose simultaneously two plaintive, inconsolable sounds.

The bugler playing "Taps" and the month-old baby crying.

One bid farewell to a comrade, the other bid farewell to a father.

The priest had said something about Afghanistan. That was back at St. Elizabeth Ann Seton Church, after "Amazing Grace" had been sung and Uncle Jim had read from Ecclesiastes and Aunt Linda had read from Revelation. "A time to be born and a time to die" and "He will wipe every tear from their eyes."

There was a responsive song and a choir song and the priest stood up. He was a good priest and he had a good spirit and he talked about the last time he saw him. He had been sitting on the left side of the sanctuary, in July, where his family always sat, proud of his Army uniform and happy with his life.

It was a perfectly pressed green uniform, with honor cords on each arm, and silver jump wings, a Combat Infantry Badge, PFC stripes and the proud patch of the 82nd Airborne. On his feet he had spit-shined jump boots. Just like the ones his Army friends wore to the funeral.

"Today he comes back for the final time," the priest said. His "tour of duty is over."

Then Aunt Abby led the prayer and Aunt Karen stood up to talk about him on behalf of the family.

She said he was a "go big or go home kind of guy," a firstborn son and a first grandchild. "He was born with a battery inside him that didn't need recharging." As a little boy, when Grandma gave him a timeout on the couch, she made him sit on his hands so he'd hold still. When he was 3 he pulled the fire alarm at the library.

When he was a soldier on a parachute jump, he called his father on a cell phone, hanging in midair under the canopy, to share the thrill of the descent with home.

It was random recollections, snatches of life that gave witness to his nature.

He collected Hess trucks, liked to drive fast, had blue eyes and he loved a dog named Duchess. Trying to impress his family with a magic trick, he accidentally handcuffed himself to a tree. Summoned to help, his father instead went back inside to get the video camera.

They had to move the trampoline away from the house so he wouldn't jump onto it from the second-story window.

He wanted to have four children, just like his parents. He had a habit of telling members of his family, every time he saw them, that he loved them.

Every Sunday morning the family gathered at the Golden Boys restaurant, three generations, all enjoying breakfast. It was a tradition. Like the military. That was three generations, too.

"I stand here so proud of how he turned out," Aunt Karen said. "He'd want us to live our lives and have fun."

As she spoke there were two large stone facades behind her, at the front of the sanctuary. When the church was built, members gathered stone from their farms and yards and brought them to adorn their church. As a boy he helped haul that stone with his dad.

The same dad who saw the two soldiers walking up the sidewalk. At first he thought they were Reserve recruiters come to visit his younger son. Then he saw the crosses on the chaplain's uniform. And he knew. But it's got to be done just so and the officer read a letter from the government and trembled as he did so.

Then the dad excused himself to call his wife and tell her that her son was dead in the war.

After the priest incensed the casket and another hymn was sung, the pallbearers took their friend out the back and the family followed and while deputies watched and veterans saluted a mile-long line of cars formed and set out for the half-hour drive to the cemetery.

There were various honors along the way. One old man simply got out of his car and held a salute as the long line passed. In his hometown, scores of firefighters and their vehicles stood at attention on both sides of the road, with their lights flashing, a giant American flag suspended between two aerial trucks in an arch of honor. A couple of homes had yellow ribbons, many had American flags, one down the road from the cemetery had a silk banner in the window with three stars—one for every member of the family serving in the war zone.

He was one of those stars. The other two were his cousins. The banner hangs in his grandmother's window.

And just down the row from where he was buried, next to the headstone of a 5-year-old named Tyler, was a holiday picture of a family of snowmen bedecked in red, white and blue with the words "United We Stand."

And united they stood in silence while they listened to the baby and bugle. Then the bugle stopped and it was just the baby. Just the baby and their thoughts.

Then the general bent down and offered his parents the folded flag on behalf of a grateful nation. A few minutes later, the congressman would give them another one, in a Plexiglas presentation case, and he would give them a hug. And the young firemen would walk away in tears.

While the honor guard from the 82nd stood at parade rest in the winter cold.

A half an hour later the cemetery would be empty except for the man who fills in the grave and takes down the tent.

Jason Hasenauer was 21.

He died in the service of his country.

A note to World War II veterans

Thank you, my friends, and good-bye.

I know it is premature, but I want to say it. And I want to say it while you are still alive to hear it.

To those of you who fought World War II: Thank you, and Godspeed.

From my generation to yours, we send our gratitude, admiration and respect. As your time on this earth fades and you go to the next life before us, please know that your great valor and vigor are known and remembered.

The time moves so quickly.

As a boy, I remember they were all vets, all the men I knew. All the older men had been in your war or in Korea or had been alive during that era. They had all fought or served and the VFW and the Legion were the biggest places in town.

But 20 or 30 years later time has worked its work and most of those men are dead, the ones I knew, all gone and the world has changed. There is no more telling of the memories they held so close or of the experiences they worked so hard to forget.

Like my stepfather.

There were two wars for him and which one you heard about depended on how much he had been drinking. If he was a little drunk you heard about the stolen ambulance and the parties in liberated Paris and the pretty French girls.

But if he had been drinking a lot you heard about how the glider came apart as it slammed into the Normandy countryside and how most of the men died around him there and then he would put his head down on his folded arms and sob.

That was the war for him.

And for the other millions it was something different.

But he is in the ground now, beneath the little brass plate the government sends out to veterans. And as you walk through the cemetery where he lies, you see dozens of similar plates above other combatants from his war.

All gone, awaiting their comrades.

And soon there will be none left.

In another 30 years there will be a macabre vigil as America waits for the last World War II veteran to pass away. It will be a handful and then a few and then two, in nursing homes probably, visited by reporters on their birthdays.

And then it will be one and then it will be none.

And then it will be too late, and now it is already almost too late. So many are gone, so much is forgotten.

Just know that we understand.

A third generation has arisen since the war, and since the might and men of America set the world aright. Many of you have great-grandchildren now, little tots whose lives and prosperity are better because of what doddering old men did as strapping boys.

Please know that we recognize what you did and value it, and are awed by it.

History asked tremendous things of your era and generation, and you did not shirk. You stood as bravely as Americans ever have, as bravely as Gettysburg, as bravely as Valley Forge.

And you stood as victoriously as Americans ever have.

You materially changed the history of the world, bringing down two supposed dynasties on two separate continents. You freed tens of millions of people from oppression and averted slaughter that bordered on and became extermination.

You liberated more than a dozen countries, preserving them as national identities, defending them when they had failed to do so themselves.

There is a France today because of you.

And a Great Britain and a Philippines and an Algeria. And so many others.

And we do not yet know the end of your good works. Because your might was not merely at the point of a rifle, it was also by the power of example.

And the future will study the Second World War as fervently as the past and present have studied the Civil War. Your courage and capacity will be spoken of and remembered, and at some future time when the American spirit is challenged, your country will take inspiration from your achievements.

Another generation will rise in need of heroes, and you will be those heroes. Both the big names and the small names. The ones learned in history class and the ones learned around the dinner table.

You saved us once. It is completely possible your good example will save us again.

And for both, I thank you.

While I can.

While we are both still here.

While your great generation still walks the earth.

Please remember, as your time comes to pass away, how grateful we all are to you. How proud we are of you and how great you have been, for our country and for mankind.

So God be with you.

As he has been all these years.

Thank you, my friends, and good bye.

Four

The only Christmas I remember

In the first-grade we were poor, in a house with three other families on a busy street a few blocks from school.

And it was Christmas.

I knew that. But I didn't know we were poor. You don't know those things when you're in the first-grade.

When you're in the first-grade and you sit in class with rounded scissors cutting strips of construction paper and gluing them around one another into hoops and eventually a long, multi-colored chain that you string around the tree your teacher brought to class. You don't know much then.

Only what your mother tells you.

And mine told me not to get my hopes up. She told me that Santa might not be able to stop. That he might be busy, and might have to come to our house later.

And that we couldn't have a Christmas tree.

It must have hurt her to tell me that. I know it hurt me to hear it. It disappointed me. And she told me not to be sad, that something would work out.

She was 24 then, and her second baby was about six months old. My little brother Sean who slept beneath me. Beneath me in a box on the bottom bunk in a closet with a brown folding door.

She said something would work out and one night she popped popcorn and opened a bag of cranberries and we sat there with needle and thread stringing them into garlands to drape around our apartment. Mostly she strung and mostly I played with the thimble. Played with the thimble and ate the popcorn and marveled at how beautiful it was.

There was a party the last day of school. The last day of school before Christmas. A party with games and songs and cookies and at 3:30 a bell to go home. It was raining that day and I had a little sweater that zipped and I got it off the hook as the other children did the same.

And the teacher stood in the middle of the room and said something about the tree. Something about how if anybody wanted it they could have it. And I stood there with the long sleeve of my shirt bunched up near the shoulder of my sweater and I looked at her. It was a green sweater and my grandmother 3,000 miles away had made it and sent it to me in the mail.

And I looked at her and for a moment I wasn't shy. And I walked up to her and I said it matter of factly.

My mother said we can't afford a Christmas tree. We're not going to have one.

And then I stood there. And she looked down at me and didn't say anything for a moment and I figured she must have been thinking. Then it looked like she was choking a little bit and she coughed or cleared her throat and she said that I could have it.

Back then they nailed wood on the bottom of Christmas trees, an X, so they would stand up. And I grabbed that X at about hip level and pulled the tree the best I could out the front door of the school, the wind quickly catching it and rolling it halfway in my hands while the little construction paper ornaments, secured with pieces of yarn, flapped madly in the breeze. I had looped the multi-colored chain around my neck.

And it was raining.

And I was about as happy as I've ever been.

And I set out, pulling that tree along the sidewalk, a step or two and then a stop, lurching it bit by bit against the wind and the hill and the fact that it was big and I was small.

And at the corner I stood breathing hard and unsure, the cars passing quickly on the street I needed to cross, my halting progress so slow. I was there a while. And a couple of cars back at the stop sign a guy watched me. And when it was his turn at the intersection he put it in park and opened his door, one of those long sleek doors that swept back to the line of the fin on the rear of the car, and walked over and grabbed my hand and the trunk of the tree and took us both across the street.

After that it was just one more block and I was home, my sweater mostly soaked through and the construction paper gone limp and torn in the weather.

Usually my mother was at work, and she was that day, and on those days I went inside and watched TV until she or my step-father came home. But I didn't that day. I stood outside chilled, with our Christmas tree, unable to get it through the door alone, unwilling to leave it outside unattended.

And I was about as happy as I've ever been.

On Christmas Eve day we were home and someone came knocking at the door. Two or three men, I think, from my teacher's church, they said, and they had boxes. Big cardboard boxes. Two of them. In one I caught a glimpse of something colorful before my step-father shushed me away and he carried it to his bedroom. In the other there were potatoes and vegetables and a canned ham, one of those with the clear gelatin that tastes so good and salty.

And a little while after that he brought out a string of lights from his bedroom, the old kind that screwed in, and strung them around the tree and as dusk came on he plugged them in and we turned out the living room lights and sat there in the red, green and blue glow.

I could see it from my bunk in the closet. Not the tree, not all of it, but the glow. It seemed to fill the room. I lay there awake as long as I could, sent to bed so Santa could come, and only closed my eyes for what seemed like a minute. But in that minute he came and as I awoke I could see the presents in the predawn, out past the edge of the tree into the middle of the livingroom floor.

And I slipped down the bunk and got my brother out of his box and ran shouting to my parents' bedroom so that they could come see what Santa had done.

In the first-grade we were poor, in a house with three other families on a busy street a few blocks from school.

And it was Christmas.

And I was about as happy as I've ever been.

Out on Willow Bend Road

I was 11, a weak child, when we lived in the trailer out on Willow Bend Road.

It was after Carl died and before the flood and we'd gotten the trailer with the life insurance money, a 14-foot-wide Marlatt on cinder blocks where the barn had stood.

I was 11 and the other three were younger and in the night I would play records to keep the monsters away.

It was different back then, before tapes and CDs, back then there were records, great flat black platters, their grooves a sheen in the quiet light. They were show tunes, some kind of *Reader's Digest* collection, maybe a dozen of them in paper sleeves in a binder. Ethel Merman and Gene Kelly and Paul Robeson. And after I got the others asleep I would stack them as high as I could, on the spindle rising up from the middle of the turntable, as many as the changer would hold and then maybe one or two more, aligning the holes so that as the stack clacked down they would settle around the spindle and take their turn under the needle.

Extending my protection.

Keeping back the night.

Out on Willow Bend Road.

The trailer creaked in the wind and settled and weeds blew against it and I could hear the mice as they snuck across the kitchen counters, and the records wouldn't drown it out, and the toilet ran and that made the pump kick on and there were a million sounds and I knew all the songs in order and I knew which album was last and as the songs counted down I knew when there would be no more click and falling record and the music would stop and it would just be the night.

In the top bunk in the first room down the hall. A kitchen and a living room and a bedroom and a bedroom and a bathroom and a bedroom, all in a line, no left or right, just one way or the other. In the top bunk in the first room down the hall with the covers tucked over my head and feet I was 11, a weak child, trying hard to fall asleep before the records stopped.

And I would awaken when they came home, laughing or stumbling or yelling angrily, a little past 1, a two-mile drive after closing time, and they would curse the playing records and come to the first room of bunks and flick on the light and I would pretend I was asleep, taking care not to swallow or flicker my eyes, until they moved on down the hall, him to the bathroom and her to the bedroom unless there was beer in the house in which case they would sit in the kitchen and drink it.

And he would fall asleep slumped forward on the table until morning or lumber off to bed, thudding against the walls as he passed, and she would turn the lights off and come behind him, leaning her head into the first bedroom to whisper, "Good night." I always responded, "See you in the morning," and she answered, "Sleep well," and I would anxiously repeat, "See you in the morning."

And she would say, "See you in the morning" and I took it as a promise.

That I would see her in the morning. That there would be a morning.

That nothing was going to end.

She was 30 then, but she had already learned that things do end. Everything ends. And it usually ends up ashes. The best you can do is hold on.

So she drank to forget the dead husband on the floor and he drank to forget how his buddies died in France and I just kept playing the records louder and louder.

Out on Willow Bend Road.

And some things never change.

From the house on Third Street

The chairs in the dining room were old and dark and graceful, and to me as a kid they were a marvel.

A circle of sedate respectability, second-hand from another era, in the middle of my life.

There were probably six or eight at the start, expertly turned and joined and sitting there genteel and worthy. A testament to an existence in which beauty mattered.

They were strangers in our home.

Out of place, and I guess, looking back, ill fated.

I think two had been broken by the time of the peanut butter.

Mostly they splintered when the shouting broke into mad, slapping wrestling and together they fell over against the table or a chair, and slipping back the wood cracked beneath them.

A clear high pop that carried to the bedrooms above.

Everything carried to the bedrooms above. Certainly the noise, and usually the fight.

And the foaming hatred and the monotony of blows that came in a flagging thud, thud, thud against your back or your arm or sometimes your head. There was a humiliation in crying that was the unspoken objective, and you knew it would feed and grow until you cried, but you resisted anyway.

And the next morning at breakfast there would be one less chair.

It was always in pieces outside the back door and come Friday it would go in the bonfire.

And you walked home from school in the afternoon hoping they were at the bar and that somehow they would have enough money to stay there until you all were in bed and could pretend you were asleep and lay there immobile until they passed out.

The peanut butter was there a long time.

There was a shelf on the wall with lanterns and models and knick knacks, and one night in a fury of profanity a big glass jar was thrown. And its shards stuck in the wall and splattered across its face.

And it stayed that way.

In that room with the chairs.

We were taken to an uncle's house one night when the .22 was fired, and we weren't there long but the cops kept the guns for a while anyway. I never saw where the bullet went but they talked about it for months.

Like the time when they were in the backyard and he was on top choking her and we were all shrieking and I ran to my tackle box and got a folding filet knife with a yellow plastic handle and ran back and told him to stop.

He did but that was the beginning of the end.

Not long after was the only fight of my life and I held him back and grappled him down and had to leave after that.

But that was almost 35 years ago and I seldom think about it anymore.

Except lately it's been harder to ignore. I seem to see reminders everywhere. Saturday night on *Cops* there was a screaming mother who brought it back and Sunday, while I was doing the dishes, there was a call on the scanner for an ambulance in East Rochester, to the scene of a family dispute.

And while I stood there at the sink wondering what that ambulance would find I thought about those chairs.

There were just two when I moved out, and on the odd Sunday when I came back for dinner, I would sit in one and he would sit in the other.

And then there was one and years later when I came to visit there were none. They each in turn were piled outside the back door and consumed in the bonfire.

The bonfire that burns all things tender.

But like I said, that was almost 35 years ago, and I guess it's silly to waste time mourning a bunch of chairs.

Though I do it anyway.

I tried to kill myself once

I tried to kill myself once.

I was 12.

I went out one winter morning and laid down in a snow bank.

I got the idea from Jack London, who coincidentally had killed himself. But I didn't know that then. All I knew was what I'd read in school from that story about building a fire. It's way up in the Yukon or Klondike or Alaska or someplace like that, and some guy's caught out in a blizzard and the killer cold and when he fails to build a fire to warm himself he freezes to death.

It said that it was just like falling asleep.

So I went out early one Saturday and laid down in the snow and waited to fall asleep.

There's no point in going over the details. But it was a tough time. What could go wrong had and I couldn't see any way out.

When you're young you lack the perspective of time, the certain knowledge that everything passes, that there's always a tomorrow and that if you can just tough it out until then, you'll be OK. Even if it is just a metaphorical tomorrow, a new day that doesn't dawn for months or even years.

But when you're young you don't know that.

Or when you're confused. When things look like they're going to crap.

It's always a failure of perspective. When people get in trouble like that, it's not a comment on their circumstance, it's a comment on their perspective. Nobody ever killed themselves because their problems were bad, they killed themselves because their perspective was bad. Because they couldn't imagine things on the other side of the hill, because they couldn't see that the hell in which they found themselves was temporary and survivable.

But my problems were significant to me.

And I had exhausted my options, and there really didn't seem to be any other way out, no way to escape.

I was wrong, of course, but that's where perspective comes in. My situation was not impossible. The danger was that I didn't know that.

So I went out and laid in the snow.

It was a hard winter day, one of those raw windy days with the winter sun at its odd angle, casting everything in stark, contrasty shadows and lights. I went out into a sometimes swampy area on the farm where my mother had grown up, maybe a hundred yards from the trailer where she and her new husband sat transitioning from coffee to beer.

I can't remember what I had for a coat but I wore a knit hat and mittens my grandmother had given me for Christmas.

And I just laid there, waiting to fall asleep.

It was an odd time for thought. I imagined them finding me there, maybe it would be the troopers or the volunteer firemen, and I played out scenarios about how much everyone would miss me when I was gone.

And I went over and over again in my head the wrongs which had been done me, feeling that I was the most misused of little boys, and listing the woes and reversals, the heartbreaks of my time on earth, waiting to get drowsy.

Which I never really did.

I just got cold, and shivered pretty good.

And then I'd stop, and later I'd start again, and it would go away and return and I'd be sure that sleepiness would be just around the corner, that certainly in another few minutes I would doze off, like in the story, and be free.

I was as sad and as resigned as I could be.

But I just wouldn't die.

And the morning stretched into midday and some flurries fell and the sun shone straight on me and I shivered less and eventually it arched over from my left to my right, riding down till it rested atop and then slid behind the hill behind my grandmother's farm.

Chickadees occasionally flitted through the bull thistles and goldenrod that grew around me.

I shivered some more and my muscles ached from it and I was hungry, and as the early dusk settled and darkened I sat up and stood and brushed the snow from my clothes and followed my tracks back to the trailer and up the steps to the door.

And my problems weren't any different. In fact, they got worse over the years that followed. A lot of things were worse over the years that followed.

But I never tried to kill myself again.

It just never made sense again, not like it did that day.

Looking back, I think I learned some things that day laying in the snow. I learned how irresistibly vital life is, how very much things want to live. Including me. It was some instinct of body and function that neither I nor the winter cold could will away.

I also began to understand the link between sorrow and selfishness, the tendency we all have to lick our wounds, to seek the consolation of feeling sorry for ourselves. I learned to be suspicious of the comfort of pain. I learned that you don't get very far in life worrying about your problems.

You have to push on. You have to persist and prevail.

You have to take it. You have to take it and come out the other side, still upright and moving under your own power.

The cold didn't embrace me that day. It didn't lull me into a numbing sleep, to take me away from the things that hurt.

Rather, it kicked the hell out of me. It made me shiver and quake, and bit at my fingers and toes and cheeks and nose and made them swell and crack. It grabbed me and stung me and cramped me and left my teeth chattering.

And after eight hours I knew it couldn't beat me.

So I got up and went in the trailer.

I tried to kill myself once.

I was 12.
I wanted a hug, and got a slap in the head instead.
Which was just what I needed.

What I would give my mother

If my mom were alive, I know what I'd give her.
Forgiveness.
I'd tell her I understood, that I was wrong, that it wasn't her fault, and that I forgave her.
I'd tell her that I had grown up.
But she is not alive, and she died before I caught on. Before I had lived long enough to know that parents are people, not gods.
Children believe they are the center of the universe, that it's all about them. And some people never really stop being children. I probably have been one of those people. For years and years I understood my raising as I remembered it—as a child, with all of the selfishness and none of the compassion.
When I was young, things were hard. They stayed that way and I left when I was 16.
And I left angry. I left firm in the belief that my mother was a failure. That she had neglected me and raised me wrong. For a time, the whole point of my life was to get away from her, and to be whatever she wasn't.
For a time, the whole point of my life was me. For a very long time.
She was 18 when I was born, dumped by a husband who ran to the Army and never came back. Alone with a baby in an Appalachian hill town, a 10th-grade dropout with a domineering mother and nowhere to live and a mushrooming mental illness. For three years I was shipped from relative to relative and then she got me and we drove to California, as okies, so she could wait tables.
Then some more relatives and finally, in the first grade, with her and her new husband in a fourplex where we could see Watts burn. There was no money and one year we moved 11 times, each time the rent came due, picking up and going to a new school and a new neighborhood and a new set of fears.

Then one day the husband dropped dead at the kitchen table and she had four kids now, little ones, and was a widow, at 29. With the insurance she got a trailer back in New York by the creek that flooded and in a couple of years she married a drunk railroader from the trailer park next door.

He got her to drinking and soon that's all they did and most nights they came home and beat us after the bars closed.

And I felt like the world was crapping on me and I didn't think it was fair and I thought it was her job to keep it from happening and she wasn't and I grew cold toward her. I grew cold toward everything. And when I saw my chance I got the hell out and never looked back. And in a year or two I was a different person in a different world and I went months and years without thinking about her.

Or anyone.

I left brothers and a sister behind and I didn't think about them either.

I accepted it as an article of faith that life had been mean to me and it was the fault of the people in that house, and mostly her, because she was my mother.

I wasted the rest of her life thinking that way.

Closed off, self-righteous and egocentric.

But somewhere along the line I had children of my own, and I did the math on her life, and realized how young she was and where I was at those ages and I saw my own failings and how easily they came, and how innocently, and how large they were compared to hers.

And it struck like a nuclear bomb. The instant and damning realization that she had not been a demon, but that she had only been human, facing a hell of her own, and had acted as humans do. And worse, she had done it without my help.

When I had cursed her for not helping me, it had actually been she in need of my assistance. But I hadn't seen that because of juvenile selfishness. I had shirked all responsibility at the same time I loathed her for doing the same.

And in the after years, for 15 of them, as her life continued to crumble and mine continued to build, I held her to the verdict of my youth—that she had failed. That she wasn't really a mother to me. And when I could have helped her or cared about her I didn't. I instead wore my early hard life like a medal of honor.

And it has only been lately that I have realized how wrong I was. It has only been lately that I have realized how much I had wronged her.

And now I wish she were still alive.

So that I could look her in the face and tell her that I forgive her. That the grudge is gone, the anger spent, the resentment dissipated.

So that I could tell her I was wrong. That I never had a reason to be mad at her, or to judge her so harshly, that the failing was not as much of her mothering abilities, as it was of my compassion and understanding.

I wish she were still alive.

So that I could ask for her forgiveness.

I wish she were alive, so I could apologize and tell her how sorry I am.

But she is not alive, and my chance is lost.

I hope your situation is different, and that you are not as selfish.

And that you don't waste your chance.

To the guy who stole my wife's car

She doesn't want it back.

The car you stole. My wife's car. She doesn't want it back.

It was the first one that had been hers, really hers, since she was a teenager. A six-year-old Pontiac with no cup holders. Hers a month and now you've taken it.

It's violated and she's violated and right now she hates it and she hates you and she doesn't think she could sit in it without thinking of you. Even if the police get it back, she will never be comfortable in it again.

You bastard.

She graduated from college in May, wanting to be a schoolteacher, now that our youngest is a first-grader. So she got her degree and she got her certification and she got her car. She is ready for a job and so she got a job car, a used one, a small one with good mileage, after a decade of mini-vans.

And she put her change where she wanted it and she put a mirror on the visor and she rigged it to hold a can of pop and she loved the way it was hers.

But it had some problems and the first two times the dealer's mechanics took it back they didn't fix them so Sunday we took it back again, to leave it with them, like they told us to do.

It had been a great day. One of our daughters gave a talk in church and then we went off for a happy and luxurious lunch at an inn on the edge of a waterfall in the heart of a state park. Then a long family bicycle ride and the 40-mile drive to leave off the car.

On the way home we got Kentucky Fried Chicken, because it's my wife's favorite.

On Monday a mechanic went out and tinkered with the car, locking it, he said, when he was done. Twenty-four hours later—yesterday—he went out to tinker some more.

And it was gone.

You had it. Apparently you took it in the night. Right off the dealer's lot. There was a string of crime through the dealership's suburban neighborhood and it looks like you used my wife's car to make your getaway.

My guess is you'll drive it until it runs out of gas. Then you'll ditch it somewhere, walk a couple of blocks, and steal another one. Or maybe you'll trade it for crack or a gun or give it to someone to pay a debt.

Either way, you will dump it like a crumpled burger wrapper. In a week you won't remember it and it will simply be a small part of what passes for your miserable life.

But it will leave a hole in my wife's life.

And right now that has her steamed.

Mostly because she is a worker. She believes you work for what you get in this life, or you don't get it. And she can't countenance a thief. She can't stand to think of your self-centered laziness. Unwilling to earn the money to buy your own car, you carelessly take what she has worked and saved for.

You take the fruit of her labor and use it to underwrite your own sloth and greed.

She might forgive you someday, but not today.

Today she thinks you are scum. Cowardly, selfish trash.

One more species in a jungle of subhumans, genetically human but socially canine. Jackals living off the weak and the elderly, picking victims for their ease and gnawing on their carcasses.

You may consider yourself sly for having put one over on the dealer, for having been able to go onto a lot and rip off a car.

But you are not.

You are not sly.

You are not superior.

You are inferior.

You are inferior to everyone who passes on a busy street, driving cars they bought with the sweat of their brow. They are all honorable, able to make a way in this society, to provide for themselves.

But you are not. You are not honorable, you are not successful. You are the leech, unable to put food in your own mouth or a car in your own driveway.

Of the teeming millions of people in America, of the great variety around us, you are part of the tiny minority too defective to fend for itself.

So you have become a thief.

And this society cannot support you.

This society will reject you.

And, perhaps if you are not lucky, it shall exact its revenge.

One other thing.

In the back seat, there's a small T-shirt, the one that says "Mount Morris Youth Soccer." That's my daughter's. The 6-year-old. Today's her last game of the season.

And she will have to play it without a uniform.

Because you have it.

In her mommy's car.

The one you stole.

You bastard.

A day in the life of an American family

Out the window in the kitchen is the rosebush, wilted and tattered, petals spent and falling.

It was beautiful once, and they saw it there, at the great-grandmother's table, while they crowded around to eat.

At 8:30 was the kindergarten graduation, up at the school auditorium, and the 6-year-old stood in the second row back, on the right, singing with the class and waving to her family and making the little "I love you" sign as they looked at her and smiled. There was applause and certificates and afterward some cookies in her room and another certificate and some pictures and a scrapbook collected over the year.

And the innocent bliss of a happy child with two missing teeth and hugs and kisses for everyone.

Innocent bliss, in a world where innocence and bliss and the honestly of love are precious and rare.

The school year ended at 10:30 and by 11 the buses were past and the three youngest were home, girls, joining their brother who was already there. The last day of school and the first day of summer and this will be the year of the bike.

Everyone has one and everyone is old enough and the mother and the two oldest have already taken long trips up country roads to neighboring towns while the children show off tricks of wheelies and slides and little hops to the left.

After lunch the oldest girl, the trumpeter, sat with the phone and a pen and a paper and wrote down methodically the name and the times at the theater to the north, wavering lines of print on a crinkled sheet of information gathered seriously and considered deeply and discussed with a friend on the phone.

Maybe a movie tonight, they planned. Maybe a sleepover after.

In the late afternoon the mother went for a walk with her friend and at 7 the boy was at the big oak dining room table, with a friend, pouring over a catalog of bicycles and bicycle gear, scheming and wanting and reading aloud.

The 9-year-old lay on the couch in the early evening watching TV with her shirt off while her younger sister painted over her back with a knobby wooden roller, massaging out the stresses of a carefree life.

America. Main Street. Where the flag flies and the children smile and the pantry is full. A poodle dog and a giant swing set and tomatoes growing in the rear.

America. Where the future lies and the sleep is peaceful and the marigolds bloom in the front.

But if you play with fire you can burn down the world, and evil is a scourge that kills what it touches and the rose petals are wilted and torn.

And the mother came home and sent the children to a friend's and then she told him with tears that he had to go.

It's enough, she said, enough and more.

And he looked at her and the edge of his vision went away and turned gray and then black and all he could see was her eyes. Beautiful eyes, broken and saddened, and he knew he had done that and he looked instead out of blankness and shame at the clock on the VCR, little devil-red numbers marking the end of his life.

The end of his life that mattered.

And all he could see was them and all he could hear was her and at 9:27 it overwhelmed him. It just cold-cocked him. The wages of sin is death, the death of a family and the crushing of young hearts and the destruction of the only woman who truly loved him and the damned dizzying realization that he had done it, all himself, thrown away everything that he had and everything that they had and that they suffered far worse than he.

I am alone in the world, he said.

And so are we, she said, and you made it that way.

The sins of the fathers shall be upon the heads of the children, he thought, and walked slowly to the door.

And there he saw her as he had seen her first, a teenage girl with a brilliant smile and big open eyes on a smooth rounded face.

I love you, he said, and she said the same.

And out he walked, the fourth generation, having failed where failure is worst.

She told them the next morning and they were confused and stunned. The two little ones cried and the two big ones sat stonily numbed and somehow everything in their life had changed, the very foundation, ripped from them and spat upon and desecrated.

By him.

And he knew it.

When Jesus comes, the scriptures say, some will wish the ground would swallow them or the mountains would fall upon them, to cover their sin and their shame.

For some it will be then and for some it will be now and the wages of sin is death.

The death of innocence and purity and light, and the sweetness of the hearth and the home.

Maybe, she said, maybe in time.

And that's all that keeps him sane.

It's a family tradition

My grandfather's name was Buster, and I wonder if he felt this way.

Well, it wasn't Buster, really, it was Royce. That was a family name, his mother's maiden name, but people called him Buster. Or just Bus.

I wonder if he felt this way.

This stone terror that comes in waves as you fight for control. This looking-into-the-face-of-hell trauma that robs your sleep and deadens your senses and makes you go panicky for no reason.

I wonder if he felt it.

They had seven kids and something happened and he had to go. And he never came back. He went to live in the barroom.

I remember there was a family reunion at my uncle's house and I was living with my grandmother then, as a little boy, and after hours of driving she wouldn't go in when she learned he was there.

She stood outside in the dark, angry and hurt, as I went inside and saw him for the first and only time. He was dark and laughing and the center of it all. He gave me my first Coca-Cola.

Then he went out to sleep in a little pop-up he'd brought with him and my grandmother finally came in the house.

She only saw him one more time while they lived.

He was in the hospital then, dying with the emphysema, and all he could say was, "I always loved you, Mae."

The saddest damned words of all.

I always loved you.

And yet it didn't work out and it didn't pay off and it forever lies unresolved and unfulfilled, a weird kind of haunting of the heart.

Buster's grandmother was a widow in the Civil War who went on to marry an old bachelor farmer up the road. She had a mess of kids right away and then he died and she raised them alone in the hills.

And some of them grew up drunks and one of them had my grandfather and he left his family and my mother never quite worked it out and now it's my turn, the circle of life.

I wonder if he felt this way.

If he got the strange twitch in his eye, that came and went and came and went and reminded him that things weren't right. I wonder if he saw it as a death, the loss of all that mattered, the failure of his essential mission.

Or I wonder if the drink took it away.

Growing up, a lot of the old railroad men told me about Buster, and his antics, strolling drunk through the streets of Wellsville, handing out hotdogs he had just bought at the Texas Hots. The men liked it when he was on the crew because nobody was ever bored and nobody ever slept.

He was the happiest man on earth.

Or so they thought.

But you can drink because you're happy or you can drink because you're sad.

He was a handsome man with a smile on his face but in all the pictures you get the sense he's performing, he's putting on an act, being the hail-fellow-well-met and never being himself. See, it's the same smile in all the pictures. The same one. That's how rehearsed smiles come out. The same. Natural ones come in different forms, depending, like the other people in the photographs.

His children remembered him two ways. Half hated him, half idolized him. And the division stood like a wall between them, and still does, even though they are mostly dead. Two of his sons have been troubled all their lives by the dissolution of their family and another of his sons killed himself in a numbed cloud when his own family was breaking apart.

It's a family tradition.

And I had hoped I could stop it. That I would be the white picket fence and the middle class life and the Ward and June Cleaver.

But I wasn't.

After a lifetime of damning my progenitors for their mistakes, I have made the same ones. Maybe that's the way life is.

But my grandfather didn't live and die for nothing, and I'm going to try to learn from him. I'm going to try to do something he couldn't. I'm going to try to put it back together.

"I always loved you, Mae," Buster told her on his deathbed.

I'm not going to wait that long.

I'm not going to let this wound to family fester and putrefy and grow fatal. I'm going to dress it and clean it and make it mend.

And maybe I can do it and maybe I can't.

But I'm going to try.

And I'm not going to stop trying.

Because I have no other choice.

For years I kept a paragraph from the first page of the baseball rulebook taped above my desk: "The team with the most runs at the end of the game shall be declared the winner."

I underlined in red, "at the end of the game."

This game isn't over, and neither am I, and neither is my family.

Maybe I can do it and maybe I can't.

But I'm going to try.

It's not parenting

Visitation is a lie.

We tell it to ourselves, to think we're still parents, to keep from going mad at our loss.

But it's not parenting. It's chaperoning a field trip.

Let's go to the zoo. Let's go get ice cream. Let's spend the weekend at my dumpy apartment and pretend we're still family.

Pretend, pretend, pretend.

We totter like zombies who haven't heard that they're dead. We scramble like beggars after bread on the floor.

This isn't parenting, this every other weekend and alternating Christmases and two weeks in the summer except during soccer camp. This is a ruse, a dishonest confusion, a babysitting service for divorcees.

I am a lonely man and I used to be your father, but things are different now and I need you to fake it. I need you to act like this is normal so your mother and I don't feel guilty. So we can laugh and smile and make good for our friends. So we can pretend for a moment that we haven't just failed at the only thing that really mattered.

It's all an act.

Because it sure isn't parenting.

Because parenting happens when they come home from school and splash in the bath and watch their favorite shows and talk on the phone and quarrel over breakfast. Life happens in the boring moments, crammed in somewhere, when things are quiet and routine and mundane. There is preciousness in the nothingness, and in the million little unremarkable happenings which are a childhood.

When the former-father is off somewhere, in his other life, eight days and 10 hours away from the next strained performance. When they laugh loud and play their roles and pretend it isn't over.

Weekends. When friends sleep over and games are scheduled and the distractions and enjoyments of life crowd in for a piece of the clock. And that's Dad's time, the breaks from school, and children must choose between natural enjoyments and a sense of obligation to someone who doesn't even live in their house. It is an unfair competition.

And everybody loses.

And nobody's honest enough to say so.

We lie about "being there" for our children, and being their confidantes, and "having a good relationship," and how they're doing fine and seem well-adjusted and various other cons we pull on ourselves and the world. It's not parenting, it's a coping mechanism, a mental game, a paliative narcotic, easing the pain of the death of our parenthood.

Once a father always a father?

My ass.

It ends when you walk out the door. You and they may cling to the memory, in the way one treasures the photograph of a departed loved one, but it is over. The "it" that really counts. Because there is no betwixt and between, no no-man's-land of life, no way to live in two worlds and serve two masters.

There is a mom and dad. There is no mom and dad. It is a singular unit, it does not exist in separation and division. Parents are not individuals, they are a couple. And if they are not, they are not.

The surviving parent is called a "single mother." The former father is called a "divorced man."

One has society's sympathy, the other society's contempt. It's cops and robbers for keeps and you always have to be the robber.

That's in the best of worlds. In the worst, the adults bicker and twist the children, swinging them like clubs to hurt one another and to substantiate their own sick sense of self. It's not about mother's rights or father's rights or what the judge says to whom, it's about Ground Zero at Hiroshima and getting in a knife fight over who gets the rubble.

Score it a loss, all the way around. No high-fives for this caper.

And there are no fixes either. No way out. No way to make it better. Families don't get over divorce. All they can hope to do is avoid it. Humpty Dumpty had a great fall and that's all she wrote so get over it and get on with it.

Get on with whatever it is you think you can salvage of your life. Whatever other lie you tell yourself.

Just don't think you're a parent. Because you're not. Not any more than a guy who goes to a zoo is a farmer. Being a parent isn't a break from life. It is life, and you don't get to play it anymore.

Except every other weekend, and alternating Christmases, when you're jonesing so bad for what used to be that you'll take whatever you can get.

And pretend it's real.

The decay begins

I am 40.

I've been that way for three days.

It happened in Canada, north of Lake Huron, in the back of my van, in the parking lot beside a little hockey barn, trying to sleep as midnight passed.

I am 40 and six hours later I ran a marathon along a river in the forest where the deer flies bite. There was no reason for it, no logical reason, and no preparation or explanation.

I just got in my van and drove eight hours with a couple of bags of chips, my running shoes, a map, the sleeping bag and two books of Hemingway. And for 42 kilometers I slogged through it, not enjoying it, sometimes cursing it, wishing it was over.

Wishing I could stop.

But I didn't. And it hurt, and as I turned the corner where the volunteers sat and saw the hundred yards remaining I knew I owned it.

No one could ever take it away from me.

My life can go to hell, and I can go to hell, and it can all evaporate and leave me old or alone or penniless or even dead and still it will be a fact. On a certain day at a certain place at a certain milestone of life I ran 26 miles.

I've done it before, a half a dozen times, but before I was always in shape. I had trained and prepared and schemed for months. But I can't do that now, with two jobs and a column, and after months of not running I did it.

Which means nothing.

To anyone but me.

It's like Hemingway. When he was a little boy, a toddler really, running around his parents' home, one of his first sentences. 'Fraid of nothin', he would say.

Afraid of nothing.

And yet he was. He was often terrified. Haunted through life by a series of demons that caused him incomprehensible fear.

That's why he seemed so reckless and daring, taunting danger. He went to his fears, to subdue them, maybe, or to conceal his shame, or to be something he wished he was, or to gain a token to remind himself of his occasional strength, or maybe it was just because he found feeling any emotion, even a negative one, better than feeling none.

He would have understood about the marathon. And the eight hours of cramped driving after, and the wasted day and the wasted weekend and the hours spent not speaking to another human being.

He would have understood.

Because it was Hemingway who helped me understand van Gogh and Mozart and Gaughan. They were all crazy as hell, barely able to function in life sometimes, broken freaks on the edge. And yet they did something beautiful, each of them, touching some aesthetic purity like it was a high tension line. It arced and gave light and was exquisite, but its creation pretty much left somebody dead.

Hemingway was a drunk, and a depressive, and he wouldn't have known adult intimacy if it walked up and bit him.

But he did make some beauty.

Like no American writer had done before, and no American writer has done since.

And he paid for it with his mind and his life. And, of course, his joy. And to make sense of it all he created a world in which the primal expressions of manhood were writing and sex, and when he could no longer do either he went into a stairwell and did what his father had done.

Van Gogh was messed up in the head, yet if you could have cured him of that would you also have cured him of his genius? Would a mentally well Mozart have been a forgettable piano teacher and nothing more?

And, at 40, if I could overcome my flaws, would I also overcome myself? Would normalcy in one area of the mind impose normalcy, and consequently mediocrity, on all areas of the mind?

If you are to use your talents for the benefit of others, are you doing wrong if you extinguish them for the benefit of yourself?

Hemingway, born 100 years ago today, couldn't answer that. And I, born 40 years ago the other day, can't either.

He was the greatest American writer, and I am a loser with a computer. But we wrestle with some of the same things. And he lost.

And I'm afraid I may do no better.

So I spent the day alone, thinking and aching, and doing this stupid run. Fighting back the things which torment me.

I am 40.

I've been that way since I was a child.

On paths and the straying therefrom

Twenty years ago I went home.

From two years in the desert, hauling water and chopping wood and knocking on doors.

We were Mormon missionaries, 19 and 20 and 21, with smooth faces and youthful dreams and a young man's faith in God. Faith in a God who had sent us out, the weak and the ignorant, to tell people what he wanted them to know.

That's what I believed then, and that's what I believe now.

And Friday night I looked back, at a reunion with the people from then, slides on a wall and pats on the back and the odd pang that only the past can give. Smiling pictures of boys in suits and ties and families dressed in white at the waters of baptism. Friendships long forgotten and places barely remembered.

Each slide a jostled memory and names mouthed automatically for the first time in years.

Embraces and tears and pledges to stay in touch.

With the people, for them, with the message, for me. To stay in touch with the simple faith that testified on doorsteps and got us through in the lonely face of adversity.

I was younger then, and better. Not in knowledge or wisdom or the lessons of life, the parrying of blows and the landing of them.

But in purity.

The blessing of God that comes from obedience.

I am not now a tenth of what I was then. And I am so sorry for that. Sorry for the failure to myself, and to others, and to the promise of those days in the desert.

I am not now a Mormon, having been rightly kicked out for bad conduct.

I am not now anything I should be.

And few things could be less relevant to you than that, except for the fact of perspective. Because mine has changed.

Twenty years ago I was on the inside looking out. Today I am on the outside looking in.

Yet nothing has changed. Nothing of value. The truth is the truth and the facts are the facts. And the things I said when they justified me are just as true now that they condemn me. The me of today could stand a good talking to by the me of yesterday.

And maybe that conversation is taking place.

And if it is it's private.

But my conversation with you is not. Because this really isn't about me, it's about you.

I have been farther down the trail, and seen the lay of the land, and I am yelling back, "Don't come this way."

It'll kill you.

It'll kill the part of you that counts.

There is anguish and pain in this direction, numbing guilt and loss, a fraying of what you fundamentally are.

So go back, and don't follow me.

Follow, instead, your conscience, the spark of divinity which was yours at birth, which can whisper direction to you if you stop to listen. Or which you can drown and extinguish, as I may have done to mine.

Follow it and have the courage to obey it, to do what your

conscience says when your desires or your friends say something else. Sometimes you will find the answers by looking within, not by looking without. Don't do what everyone else does. Do what you feel good about.

And let the measure of every decision be the approval of your own conscience.

And keep your faith. Or find one you can. Be honest and open enough to look for what God wants you to find. Be humble and childlike enough to admit—if only to yourself—that there is a God.

Because there is.

I know that.

And so do you.

And I know that the only joy in this life or the next comes through faith in him and obedience to his word.

I know that.

And so do you.

So do something about it. Do not let that knowledge lie fallow, as I have done, to your own chagrin and sadness.

Instead, enthrone it, and make it the center of your life, and feel the sense of peace and integrity which will follow. Gain the strength which comes from doing what you know is right.

You think about it, and pray about it, and decide for yourself.

And do me a favor.

If a couple of Mormon missionaries come knocking on your door, let them in. Give them a glass of water and a couple of minutes of your time and see them for the people they are.

Because I think you'll like them.

And I think you'll like what they have to say.

And you stay on the right path. And I'll see what I can do to get there myself.

On the subject of having a very bad day

Sometimes, when the storm rages, you must rage back.

You must clench your fists and face the brunt of it and howl. Howl and yell and curse it. Just curse it all to hell.

And know that there will be peace soon. There is always peace coming soon. Or at least you have to believe that.

Believe that if you put one foot in front of the other you will eventually get where you need to go. And if you are lucky you will recognize it once you get there.

But if you are not, if you are like so many, you will walk right through and never know, leaving footprints and broken sod and the ruts of callous passage. Like a pet rat on an exercise wheel, running and running and running, in a cage from which there is no escape.

A cage in which you were born and in which you will die and freedom will come briefly and too late, as you are cold and stiff and dropped disdainfully into the flushing toilet.

Ashes to ashes, dust to dust, enjoy the view along the way.

And you run your hand through your hair and think hard and can't quite remember the point. The what's-it-all-about. The raison-d'etre. The who-am-I-and-what-am-I-doing-here.

And you shake it off and you smooth the hair back down and you walk through the door and you smile and shake hands and laugh loud and everybody's happy. Everybody but you. But that's not such a bad percentage. That's a good success rate, that's way above average. I'm doing great. How about you? You're looking good.

And you gaze over their shoulder as they talk and you lose focus for a moment and your face goes kind of flaccid and everything's still. Just a little buzz and then you laugh loud and slap them on the shoulder and make a joke.

Score that a win. Two thumbs up.

And push yourself till you drop, and leave the volume high so you can't hear anything in the quiet moments, if you can't avoid having them. Just play life loud to drown out what you don't want to hear in the quiet of the night when the morphine drip of sleep refuses to come.

Run and run and run.

Like a rat in a cage.

With too many acquaintances and not enough friends. With no friends, really, no intimates. No one to whisper to when it is the sun or the rain. When exultant or humiliated, in victory or defeat. Just taken out by the scruff of the neck sometimes and petted, and then returned to the stink of the cage, fouled by the waste of life, behind bars of your own making.

No, sometimes all you can do is rage at the storm. To defy it as it swirls around you, ripping and blowing and drenching as the world retreats to the safety of the storm cellar. And you stand alone bracing yourself against its onslaught.

That's just how it is.

And you stand there and you think things about God and Jesus and the valley of the shadow of death and now-I-lay-me-down-to-sleep and it's "Why hast thou forsaken me?" as you run as fast and as far from God as you can.

And sometimes you just have to take the hit, to tough it out, to cover your face and rope-a-dope and try to come out of it without any scars.

Or at least any scars that show.

But sometimes it knocks you on your ass. Flat-out sprawled, looking up in a cloud, dazed and down, hoping it doesn't stomp you. Hoping it doesn't kick in your ribs while you're there defenseless on the ground.

But that's how life is. Ward and June don't live here anymore and Aunt Bea doesn't have dinner on the table. Fry your own damn chicken, Andy, and watch out because the grease is going to splatter and it is going to burn and if you're going to put dinner on the table somebody's going to have to pay.

It's the American way. It's the way of the world.

And the storm rages around you and you give as good as you get, a speck in revolt against the universe, cursing its place in the cosmos and the fate of its own creation.

But peace is coming soon.

Peace is always coming soon.

It is on the other side of the storm, when the dark clouds break and the eye recoils from the brilliant sun and the drenched and pruned forest stands scoured by violence of its dead wood and weak limbs. And it stands somehow stronger because of the beating.

At least that's what you have to believe.

When you feel the whirlwind reach down to consume you.

And your shouts of resistance are lost in the din.

When your strength is your weakness

The thing about hitting rock bottom is that it doesn't always happen.

In fact, it's probably only the weak ones who ever hit it. Who are caught up short and shake their heads and whisper, "Oh my God, what am I doing?"

The rest just wrestle it into the grave, struggling in a death grip with whatever it is, assured in their ability to retain control while it drives a stake through their heart.

The undead, uncomfortable in the light of human society, creatures of a night of their own creation.

And demon possession isn't about spinning heads and puking pea soup, it's about being the host to a homemade parasite, about carrying around a burden freely picked up and unconsciously enlarged.

Until what you do is shoulder it and nothing more. It cheats and eclipses everything you should be or want to be and one-by-one it kills everything of value to you.

Rather, you kill everything of value to you.

Because the only enemy to fear is the enemy within, the demon that speaks in your own voice, the assassin in the mirror.

And the stronger you are the stronger it is. And if you're lucky it will break you early, because if it doesn't it will eventually break you eternally. And you become one of the pathetic derelicts of life, the teetotaling wino scrounging quarters for the next bottle.

Only a wino has a real bottle, a vessel of destruction, and you can see it in his hand and smell it on his breath and notice it in his walk.

But it's not always that way. It's not always alcohol. Or pills or anything they can test you for. It's sometimes just a fire, where your soul used to be, and you spend your waking hours tending it, jonesing for something to give you that nervous and energetic feeling, to fill in for the life you're not living and probably never will live.

And the weak ones crumble before it becomes them.

They hit their bottom and shed their tears and go off to rehab or the psych center or to the nightly meetings and then sally forth with a coin in their pocket and a count of days in their mind.

While the next guy mocks them and their convert's zeal and staggers at a misstep under his burden.

Because if you're the kind who can't be beat, odds are you're the kind who can't be saved. And the great stamina and power of the indomitable soul is the sword upon which it falls. And just as life's greatest triumphs require the ability to never quit, to endure all, and to march when others faint, life's greatest failures are likewise dependent upon those same characteristics.

And you can't truly crash if you never truly had prospects of flying.

Which makes it all the more a waste. How are the mighty fallen indeed.

They are fallen at their own hand.

And like a pressure that builds but does not alleviate, it all swirls ever faster around the drain, going down with fire and spark, but going down nonetheless.

And in the wee hours of an exhausted night you push and crave for more, unsated and insatiable, and freedom of thought is given over to the voluntary bondage of the burden.

And the burden is life, and life is dark, and you smile and talk fast and nobody notices. And if this mind can do this for good, what can this mind do for evil, what can it do for its own debasement.

But there are no physics of destruction; there is no terminal velocity in the fall of a human soul, there is only faster and faster and beyond that I don't know. There are no bottomless pits. There are only the crevasses of personal destruction, stained and rank with the shattered remains of the men and women who dug them, babies once in their mothers' arms, pure and sweet and close to the angels.

Now ripped apart by the demons.

Ripped apart by themselves.

Ashes to ashes, dust to dust. It's just that some don't wait until they die.

They just burn up and they burn out and they never quite hit bottom. They never reach the place where it breaks them, even when they are well past the place where it ruins them.

And that's how it is. That's the report from the front. That's me, that's you, that's the drunk on the corner. Addicts all.

Sometimes you just don't wake up and smell the coffee.

Sometimes they have to tap you on the shoulder to tell you you're dead.

And sometimes you just shake your head and wonder how it all got so sideways.

Good-bye, Ike, I love you

Good-bye, Ike, I love you.

You were a good dog and I will always miss you.

And I will always regret that I could not save you, and that I did not more freely return the simple love that you had for me.

I suspect that I will sit on the couch sometime and cry, realizing that you don't come any more and nuzzle me and drop a wet tennis ball in my hand. I will cry because you are gone and I will cry because of the disappointment you must have felt as I pushed you away.

A toss or two and I would grow tired of the play and when you plopped it back in my hand I would ignore you, watching the television, as you stood there, expectant, happy, and then nudge it toward me with your nose, trying to stir me. Then you would pick it up and move to the next person on the couch and try there to recruit a friend.

You were the smartest dog. A big black standard poodle, big as a collie, shaved skinny or shaggy and full with hair.

And all I had to do was say, sometimes in a whisper to test you, "Let's go to the woods," and you would sprint with delight to the door, bounding and whirling, your tongue alive and lolling, your tail whipping with zest and joy. "Get in Daddy's van," I would say as I opened the kitchen door and out you would run, flat as fast as you could, and sit expectant by the truck, wishing I would hurry.

And in the rear view mirror as I drove you would sit there, in the back seat, politely, watching out the windows, waiting for the freedom of the forest and the trees, the snow banks of winter and the cool ponds of summer and the license to run as far and as fast as you chose.

And sometimes we did run, on this five-mile loop through the hills, you circling me and darting off at the start and then falling in at my heel in the sun and the shade, the sound of your breath as loud as my own. Through the same woods where you came squirrel hunting, my son and I stone still and silent as you dashed and dove through the loud dry leaves of autumn. And though you were a natural retriever you just couldn't see the sense of game in your mouth, and I'd put it there and you'd drop it and I'd put it back and you'd drop it and you were too smart not to get it so I always figured you just didn't like it.

Because animals were your friends. In a fashion of your own.

You wanted to play. And you would bark a happy bark and wiggle your tail and circle them and playfully snap and rough house a bit, like a friend.

That's what you did with Rachel the cat, all those years, her on the kitchen counter or livingroom couch or dining room table, reaching down to swat at you, completely unamused, while you circled and yipped and wagged.

And that's what you did that day winter before last, on the ski trek through the woods in the hills. For three hours we had been out, you and my son and me, and were finally within sight of the road.

And that's when the skunk came out. Ambling quietly across our path. I yelled "freeze" and you didn't know what that meant and you went to greet your new friend and I could see the instant he sprayed.

Not by what he did but by what you did and the odd leap into the air you took. And the running and rolling and the headlong dives against the snow. My poor baby, how you stunk. And how we grew closer on the ride home and in the bathroom as we shampooed and shampooed and shampooed.

You were a good boy, Ike, the best dog I ever had.

And on Sunday afternoons I would lie on the dining room floor to take a nap and you would come and lie beside me, your head on my arm, on your back, your legs splayed outward in a most ungentlemanly fashion.

And when I would come in the door, after hours or days, you would be so happy and squirmy, so loving and kind, running to grab a shoe or a pillow to hold in your mouth. You always greeted people with a gift.

And you guarded my children at night, and slept beside them in their beds, crowding them for space or plopping flat on the floor or simply standing and staring or maybe licking once their faces.

You loved them, Ike, and they loved you, and they miss you terribly.

I'm so sorry, Ike, for them, and for you and me. But I guess you must have been what they meant by "furniture of the primary residence" in the paperwork.

And now you are asleep and I wish you weren't. You are asleep and I wish I could get it out of my head. I wish there was a dial I could turn up, the volume of life, to make it drown out the memory and the loss and the damn sad fact that you're gone.

But I can't. I can't even close.

But I hear it's a long walk to hell, and maybe someday God will let you walk me part way. We'll go through the hills and maybe just stop for a while, in the deep forest, and live for a season you and me.

Until then, my friend, I will think of you and treasure the memory, and picture you alive in the trees.

Let's go to the woods, Ike.

Get in Daddy's van.

Godspeed, David

Unknown in life, unrecognized in death.

This is the story of a father and a son.

Specifically, my father and me.

Father in a biological sense, if nothing else. The man who got my mother pregnant. The man who ran out on her. The man who ruined her life.

With my help.

A picture of them came in the mail the other day. One of those old black and white pictures, square, with scalloped edges. It was developed in December 1958 and taken the summer before. He is in a suit with a kerchief and his hair slicked down. She has on a wedding dress and is holding a corsage.

They are outside, on a front lawn I don't recognize. She is 17. A year later, she would have a newborn, he would be in the Army and they would never see one another again.

On the back in blue pen is written his name and the words "and wife."

Her name was Natilee. The shotgun annulment—something his family's lawyer pushed through—gave her back her maiden name and that's the name I was given at birth.

I was the bastard son of a bastard son.

His mother lived in the state asylum, dropped off when she was 14 because she had fits or depressions or because her family had seven kids and it was the Depression and she was one less mouth to feed. She had him when she was 21, there at Willard, all alone, and something killed her three years later and he went to live with an aunt and uncle.

It was ironic in a way because my mother was in a mental hospital herself by the time she was 19. It was all too much for her, I guess, and she broke down. I think she was still in there when she turned 21.

Anyway, you don't miss what you've never had, and I didn't know what it was like to have a father so it didn't bother me. Except in town. In our little town where everyone knew everyone and often to connect the genealogy the question would be, "Who's your father?" Back then people had fathers. Back then if you didn't you were a bastard. Not maliciously, just as a matter of fact. And when it was too awkward to answer "Natilee" when they asked me, "Which Lonsberry are you?" I'd say one of my uncles' names, or pretend I didn't hear.

It was that way until I graduated and moved away.

I knew his name and I'd seen a picture like the one that came in the mail, and the clipping of the notice in the paper, and I knew that he ran away to the Army. But beyond that there was nothing.

I just didn't think about it.

Though as I became a man and started a family of my own I found myself looking for his name. In phone books as I traveled, once on the roster of teachers stapled to a school bulletin board. And once almost accidentally at work as I tried to make a computer look up a driver's license. I was confirming someone's identity for a newspaper story and the computer wouldn't work and an editor suggested I try another name.

So I typed in the name of my father.

For no reason at all. I was frustrated at the computer, I needed to get the story done, I just wanted it to work.

And it did when I typed in my father's name.

It gave his name and address. His phone number was just a few pages away from mine in the white pages.

I didn't want to call.

But my wife did. So I sat on the stairs, out of sight but listening as she apologized for calling and said this might seem strange but are you so-and-so?

And did you have a son a long time ago?

Robbie? he responded, and started crying.

He and his wife came over a few nights later. And an older, pot-bellied me walked up the steps to introduce himself.

He was a good man.

And for a couple or three years we stayed in touch, visiting one another, but then we didn't. I'm not sure why. His wife hadn't been able to have children, so they adopted a boy, and I think bringing in a blood son and blood grandchildren was uncomfortable or unsettling for some. And I don't think we had much in common. We were different people, we were strangers.

And the things you go to family for, for connection and memory and common assumptions, he couldn't give me and I couldn't give him. He was just some middle-aged guy I met when I was 30. And I may have been a reminder of a part of his life that hadn't gone so well and of which he hadn't been particularly proud.

I knew him in the waning years of my mother's life. And I couldn't help but think how things would have gone differently for her if he hadn't run out. If he had stayed and she had had some stability and if she hadn't been left pregnant and alone in a small town in 1959. If she'd had a fair chance at life.

So many times she said all she'd wanted from life was a home and a family, a husband and love and peace and quiet.

And he kept that from her.

But I don't blame him. In life we do what we do, we follow our best lights, and people don't set out to hurt one another, they just do. It's life. And I forgive him the way I hope others forgive me. We're all a bunch of screw-ups, stumbling through life, learning to have a good heart.

That's what my father taught me. At least that's the lesson I chose to learn.

He died a month ago of cancer.

My children and I are not listed in his death notice.

But somebody clipped it out, to let me know he was gone, and sent it with a funeral card and the picture of him and my mother on their wedding day.

There is sorrow in life sometimes. If not for what is lost, then for what could have been.

Like my father and me.

Unknown in life, unrecognized in death.

What I did on Christmas

I was sad on Christmas, and feeling sorry for myself, withdrawing into a gloom I sometimes find inviting and easy.

Work had gone well, a radio show in the morning, but then there was nothing. No plans, no family, no nothing. Spit out at noon with hours on my hands and the empty stillness of a city at Christmastime.

So I lay down and took a nap. On the couch at work, a comfortable leather thing with my coat across my chest as a blanket.

And an hour later my phone rang. The little silver flip phone in the pocket of the coat. It woke me with a start and I fumbled with the coat and lifted it up and looked at the screen. The caller I.D. screen. It was my number.

Or what used to be my number. Back when I was married. Back when I had a family. Back before the divorce.

It was my number, and I knew who it was. It was my son. My 15-year-old son. He was calling to invite me over, to tell me to stop and see him and the others, to ask me to Christmas dinner. But I put it back in the coat and wished for it to stop ringing, for him to give up. It rang and rang. And eventually it stopped.

He wanted me to come to dinner and his mother did not, and in the weeks before the holiday there had not been an invitation and it became obvious there wouldn't be one and I wasn't going to ask for one. And so I withdrew. And the phone stopped ringing and I got up and rubbed my eyes and went to the restroom to brush my teeth and 10 minutes later in the cold of the parking garage it rang again, in the pocket, the little silver flip phone, with the same number on the screen.

I had forgotten to get gas the night before and coming out onto the Interstate the gauge was below E and the orange warning light was on and I made for the nearest service station. But it was Christmas and it was closed and I got back onto the freeway and headed around town to another big one. And as I got close the phone rang again, a high-pitched nagging, incessant, my son, wanting to talk. Wanting his father on Christmas. And I turned the radio up and tried to drown it out.

And the gas station was closed. Like the next one I tried. And I was 20 minutes into this and one more unanswered ring and then I remembered someone on the radio had said there was one open out this road a ways and so I headed that direction.

And I felt miserable, in a selfish, martyr kind of way. My pain had a sweetness that swallowed me as fast as I swallowed it. It was a mix of self-interest and self-loathing. And I was alone and I wanted to be alone and I resolved not to speak to another person the rest of the day. Not the people I love, not the people who love me. Nobody. Nothing but dark seclusion.

And the phone rang again, and it almost killed me, as I thought about my son, on the phone, miles away, wanting something, having faith in me, and me disappointing that faith and spurning that love.

But I didn't answer.

And I drove on and it was about 10 degrees outside and the road was deserted and I only had a light coat and I was all but out of gas. And I prayed. One of those silent unthinking prayers. Thrown off in an instant.

Heavenly Father, please help me not to run out of gas.

And at that moment, instantly, in my mind I saw it. The old Gaseteria. A literal picture in my mind. It was there and I recognized it and it was gone. A station that was out of business the last time I knew. And I put on my signal at the next intersection and turned toward it. And quickly, a couple of blocks away, I could see it, and the cars, coming and going. It was open.

And it struck me.

I had—in my unworthiness—asked my Father for something, and he had instantly given it. My son had—in his innocence—asked his father for something, and I had denied it.

I had denied him. I had turned a deaf ear to a little boy wanting his father on Christmas. I had thought of how bad my Christmas was, and not how bad I was making his Christmas. I had been a bad father, and I had been shown how a good father should act. My Father had set for me an example.

And that's what dawned on me as I turned into the gas station and the phone rang.

And I clumsily fumbled for it as I brought the car to a stop.

It was my son and I told him Merry Christmas and he wanted me to come over for dinner. And a few hours later I was beside him on the couch as he handed me the present he had gotten me and his sisters and mother happily laughed and played. And there were little hugs and kisses and four children who had had a wonderful holiday, presents and companionship and pure childhood joy.

And I had not ruined it.

I had not let my failings as a father and as a person drag me away into self-pity and stupor to the detriment of my children.

Because my Father had taught me better. By not ignoring me. He taught me a lesson, with a silly tank of gas.

And I will try not to forget it.

I was sad on Christmas, and feeling sorry for myself, withdrawing into a gloom I sometimes find inviting and easy. But I got out of it. And the day ended well.

And I thank God.

What do you do when you crash your plane?

When the plane crashes, what do you do?

When it's strewn all around you, blown apart by the impact and the consequence and the sheer force of misguided powers, what do you do?

You get up and walk away.

You unstrap yourself and kick free of the debris and walk away.

Even if you crashed it.

If it's you who misjudged and failed and brought it down in a heap.

You go on.

You hope never to come to that juncture, and you fight to keep it aloft, and you struggle until it hits, end over end in the collapse of flight, the magic gone and the physics taking over and it's consumed in flame and smoke and noise.

Your greatest failure.

A pilot in the rubble in a field.

But you get up and walk away.

It's one of life's hard lessons.

How to handle failure.

Catastrophic failure, the kind that changes all the rules and all the givens and turns the best of dreams into a monument to smallness and stupidity and evil. It crashed and I did it and it's a pile of ruin and waste.

Damage to yourself and to others and to many.

Yours of your deserving and theirs of their innocence.

I own this. It is my fault. Write it down in my book.

But I'm not dead yet. And life goes on.

And between the grief and the shame and the hard-sobbing loss you put one foot in front of another.

You're either an animal or a child of God or some combination of the two and either way there is an imperative, a command, a necessity to live, to breathe and eat and survive. And to go on. To just somehow go on.

You see it all around. At the prisons and the bankruptcies and the divorce courts. Standing there with a pink slip or a good-bye note or a diagnosis from the doctor.

It's in the wind, all of it, blown to smithereens, by the explosion of bad fortune and bad conduct, and the fault is in the mirror.

As ye sow so shall ye reap.

And it is a bitter harvest. And you force it on others by your collapse.

So this is the bottom?

The bottom you hit, the bottom where you stand up or expire.

The bottom where there's nothing left but grit and instinct. A place where the tone goes out of your face and you stand there flaccid and weak, but you're standing, and you go from there.

If you're lucky.

Because some aren't. Most aren't, in fact. Most never get it off their backs. Like a festering wound it cripples them and dominates them and fills their minds. They live out their days in regret and retreat.

But I'm too selfish for that.

I'm too selfish to fold tent.

Too selfish to admit defeat and disgrace and disrepute.

Too selfish to say it's over, that my turn is used or that my energy is spent.

So I get up and walk away.

It didn't work. It didn't work because I ruined it. I destroyed it.

But the mountains won't fall on me and hide me and the earth won't swallow me and conceal my shame so I must go on. And I won't be the first.

Not the first or the last or the worst. Just one more battered hulk who has soiled himself and his world and his future.

There is no excuse and there is no forgiveness but there might be hope.

Because where there is life there is hope.

And must be God knew we would walk this way sometimes, for he gave us legs which don't buckle and desires which don't die. He made it so that when you're flat on your back you're still looking up.

There might be a hell, but this isn't it. This isn't the end or the last or the pit.

So you kick back the debris and unfasten your belt and crawl bloodied out the side of the wreck. Do-over, you say, do over, you hope, do-over, you kneel and you pray.

I walk through the valley of the shadow of death because I chose this path, freely and foolishly and arrogantly, them not me, I can get through, when I walk in the mud it won't stick.

But it does and it covers and eventually it defines.

And I stand now in need of a bath.

Caked hard with the waste of the earth and the offal of my own device, but I stand and I breathe and where there is life there is hope.

And where there is hope there is life.

At the prisons and the bankruptcies and the divorce courts. Where tattered failures stand stripped of their pride, shown for their choices and destructive desires.

When the plane crashes, what do you do?

When it's strewn all around you, blown apart by the impact and the consequence and the sheer force of misguided powers, what do you?

You get up and walk away.

You survive, the best you can.

But you go on.

Do-over, you say, do-over, you hope, do-over, you kneel and you pray.

To move in, you must first move out

The first thing I did was get the kayak out of the kitchen.

And the bike and the Rollerblades and the pile of clothing where the stove is supposed to be.

It has taken me a year to do this but I am doing it now and it is going well.

I am moving in. Really moving in. Not just to sleep on a cot and shower sometimes and step over the growing clutter of a bachelor hermitage, but to unpack and organize and hang pictures on the wall. To put up book shelves and deodorizers and stack cans in the cupboards and buy a refrigerator.

I have silverware now, a setting for 12, and Windex and a throw rug and 70 plastic hangers. For half a week I have prowled Wal-Mart, buying a computer cart and a salt shaker and washcloths and waste baskets and the countless other necessities of life.

I even had the electricity turned on.

In a week or two they'll get around to hooking up my phone, and my TV cable, and I think I'll get a birdfeeder.

Because I am moving in.

And that's hard because first you must acknowledge that you've moved out. Not to anybody else, but to yourself. And not at an intellectual level, in the conscious mind, but somewhere far away in the soul where such things don't register. If you move in, that means you have moved out.

So you don't move in.

You live in this limbo. You sleep where you can and eat where you can and maybe you crash there but you don't live there, not really, not the way people live. And you ignore the growing heap of letters beneath the slot and you come late and leave early and you don't attach. It's not your place. It's not your home.

And I don't know how long that lasts for different people. I don't know if everybody gets over it. I don't know if it doesn't reach up and hold some people and never let them free. I think I know how those kooky people who keep to themselves come to be. I think they're simply folks who never escape, or who never come home, whose lack of true home becomes the defining characteristic of their lives.

You learn these things. You learn them or you lose.

Like about the laundromats. There are laundromats for welfare people and there are laundromats for divorced people. If you go to the wrong one, you will feel out of place, no matter who you are. And after 20 years it can be odd to dump your basket into a cart and then feed it into a big machine that takes eight quarters for a double load. And at the divorced laundromats they know that.

So the lady will tell you that you can drop it off and pay by the pound. That she will wash it and dry it and fold it and you can pick it up like any other business transaction.

And that's good because sometimes it comes up behind you and crushes your skull. Just one of those sucker punches. The damned odd loneliness of it all.

Like in a restaurant when you're eating alone, or when you're in the laundromat waiting on the machines. So fundamentally out of place and alone. And you get this realization of panic and you go dry in your mouth and you know that it's all just fallen apart on you.

So it's better if she washes it. But you bring it home and leave it in the basket and paw through to pull out what you need.

Until you move in.

Which I did this weekend.

One foot in front of the other.

It was the prettiest cake you ever saw

The groom was from out of town, from across the valley and the continent and the culture, an easterner in a cowboy town, come to take a bride.

It's not much of a place really, a few trailers and humble houses on a couple of side hills where the canyon cuts through the mountains. Some deserted mines and a bunch of pick-up trucks and an old courthouse where they used to hang men from the balcony.

That's where they held it.

Upstairs in the courtroom.

It was a family affair, put together by a couple of aunts and a mother, with the men hauling tables and roasting beef and making chili in a line of cast-iron Dutch ovens. It was cold in the morning but the skies cleared and, though it looked like the wind was going to blow the cake over, it was warm enough to eat outside after the ceremony.

The groom dressed off by himself in an empty house that belonged to a great-grandmother. A lady named Clara who ran a bar. A polyester tuxedo and some Wal-Mart shoes and a black bowtie. Standing up while he waited so as not to wrinkle the pants.

The bride got dressed in the room outside the jail cells at the courthouse. Little holes of wrought iron and stone piled high now with Christmas decorations and papers from the clerk's office.

She did her hair at her mom's place with her sister and niece helping, a team effort to put on the make-up and the veil and then drive over in jeans to the courthouse to put on the dress. It was an off-white thing, something like ivory, with a train and an embroidered bodice and sleeves she had sewed on to make it modest. It was Cinderella time in a cowgirl's world. A bouquet and a smile and a walk up the stairs.

The niece went in first, in her Sunday dress, with a basket of rose petals she scattered along the way. In the courtroom door and through the swinging gate where the defendant usually sits and up to her place in front of the judge's desk by the bishop and the groom. Then her brother came in, in a new shirt and tie, carrying a pillow with a couple of rings tied to it with tiny ribbons. It was heart-shaped and pink, and had a border of lace all the way around.

The bridesmaid was the mother of the ring bearer and the flower girl and she took her place beside her daughter.

There was music from a CD player and in regular strides the bride walked in on the arm of her stepfather. He wore jeans and she wore a glow and after taking her to her place he stepped to the groom's side to be a witness and stand-in best man.

Then there was some singing and some talking and some kissing and the thing was done.

But before it was they looked back and forth at one another and broke into broad and winking smiles before they averted their eyes to stay dignified for a few moments until they met again and smiled the same way. The bishop might have said something good but they didn't hear him. They were distracted by the fact they were two "I do's" away from being where they were born to be.

And then they were there.

And the people came by hugging and hand-shaking on their way out of the courtroom and down to the reception to take pictures and visit and get to the salads and deviled eggs.

They forgot to fling the garter or throw the bouquet but they did cut the cake and he did push her in the wheelbarrow.

Nobody knew when it started but it went back four generations that they could count and it had always been the same wheelbarrow. Tarnished now and wobbly, from the ranches or the mines, with a blanket draped across it to protect her dress. The bride gets in and the groom pushes her down the center of Main Street to the bar where they celebrate.

They didn't go to the bar but they did take the wheelbarrow ride on Main Street and a vanful of passing Californians honked and waved and smiled.

And in a couple of hours people were mostly gone and the tables had been put away and they slipped off to be alone.

Their first dance was that night, at the bar between pool shots. It's kind of where the town gets together and most of the family showed up and reminisced. Some few were drinking, but most weren't. Most were just lengthening out a springtime desert day, not wanting it or its new beginning to slip away.

He put a quarter in the jukebox and it played a slow song. She passed off the pool cue and stepped into his arms and between her waltz and his clumsiness they walked little circles together in the back of the bar.

Their first dance, and the people around the pool table stopped to watch.

It was a Jim Croce song, the one about saving time in a bottle.

I walked through a blizzard once

I walked through a blizzard once.

It was a big one. Maybe the biggest I ever saw. Blinding,

falling, blowing, drifting. Hellacious snow, choking and stopping everything, bringing down wires and communities, freezing the Northeast in its tracks.

It was a big one.

And it came on a work day. On a day when it took three-quarters of an hour to shovel a path out the driveway and into the road. A day of shoulder-high drifts and numbing cold.

It was a big one.

And on my fifth try I got the van into the road, crosswise, bottomed out in the snow. But with some pushing and shoveling and rocking it slid sideways off the crown of the street and got traction in the ruts of the last vehicle to pass.

And up Main Street I went, not stopping for lights on the deserted road, building up speed on the downhill to plow through the snow at the bottom. It was hard going across the flats to the expressway but I broke trail and got up the ramp and nursed it faster and faster to gain momentum for the big climb out of the valley.

It's funny, at a time like that, speed saves you and speed kills you. If you give it too much gas, pushing through maybe a foot of snow atop the Interstate hard pack, you lose traction and slide off into the median or the shoulder. But if you don't give it enough, the plowing holds you back and bleeds your momentum and you come to a halt, halfway up some hill in the middle of the road in the blizzard to end all blizzards.

So you nurse it. And you pray. A constant "Please, help me. Please, help me." You swing the wheel coolly when it starts to slide and you ease the gas slightly when it starts to spin.

It's really hard. And you don't notice at the time how tightly you're gripping the wheel, how badly you're wishing the windshield wipers wouldn't cake up, how desperately you want to make it to the top of this hill.

And somehow you do it.

At least I did it.

Past the cars and the trucks slid off and drifted over, beyond where the tracks ended and where the only cues were topography and memory.

And I kept on driving. I turned the defroster on high and bent down to peer through the semi-circle where the blowing, caking snow was melting as it fell.

It was two hours like that.

Maybe 10 miles an hour, trying to gently skirt drifts across the road, or to at least strike them where they were thinnest, repeatedly spinning 30 or 45 or 90 degrees out of true, steering out of them and nursing the gas pedal and pushing on.

I passed a highway plow in the ditch, and two sheriff's cars, and the various motorists and truckers of the night. Each had lost the fight, each had slid out of control, each had become the genesis of a new drift that stretched on the leeward side another car length or two or three.

The snow got me in Avon. There was too much of it and not enough momentum and the van settled to a stop with snow to the middle of the grill.

I couldn't see much through the van's windows. They clouded up and frosted up and it got cold. And I knew that turning the engine on would just fill me up with gas and make something that was merely frightening truly dangerous.

It was an old van, about a dozen years then, and I'd taken the back seats out to make room for my gear. Skiing gear and hiking gear and hunting gear. It was all back there. And I thought about what to do.

And I knew I couldn't go back, and I didn't want to stay there, and the only way out was forward. So I stripped off my office clothes and put on some thermals and an insulated coverall and pulled knit caps over my head and laced up my hunting boots and put mittens over gloves and pushed the passenger door open against the drift.

And I stepped out, up to my hind end, into the snow.

And the howl and the cold and the wind that took your breath away.

And I began to walk, to wade almost, stepping over drifts when I could, plowing through when I had to, looking for areas where it had blown shallow and stopping at underpasses to get out of the wind.

People yelled at me to get in, to come out of the cold, that it was dangerous and foolhardy. But I didn't stop. I kept walking. And I stopped at trapped cars, to see if everyone was OK, and a few times I borrowed cell phones to call into work.

It was very tiring, and my legs and lungs burned and the snow built up on my brows and encrusted my mustache. The snow came and went and came again, and in the high areas scrubbed by the wind I trotted to build my body temperature and at the bridge over the thruway I stopped to look in shock at the scores of cars in each direction, snowed in and trapped, their drivers running the engines for minutes at a time to stave off the cold and charge the battery to listen to the radio.

It took about five hours to get into town and climb up a ramp and wave down a passing state trooper. He took me back to the substation and we got warmed up and then he drove me as best he could the rest of the way to work.

I had come 40 miles, about 12 of them on foot. I did it because I had to. Because it was the only way. Because it was my job, because it was my duty, because I wanted to see if I could. Because I knew I couldn't give up or quit.

I walked through a blizzard once.

And now I've done it again.

Five

At least I have my health

I think I have monkey pox.

I have all the symptoms.

I don't know what they are, but as soon as I do, I'm sure I'll have them.

I get all the diseases. I'm just now getting over mad cow. And SARS. And I still have nightmares about ebola. I've applied for rickets and have toyed with South American parasites.

That's been hard, of course, because I'm plagued by the chemicals in my carpet and the arsenic in the pressure-treated lumber swing set at the town park. And, of course, the perfume this woman wore the other day at the supermarket. I've been sneezing for days and have unsightly blotches.

Which, naturally, led to clinical depression, which I am treating with a variety of nutritional supplements and Chinese herbs. I carry them in a little bag with my crystals.

But sadly that's done nothing for my gout and elephant man's disease. Or the nasty case of malaria I got after reading a fascinating history of the digging of the Panama Canal. It's amazing that the chlorine, fluoride and other poisons put in the water supply by various government conspiracies haven't killed me already.

In fact, I was saying just the other day at my lupus support group that if it wasn't for the fascinating world of auto-immune disorders, there'd be no reason to live. Except to get revenge on my drunken great-grandfather for making me the adult child of an adult child of an adult child of an alcoholic.

But, like they say, one day at a time.

Which reminds me, I've got to get some of that Zoloft stuff I saw on television the other day. And some psyllium powder, and some Paxal, like my neighbor has, and a few of these herbal Viagras I got the e-mail about. Though the other stuff, to make my breasts larger, I think I'll pass on that. Seems like it would make it hard to run.

Which is difficult enough with my carpal tunnel syndrome.

And dwarfism.

And frequent alien abductions.

Not that I get out much since I caught West Nile virus. And Lyme disease. And the hepatitis. But I sure try.

If I can get past these filthy cigarette companies and their unfair enticements to smoke more of their products. Granted, it's hard feeling like the Marlboro man now that I'm morbidly obese, but if I ever could squeeze my way through the door of the apartment I share with my 47 cats, I'd probably fall prey to tobacco and fast food.

Which is a real problem for us lesbians.

Us dyslexic Hispanic lesbians with ADD.

And bi-polar irritable bowel syndrome.

Which has gotten a lot worse since I caught that bug on the cruise ship, on top of my Gulf War syndrome and premature menopause.

Which was kind of a bad news, good news thing. The bad news is I grew a mustache. The good news is the alopecia made it fall out. It was either that or radiation sickness. I'm not sure, but I bought these barrels on eBay from some guy in Iraq and they kind of glowed.

Which was pretty traumatic, since the hormones they give dairy cows have caused me to grow two extra breasts. And that's no fun for somebody with a Twinkies addiction and seasonally affected disorder.

Or periodontal disease.

And a rash I'm fairly certain is anthrax.

But I can't worry about that now. I've just been bitten by my pet prairie dog, which caught a sniffle from a Gambian giant rat, which was once the subject of product testing by a giant cosmetics company.

Owned by George W. Bush, Rupert Murdoch and the Illuminati.

Does Triple-A do plumbing?

Sometime last year I hung a picture.

It was a significant accomplishment and a rare occurrence in that it included a hammer and a nail and me.

I am ashamed to say that, though heterosexual and male, I'm not handy.

I don't now how to fix things. If it backs up, burns out or falls down, I'm pretty much screwed. This fact has caused me no small amount of difficulty in life.

Whereas other men seem genetically programmed to use circular saws, I view construction and home repair as miraculous undertakings somewhat akin to the parting of the Red Sea by Moses. I know that things get built, but I don't know how. My best theory is that elves come in the night while we are asleep.

I chalk this up to my illegitimacy. I was born out of wedlock. There was no dad. Had there been a dad, I assure people, I'd be completely normal. I'd be changing oil and hanging drywall with the best of them.

It's not true, of course. I don't believe any amount of fathering or instruction could have made me turn out any different. Had there been a father around, with my lack of ability, I'm afraid one of us would have been killed in a nail gun accident. I'm just defective that way.

There are books for people like me. Usually they're published by *Reader's Digest*. They have chapters on changing light bulbs and making the toilet flush. They even have advanced texts on cleaning the eaves gutter and installing light switches.

These should be avoided.

At least by me.

It's just not in me. I picked up a paint brush once and had nightmares for weeks.

Understandably, this has caused me quite a bit of difficulty in life. Particularly with women. Women presume men can fix anything. And when men can't, their masculinity is called into direct question.

For example, if the car chugs or whistles or burps, the woman turns to the man and asks, "What's wrong with it?'

The man, of course, thinks, "How on earth would I know?"

He instead says, "I'll take a look at it."

That means he will raise the hood and stand there in front of the exposed engine with his hands on his hips. He does that because he knows that there are moving parts in a car engine and that if he touches them he will be pulled in and excreted out the exhaust pipe.

Sometimes, the daring man will actually reach into the engine compartment and tighten the nut on top of the air cleaner. If the car has no visible air cleaner, he's screwed.

Men will also check the lid on the reservoir of windshield washer fluid. Not that a car has ever stalled or malfunctioned because of difficulties in the windshield washer fluid reservoir, but it's the only thing he knows what is, and he's fairly certain that, as long as he doesn't lick his fingers, it can't hurt him.

All I know about cars is, if they don't work, you have to call Triple-A.

Then Triple-A hauls them off somewhere so that elves can come work on them at night while we sleep.

My 11-year-old daughter bought a light-switch cover recently. While I looked up the phone number of the electric company, so some of those guys in those giant trucks could come out and install it, she did something with a screwdriver to put it on herself.

I've been afraid of her since.

Five months ago people came to put new windows in my house. I haven't been able to watch TV in my underwear since. I can't figure out how to get the curtain rods back up.

I got a DVD player from my kids for Christmas two years ago. My wife hooked it up last week, because I couldn't figure out how.

And yet, as a man, I'm supposed to know how to do all these things. And when I don't, it's embarrassing.

Like when the toilet backs up.

Why is it if somebody puts too much of something down the toilet it becomes my business?

"Honey, the toilet's backed up."

How are you supposed to respond to that? Beyond recommending a diet higher in fiber, I have no idea whatsoever where to begin.

So in I go, plunger in hand. And there I stand, looking down on way too much information about the family's digestive habits. And I plunge, plunge, plunge.

I don't know what this does. But I do it gingerly. I've found in this situation, making too many waves is not a good idea. I've also learned that when you pull the plunger back up, after it's all but turned inside out, it's going to snap back into shape and throw "water" on me.

I don't like that.

So here's what I do. When the toilet backs up, I just turn off the light, close the door, and drive to McDonald's when I have to use the bathroom.

If you ignore it, it will go away.

Or your 11-year-old daughter will go in and fix it.

The day I became a man

I remember the day I became a man.

I thought my head was going to explode. As the pleasure swept over my body and I started to lose control, I knew this was what I had been put on earth to do.

I could feel my toes curl, pressing downward automatically, as I held on tighter and the two of us bucked and bounced, plowing almost, deeper with each lurch, so loud I'm sure the neighbors heard, but so engrossing I didn't care.

It's different with different cultures.

In primitive societies, I think they have to kill a lion. For ancient Native Americans, they often had to do vision quests, or cut off some guy's hair, or castrate a buffalo on the run.

For others, it is the mastering of long poems or sacred texts or the completion of difficult pilgrimages.

But I'm an American and we define our manhood in a more earthy context.

Either you've done it or you haven't.

And I remember the first time I did it.

It was up on top of a hill, down in the Southern Tier, where the Appalachians string off as far as you can see and there is neither pavement nor electricity.

It was about 2 in the afternoon.

The leaves had turned and the hillsides were as beautiful as the event, and it seemed right that something so natural should take place in nature, in an old hay field, where the fertility of the soil called out to my own.

And she was beautiful.

All in red, so smooth and sleek, with the biggest headlights I'd ever seen. A good front end and a solid backside and kind of a purr that turned to a roar.

And I did it with her.

I became a man.

I goosed her a bit, I put it in, I felt her respond and I held on tight.

It was my first time.

And it was so vigorous that it took my breath away and I felt a little dazed, carried away in it all.

"This is awesome," I said to my son, in the next seat over, watching closely every move I made.

He became a man later the same day.

In the same truck.

That's how it is with four-wheel drive. It changes your life. It transforms you.

It makes you a man.

One minute you're in two-wheel high. Like a woman. Driving along, incomplete.

Then the road ends. But your wanderlust doesn't. So you stop on the edge and breath deep and push the "four-wheel low" button and feel the gears kick in.

It's about to happen.

The forbidden fruit is about to be yours.

She jerks as you give her the gas, and rolls off unstoppable across the countryside, out where the deer walk and the tractors toil.

Around things at first, tentatively, then bolder and more aggressive, going over them soon, weeds and ant hills and anything else foolish enough to get in the way of man and machine.

Through mud and up hills and between trees and any damn place you please.

"We're in four-wheel drive now," you nonchalantly tell the person beside you, as he holds on, desperately trying not to knock his head against the window or doorframe as you bounce and bob over nature's contours.

I remember the day I became a man.

And I remember recently, when my 12-year-old daughter took her first turn behind the wheel. Peering up over the hood in four-wheel low.

Five-miles-an-hour across an old alfalfa field under a gray autumn sky, laughing hysterically at the fun of it, trying to remember which pedal was the brake and which was the gas.

Thanks goodness her mom doesn't read this column.

I hear they make good fertilizer

I'm not saying that cats should be outlawed.

But I'm willing to discuss it.

I think it's the most humane option. And a lot quieter than a shotgun.

Don't think I'm heartless. I used to like cats. I've even owned them.

For non-culinary purposes.

I have petted them and heard them purr and baby-talked to them and picked their hair from my food and smelled their litter boxes and put up with that odd habit they have of walking around with their butt holes showing.

So I'm not some cat hater.

I just think they should all be gathered up, put in some sort of rocket ship and fired into the vast emptiness of intergalactic space. I'd suggest a burlap bag thrown into the river but I recognize that that would be environmentally irresponsible.

I don't have much of a life, but right now what little there is of it is centered around cussing the 14,000 stray cats that live in my neighborhood and crap outside my window. They are filthy loathsome beasts that think my birdfeeder is their buffet.

And rumor has it that most of them are going to vote for John Kerry.

Outside my living room windows I have three birdfeeders. Squirrels and birds eat there. So do the cats. They eat the squirrels and the birds.

No matter how much I cuss at them.

No matter how many times I run up to the window shouting and screaming like I was John Wayne Bobbit waking up from a bad dream.

They just look at me, mutter bad words in French, and then walk away with their butt hole showing.

With one of my birds in their mouth.

I take it as an affront to our species.

We take these creatures out of the wild, we teach them to crap in boxes in our houses, we feed them stuff that smells like menstrual salmon, we let them sit on our furniture, and still they treat us like we're idiots.

I mean, they don't even catch mice anymore.

They just sit around and lick themselves and sleep.

Which, granted, sounds rather pleasant.

But it's our planet, not theirs.

As evidenced by the fact they have names like "Muffin" and "Snuggles" and we have both nuclear bombs and the Marine Corps.

Anyway, I want the highway department to come along with a dump truck and some pitchforks and chase these cats down and get them out of here. My neighbors had to build a chain-link fence to hold their beautiful dogs but everybody else on God's green earth can let their skanky cats run loose.

Maybe a one-day amnesty on the leash law, so the dogs can run around and clean these cats up. Seriously, I wouldn't mind the occasional child maiming if it meant no more cats. I mean, we've got these crack heads downtown with their pit bulls and rottweilers. It just seems a waste to let all that cat-crunching power go unused.

I think this is one of those areas where our Asian friends are miles ahead of us.

I mean, it's not just sticking needles in people to cure what ails them. It's a whole lifestyle they have over there. China isn't just communism anymore. It's also eating weird things other people consider pets.

Like cats.

Sadly, when they eat their own cats, they get kooky jungle diseases from them. Which I think offers an opportunity to solve our cat problem and address the troubling trade imbalance.

I say let's ship all our cats over to China and let those people fricassee them.

I hear it tastes like chicken.

Now, if we try to gather up all the cats, some people are going to be upset. I'm talking mostly about those nut-ball women with the dozens of cats that will eat her fingers off after she dies like she lived—alone and forgotten.

So what we've got to do is come up with a plan to get the cats when their owners are distracted.

Like when they're doing a special makeover program on the Dr. Phil show. Or when Marie Osmond is on that shopping channel hawking those dolls.

Or when the new Harlequin shipment comes into the bookstore.

But that's just an idea. Mass abduction may not work.

Which is why I'm exploring the possibility of exploding kibble.

I mean, honestly, I'm thinking of starting an ad campaign to convince the Palestinians that cats are Zionists. Maybe if they could take a break from strapping suicide vests on children they could fit one to a mouse or something.

Seriously, of all the things these Jihad boys insanely hate, how is it that cats escaped their attention?

Anyway, I can't write any more. I'm going out to sit on my front porch.

With my BB gun.

I'm teaching the neighborhood cats to dance.

Reefer madness

I'm writing this slowly.

Very slowly.

When I'm done I have to mow the lawn.

It's that time of the year again and the grass has grown shaggy out in front of the house. It's time for man to do the work of sheep.

Don't get me wrong, I like a nicely mown lawn. Each time I pass one I remark upon it admiringly.

Something like, "I wonder what poor, obsessed sap lives there?"

I wonder what proud human has been reduced to the drudgery of slaving over a few square feet of turf. Given the amount of time a good lawn requires, it's a wonder people don't carve it on headstones: He kept a good lawn.

Usually, I hire somebody else to do it.

Unfortunately, they want to be paid for it.

The day of the neighborhood kid mowing your lawn for five bucks is long since gone. I had one who did it a couple of years back and I calculated, timing his efforts on my behalf, that he was pulling down $32 an hour for his efforts.

Fortunately, he dropped me from his client list.

The one downside of using neighborhood kids is that how often your grass gets cut is determined not by how long it is, but by how much they need money. If they're planning a trip to the amusement park, you can get the full-service cut two or three times a week.

Used to be I had a mentally handicapped man cut my lawn. He was a pretty good guy and I was glad he came over. He kept mowing over my newly planted fruit trees and lilacs, however. At first I figured this was because he was mentally handicapped. Later I learned that he just didn't like fruit trees and lilac bushes.

But he's passed on now and the place is like a jungle out there.

I find it doesn't bother you too much if you just don't look out the window. And avert your eyes when you drive by.

Sometimes I tell myself that I'm making a wildlife refuge out there, that the whole jungle thing is something I do because I love the environment.

But, actually, I own a chainsaw and I like snowmobiling, so I'm not that into the environment.

I don't cut the lawn primarily because I'm lazy. And also because I don't have a lawn mower.

My former wife does, and she will loan it to me, but I have to mow her lawn first. Which, from the lazy man's standpoint, is not a good deal. I'm sure I get brownie points in heaven and it will help my tan, but her yard is a lot larger than mine—divorces usually work out that way—and somebody's going to have to pick up the sticks that blew out of the tree over the winter.

Now, some guys love this stuff.

They've got MiracleGro in their veins.

Personally, I'd prefer to go fishing. Or running or bicycling or hiking or shooting or television watching.

Plus, I live in a part of the country where there are only three or four nice days each year. All the other days there are tornadoes or earthquakes or blizzards or something. And this poses a dilemma. See, if it's a nice day, I figure I'm a fool to waste it cutting the grass when I could be out in the kayak.

And then, when it's too gloomy a day to go play, it's probably raining or snowing and it's too gloomy a day to cut the grass.

Which brings us to today.

It's nice out there, and I can see the grass in my front yard waving beautifully in the wind, and the tops of the neighbor kids' heads as they play hide and seek in it, and I'm torn. Every other house on the street has a perfectly manicured lawn.

And mine looks like a meadow.

And part of me thinks I should mow it.

And the other part of me thinks I should go for a run. Or go get a soft-serve ice cream cone. Or see if there are any new titles at the bookstore.

Conveniently, I have to write the column.

Unfortunately, it is almost done.

Granted, I haven't said anything of worth or substance, but I have delayed cutting the grass by more than half an hour. Another eight hours and it will be too dark to mow.

So I should sit and think and deliberate. Perhaps I'll ponder.

Or maybe I'll stand up resolutely from this keyboard and march out there to do my manly duty. I will show this lowly patch of grass once and for all—or at least for another week—who's the boss around here.

That's one option.

The other is I could just go take a nap.

Or buy a sheep.

Or close the curtains and ignore it.

Or just keep typing meaningless little lines to delay the inevitable.

Maybe I'll just get a litter box

I don't believe in plumbing.

I used to. But not anymore.

I think it's all a hoax.

I mean, think about it. You can sit on this porcelain thing and do your business and jerk a little lever and somehow it magically disappears. No muss no fuss?

Come on. Get real.

You can just stand there in the shower and run all this water over your amazingly firm and muscled body and it all just runs down some little hole into oblivion?

I don't think so.

But I'm trying to get my faith back.

The plumber is helping me.

It started innocently enough. I noticed that when I ran water upstairs, smelly black gook came up the sink downstairs.

That didn't seem right to me.

So after a few months I was at a diner and there was a business card for a plumber by the cash register and I figured, hey, he must be good if he's eating here.

Anyway, he came over and I figured he was some sort of miracle worker guy who would flip a switch or snap his fingers or wave some sort of electrical device and, wham-o blam-o, I'd be flushing just like the rich people.

Sure, it costs money. Big money. But I figured I'd make up for it by what I saved on AirWick.

And I'd get to use the backroom again.

Because the black gook was coming up there, too. Into the washtubs. Gallons and gallons of it. And odd sorts of creatures loved it. And that scared me. Because who wants to live with anything that eats crap and asks for seconds?

So over came the plumber.

He didn't know what he was getting into.

Turns out there's supposed to be this thing called a "clean-out." Kind of a big pipe thing that you unscrew when you need to get into the sewer.

Now, personally, I hadn't ever figured that I would need to get into the sewer.

I've always been able to satisfy myself just fine by getting into the gutter.

Anyway, the clean-out.

I don't have one. Neither does my house. And the plumber and I discovered this after rooting through every cobweb-choked corner of the basement we could find.

See, I have one of those old homes that someone's grampa built for someone's grama as a wedding present back in the day, only grampa was really dumb about building houses. I believe the architectural style is known as "early crackerbox."

And there's no clean-out.

But the plumber figured he could go in through the closed off pipe to a toilet that used to sit in the backroom.

Only he hadn't anticipated the crap geyser.

At first it was clear water, just a little bit to bleed off, make some small talk about plumbing and soccer and then all of a sudden I'm Jed Clampett. Up from the ground came a bubblin' crude. Real crude. Black gold.

But he lunged, Audie Murphy-like, into the gook, tightening some kind of thing-a-ma-jig to save us both from the dry heaves.

We decided that maybe this required some special equipment.

Which was good. I believe in equipment. Machinery is our friend.

And a day later he was back with some huge kind of snake thing. A thick wire that plows down through a pipe, turning and scouring, bringing up the various things that can block a sewer pipe.

Think about that for a moment.

The big problem is roots. Apparently if you've got a big healthy tree out in front of your house it's not your green thumb, it's your brown behind.

And I've got some really, really healthy trees.

So he comes over the second day with his huge snake—you can't know how uncomfortable I feel typing that—and he set about cleaning the pipe.

I went for a run. And to dinner. And I hung out with my kids. And I went to the store. And I watched *Survivor*.

And five hours later I came home.

To the most forlorn-looking man you'd ever want to see. Down there on his knees, spatterings of black gook all around, this big wire feeding down into a pipe, a foot-high pile of fibrous tree roots beside him. He said he was halfway to the main sewer.

So I sent him home.

And took a shower upstairs.
While black gook came up the sink downstairs.
I've lost faith in plumbing. I don't believe in it. It's a fairy tale, a fantasy, a myth, a hoax.

Facts for fogeys

There's nothing wrong with getting old.
As long as somebody else does it.
As a personal-participation project, however, it leaves a great deal to be desired.
Don't ask me how I know.
And don't think this has anything to do with the fact that two of my children are adults now. I'm doing this merely as a guide for those unfortunate few among us who actually do remember where they were when John Kennedy was killed.
Or did at one time.
This has nothing whatsoever to do with the fact that I've got floppy boobs. Or a floppy belly. Or a floppy backside. Or that bounding down the stairs leaves me quivering in seismic aftershocks for several seconds.
What once was held steadily in place by some long-forgotten mystical substance known as "muscle tone," has been left to its own designs. Designs which look a great deal like mashed potatoes.
No, this isn't about me.
It's about my desire to help old people.
A group with which I have absolutely nothing in common and for whom I have no understanding.
I'm too busy trimming the hair growing out of my ears to worry about the needs of a bunch of geezers.
I'd leave the hair there, but I hate it when the Tolkien crowd hounds me for autographs.
And the sound of the wind whistling through it is annoying.
What little of it I can hear.
How am I supposed to go around making old people feel good

about themselves when everybody I know has taken up whispering and mumbling? I want to get a T-shirt that says, "Speak Up."

And on the back it would say either "Get a job" or "Get a haircut."

Or maybe, "Why do you have an earring in your eyebrow?"

I'd cup my hand to my ear, but it just draws attention to the hair.

Now, I don't want to brag, but I used to have legendary bladder capacity. People from far and wide marveled at it. And who could blame them? I went when I wanted to, not when some hollow organ wanted to.

How many times did I tap my head and say, "The only sphincter that matters is right up here"?

But now I'm on a world tour of urinals.

I can't pass an Interstate exit without searching for a McDonald's, which is where America goes to take a McWhiz.

This is particularly entertaining at night when toe-stubbing expeditions in the dark leave one calling for a return to the days of the chamber pot.

Though, the passing years have enhanced my understanding of poetry.

Particularly the oft-repeated line, "No matter how much you jiggle and dance, the last few drops go down your pants."

No, this isn't about me.

It's about my desire to help old people.

A group with which I have absolutely nothing in common and for whom I have no understanding.

A group which tends to repeat itself.

I'd read up on the subject, but the print's too small.

And they're using some kind of odd ink that is indiscernible at near distances. For some reason, it doesn't become clear until you hold it out at arm's length.

Or maybe arm-and-a-half's length.

They use it on the label of these jeans I wear. Which is too bad, because if they didn't, I'd get the address of the company off them and send in a letter of complaint.

Ever since they stopped using preschoolers in Vietnam to make my pants, I've noticed they're a little snug in the seat. And around the middle.

I've been wearing a 31-inch waist for 20 years and now. With the quality control all gone to heck, they don't fit anymore.

Probably has something to do with NAFTA.

But my advice to geriatrics is to quit complaining. All you guys ever do is whine about how your parts don't work anymore.

Though I do think Bob Dole makes a good point.

So buck up and stop bellyaching.

No, this isn't about me.

It's about my desire to help old people.

A group with which I have absolutely nothing in common and for whom I have no understanding.

Though I do believe they're onto something when it comes to regularity.

Last night in the park with the kids

I don't know where I went wrong.

But my daughters are cheerleaders.

I'm not kidding. Thanks to the twin wonders of American ingenuity—laptop computers and folding chairs—I am writing this while sitting halfway between the two squads of practicing York Knights cheerleaders.

To my left the C Squad, girls about 8 years old, are receiving a stern talking to about looking professional.

Genuine cheerleader tip: Purple pom-poms go in the right hand, gold pom-poms in the left.

Looking professional is very important in youth cheerleading. So, too, I've discovered, is stern talking.

Which is all a surprise to me because I thought cheerleading was mostly about avoiding blow dryer injury and shouting complex phrases like, "Go, fight, win!"

Another genuine cheerleader tip: All sentences end in an exclamation point.

On my right, the B Squad—with its 11-year-old girls—is shaking its pom-poms while counting to eight, over and over. All of this occurs to a complicated choreography known in the medical community as "grand mal."

I think all the counting to eight is to make sure they don't swallow their tongues.

The quivering and shouting are punctuated by periodic bouts of stern talk. Over at the B Squad one of the coaches is telling war stories from some sort of cheerleading competition last year. The tone is reminiscent of those stories the drill sergeants told us about Charlie over in 'Nam.

There is a momentary lack of professionalism going on in the C Squad, it seems. While engaged in precision pom-pom waving, as they sing a song from *A Very Brady Movie,* three girls in the fourth row have leaned left when they were supposed to lean right.

Genuine cheerleader tip: 'NSync rules.

See, this is all troubling to me. Because I hate cheerleaders. And I don't know if I can get over it. Through four years of high school, and innumerable requests and pleadings, not one cheerleader went out with me once.

Not once.

More on the Brady Bunch: Marcia if you're talking right now, Jan if you're talking after another couple of years.

But back to my pain.

While I realize the girls of B Squad and C Squad are not high school cheerleaders, they will be. I mean, unless they get acne or good at math. They will grow up to be just like the cheerleaders who wouldn't give me the time of day.

I'm waiting for the part of practice where they teach them how to say "no" to scrawny guys with glasses and cracking voices.

Genuine cheerleader tip: Just tell him you like him as a friend.

The C Squad has broken out of its ranks and files and formed into facing lines, the girls interlocking their arms and pom-poms in some sort of Rockette chorus line, kicking this way and that, and now it has broken apart and reconfigured in lines and rows, all the while singing that Brady song, and gone seamlessly into its lean-left lean-right thing.

OK, so that was impressive.

Over at B Squad they're still counting to eight and the coach is speculating on the weather Saturday morning and whether it would be wise to change the practice scheduled for then to Friday evening. Apparently rain and cheerleading don't mix.

Genuine cheerleading tip: Waterproof mascara?

Now the B Squad is spelling g-o-o-d-l-u-c-k over and over after turning individually and shouting their names and announcing that the Knights are back.

Which is good.

Because that's what cheerleading was like when I was in school. Just a lot of group spelling. That, and that na-na na-na song. Hey, hey, hey. Good-bye.

Now there's the final Charlie-in-'Nam lecture and all kinds of happy shouting, clapping and spelling back and forth, the girls lifting one another into the air and walking to the minivans in the parking lot snapping their arms like Egyptian tomb paintings while counting to eight.

Several of them are air kissing and doing wobbly lopsided cartwheels that are a lot better than last week's.

And they are greeting their parents and asking about pizza and school tomorrow and doing bits of routines for siblings and grandparents.

It's a little bit of America.

And my daughters are cheerleaders.

And I'm going to pretend to complain, while I beam and strut like the other parents, smiling inside and out, and decide how many copies of the squad picture I'm going to need.

Genuine cheerleading tip: It could be worse; it could be my son.

Living in harmony with nature

Personally, I'm opposed to mice.

Unfortunately, mice are also opposed to me.

Which makes it a very good thing that I know how to set a trap and they don't.

It's time for a personal confession. There are mice in my house. Fewer than there were last week at this time, but they're there. I don't know how many, but I suspect it's something like several thousand.

Either that or it's just one, and he really likes to crap a lot.

Anyway, I got married a while ago, which means there's a woman living with me now. And women are incapable if ignoring mice. Or their crap. Men, on the other hand, are pretty good at ignoring things. Particularly things involving hygiene or work.

So I suppose I've always had mice, but it took a woman to bring them to my attention.

Which she does. Often. At a fairly high volume.

See, women are prejudiced against mice. Men are a little more thoughtful on the issue, taking into consideration the important interests of biodiversity and how God made all the little creatures so they must have their place and, in the words of Hotrod Rodney, "Can't we all just get along?" So a man can co-exist with a mouse. He probably can co-exist with lots of mice.

But women are different. They don't care a bit about biodiversity. They just want the mice killed. All of them.

They shriek and scream and breathe funny and wave their arms in the air. This is if they see a piece of mouse crap on a counter or in a drawer. I expect that if they ever actually saw a mouse itself they'd have some kind of seizure.

Anyway, I know this because I have a wife now and because I have mice, which means I have a fair amount of shrieking and screaming and funny breathing and arm waving. I'm sure we talk about other things, but I can't really think of what they are. Right now, everything seems to revolve around killing the mice.

Which is my job.

That's just what a man does.

And, with the assistance of the Victor mousetrap company, I've been able to do my manly duty. It's almost like clockwork.

Just before bed, the Princess Bride asks me if I've set the mousetrap. I, of course, have not. Men don't do things until they've been reminded a couple of times. So I plod down to the kitchen, mostly because I've learned as a newlywed that it's, from the man's standpoint, wise to be very agreeable just before bedtime.

Anyway, I plod down to the kitchen, grab a butter knife and pull down the jar of peanut butter. I open the jar and stick the knife into it and pull out a big blob of peanut butter. Then I put it in my mouth.

Hey, I don't work for free.

Anyway, then I get the trap out and put a smidge of peanut butter on the pan—which is the official trapper word for it, by the way—and with great trepidation try to set the thing.

I say "try to set the thing" because I think our trap is defective. Because half the time it doesn't set right. Instead, it snaps shut in my hands, flinging a wad of peanut butter across the kitchen. This gets messy. But, remember, men are pretty tolerant of hygiene problems. So I never look around to see where the peanut butter landed.

I figure, if any body asks, I can just say, "The last I saw it, it was on the trap. I don't know how it got all over your curtain. Those danged mice."

Anyway, I lube the trap with peanut butter and it snaps shut a couple of times and finally I get it to hook up right and I gently lay it down on the countertop, where the offending mouse crap was discovered, and push it into position with a convenient piece of silverware.

Then you have to sneak out of the room, walking lightly for fear of triggering the trap, turning the lights out behind you.

That's when it gets dangerous for the mice.

From their standpoint I can see how it looks a little devious. I mean, you're a rodent, minding your own business, taking a crap on the countertop, when all of a sudden you see a big glob of peanut butter. Creamy peanut butter. And you start nibbling on it.

That's when things get really unpleasant.

Especially if your wife hears it.

Because you, having retired to bed, having been purposely nice for almost 20 minutes, being a man, had kind of hoped that the day might not be over as soon as the prayers were said, if you know what I mean. And it looks like things might be headed that way when, snap, some little rodent sees his body lying mangled on the counter and feels himself being pulled toward a bright light where, undoubtedly, dozens of his little mice ancestors await.

Anyway, there is the snap, barely audible upstairs, and your wife says, "Was that a mouse?"

"No, honey," you lie. "I had gas."

Which, odds are, you probably did.

But that's not what she heard.

She heard Mister Whiskers taking one for the team.

So you have to go down to check. At least that's how she sees it. You have to go down and check and, if you got one, dump it in the toilet and reset the trap.

Few things excite a woman more than the chance to kill two mice in one night.

So there you are, all romantic, carrying a trap dangling a limp mouse with a newly bisected head.

Chicks dig stuff like that.

Anyway, that's the report from here.

As it stands, I'm up 4-0 on the mice.

Abandoned husband bemoans woes of single life

I realized my wife was gone when I ran out of socks.

That's not true, exactly. I knew she was gone before then. It first came to me when I went to the kitchen and sat down for dinner and there was no food.

There wasn't even a plate and a fork.

I knew something was wrong.

Then it occurred to me that she was away for the week. That she had gone camping with the teenage girls from church. They were eating s'mores and I was starving.

And that was just the first day.

I'm not sure I like girls camp. She's off swatting mosquitoes and talking to adolescents about God and I'm here staring at a frozen roast wondering how she turns it into food.

I know I've lived independently before, and not that long ago, but I've forgotten everything I ever knew. I'm wandering around my own house wondering where the spoons are. I'm calling strangers in the phone book to tell them I'm out of Frosted Mini Wheats.

I kept peeking out the window wondering when she was going to come home and mow the lawn. Caught up in a fit of self-reliance, I mowed it myself. In my pajamas.

Isn't it her job to remind me to get dressed?

And to pick up these newspapers?

I get up early and read *USA Today* and put it in a stack. When she gets up, she picks it up from atop the stack and reads it herself. Then it magically disappears.

But with her gone, the whole system has come apart. The stack is almost too high to step over and I'm not sure what to do.

I might call back those people I told about the Frosted Mini Wheats and see what they think about all these newspapers.

The only good part about her being gone was I could sleep diagonally in bed. That's how rich people sleep. Rich people have giant beds. Anyway, without her there I was able to sleep diagonally across the bed, spreading my arms and legs and thrashing about all I wished.

Which messed the bed up pretty good.

Which led to another problem.

When I wanted to go to sleep the next night, the bed wasn't made. It was all messed up. It looked like somebody had been sleeping diagonally in it and thrashing all about.

So I slept on the couch.

With a bowl of Frosted Mini Wheats.

The next night, when I discovered that the bed still wasn't made, and I came back to the couch with a bowl of Frosted Mini Wheats, I was able to begin stacking my dirty bowls.

The people on the phone said I should spray the bowls so they don't attract bugs.

All I could find was Jovan Musk for Men, but I sprayed them pretty good with it. And I liked the smell so I kind of sprayed it around the house, on the curtains and such.

Then I ran out of bowls.

I kid you not. I opened the cupboard, and there weren't any bowls. Usually there's a stack of them in there, but there wasn't. It was just empty space.

Fortunately, I still had the saucepans.

But I hadn't used more than three or four of those before I was out of Frosted Mini Wheats and milk. Then I remembered that in parts of Africa they don't have cereal, either, so I tried to think what Africans eat and did I have any of that.

Well, I remembered hearing Sally Struthers say once that African people need rice and powdered milk. I don't know what powdered milk is but I found some rice in the canister.

At least I thought it was rice.

It was like rice only it was really, really hard. I poured myself a saucepanful out of the canister and put some soy sauce on it and stepped over the stack of newspapers to go out to the couch and eat.

But I couldn't get more than a spoonful or two down because it was so hard to chew. I think I chipped a filling.

That was about the time the guy from the mortgage company called. He wondered where this month's payment was. I asked how he thought I should know. He said my name was on the mortgage. I said my wife handles the money. He asked where she was. I told him she was at girls camp. He said he felt sorry for me and he understood and he'd call back next week.

Then I asked him if he knew why my rice was so hard.

He said he didn't know but he'd ask his wife when he got home.

Eventually I ate canned peas. Until the forks ran out. Then I drank canned peas. If you open them up and tip them back gingerly just a few of them will go into your mouth at a time. Property done there isn't much of a mess at all.

So I was doing pretty well, all things considered.

Until the toilet paper roll ran out.

It mystified me. It was just like, all of a sudden, there wasn't any more paper on it. I didn't know that could happen.

When I asked the people from the phone book about it, they told me not to call them anymore.

Fortunately, I had that big stack of newspapers.

And fortunately my wife is coming home soon. Things are starting to stink around here.

The saga of Dave and Lamar

Let's hear it for Lamar and Dave.

Or Cody and Lobo, or whatever chick names the Princess Bride forces on them.

Forgive me for telling tales out of school, but there are troubles at home. The Princess Bride and I are having a disagreement.

This is a consequence of me being right and her being wrong.

To whit: She says I can't name my son Lamar or my dog Dave.

Maybe I should start at the beginning.

I got married this spring. Subsequent to the wedding we may or may not have engaged in certain adult married-people activities which may or may not have resulted in her being knocked up.

I don't think I need to elaborate.

Anyway, the home pregnancy test was verified by insanely expensive screening done at the doctor's office. Subsequent to that, we were sent down to the sonogram place to find out how many were in there.

It was just one.

A little inch-long guy doing calisthenics. A dancing peanut.

Anyway, as soon as you get pregnant, you have to start thinking up a name. Usually you take Bible names and family names and fling them against the wall and keep whatever sticks. As part of this process the Princess Bride and my 14-year-old daughter, Hannah, were putting together combinations of family names trying to come up with something new and different.

This is very dangerous.

As Shaquille O'Neal's mother learned.

Anyway, my middle name is Lavern. The Princess Bride's middle name is Marie. Drunk on estrogen, the two of them laughingly took the first syllable from each name and came up with "Lamar" and "Marla."

Lamar in case it was a boy and Marla in case it was the other kind.

Which we'd take back, anyway, before the warranty expired.

Impressed with their cleverness, they told me these names. They appeared uncomfortable when I told them I liked them both—especially Lamar.

Since then I have referred to the as-yet-unborn Lonsberry as Lamar the Dancing Peanut.

They laugh.

But I'm serious. I like "Lamar." It's a cool name. Kind of old fashioned and rural.

Or, as all my wife's friends say, kind of black.

To which I respond: Since when have names been black or white?

To which they respond: You can't name your kid Lamar; it's against the law.

So that's a stalemate. I figure it's going to have some kind of soap-opera name unless I can fill out the paperwork before the Princess Bride comes out of the anesthetic.

Speaking of which, I don't think there's going to be any anesthetic.

The Princess Bride is a Democrat and she wants to use a midwife. At our birthing class I'm learning how to beat a drum and chant.

Anyway, I figure maybe I won't get to name Lamar Lamar, and I can live with that.

But she's not letting me name the dog either.

I've talked her into letting me get a dog—an English springer spaniel—and it, too, will need a name.

I pick "Dave."

Because Dave is the perfect name for a dog. Science has proven it.

But there's a problem. She used to have a boyfriend named Dave. And she figures that if she now has a dog named Dave, all her friends will think that she's not over the boyfriend.

I knew you couldn't name children after former significant others, but I didn't know the rule applied to pets, too.

I told her I never met the boyfriend and I don't care and I want to name my dog Dave.

If it would help with her friends, I'd be willing to get a female dog and name it Dave. That way, metaphorically, I'd be making Dave my, uh, female dog.

But I guess it's enough that I ended up with the girl.

Anyway, the Princess Bride is one of these people who makes lists, and she has a list of approved dog and child names. Sometimes I can't tell them apart. But either way, I think it'd look dumb if I named my dog or my son Lobo, or Scout, or Cody.

I prefer Dave, and Lamar.

Some have suggested that I name the dog Lamar, but I figure that won't work out.

Because at some point the child would learn that the dog got the cool name and it was stuck with the dull name and there would be resentment toward the dog.

So that's where things stand.

I've got a child and a dog coming, and I don't know what we're going to call either one.

Though they're both going to call me "Daddy."

With the child, I expect, eventually pronouncing it a little better than the dog.

My son is full of crap

My son can't take a crap.

Jack. Jack the Night Howler. He's become Jack the Constipated.

Not yet four months old and already he's working on a world record for longest time between bowel movements.

I'm not saying I'm disappointed in him, but if there's one thing our family's good at, well, apparently he's not good at it. Honestly, I set my clock by it.

But this isn't about my colon. It's about his.

And by now I figure that that colon has got to be about the size of Rhode Island.

And the shape, I figure, of Florida. Or California. Or maybe that island part of New York.

Anyway, it's apparently no fun holding onto your feces for weeks on end. I've gathered this from watching him lay there and make this strange grunting sound. He seems to be laboring over something.

The last time I saw this, his mother made a terrible mess on the sheets and he popped out.

But I'm too young to be a grandfather.

So I'm sticking with my constipation diagnosis. I think he just needs to take a good crap for himself.

I don't know why, but that always seems to make things better.

Anyway, back to the boy's behind. His mother, the Princess Bride, reports that his last bowel movement was on the beach at Lake Tahoe on their trip out West last week. And by "last week" I mean seven full days—one fifteenth of his life. Since then he's been packing.

And we're not sure what to do.

The doctor said to rub his belly. Especially on the left side—his left side, the baby's not the doctor's—and encourage him to go.

Which is something I don't know how to do. How do you encourage some little baby who can neither speak nor understand English to, uh, "make big stinky"? I'm not sure this kid knows I'm anything other than a bigger version of the dog. And I'm supposed to somehow communicate to him that he is to release his bowels?

How in the heck is that supposed to happen?

Do I diagram that? Or act it out? Is there a picture book I can purchase?

Who'd have thought I'd need to teach my kid how to take a crap.

Anyway, the Princess Bride is pretty worked up over this. She times and weighs his various bodily functions and excretions and the disruption of his schedule has disrupted her schedule. I picked her up at the airport night before last and for all of the hour-and-a-half ride home she was talking about his mysteriously empty diapers.

Not that it's not an important topic, but after, "My son can't take a crap," I kind of run out of things to say about it.

Anyway, she called the doctor.

That's one of the reasons I never went to medical school. I don't want to be taking calls in the night from ladies whose kids won't crap, and I don't want some old guy bending over a table waiting for me to check his prostate.

And I'm not too keen on that look-in-people's-ears thing either.

Anyway, so she calls the doctor and the doctor says give him some prune juice.

I think that's the circle-of-life thing. When you're old, they give you prune juice. When you're young, they give you prune juice. When you're in the middle, and can fight back, nobody gives you prune juice.

Sometimes, if you're a sadist, you give prune juice to other people.

Anyway, the doctor says give him prune juice. And if that doesn't work, well, that's when it gets nasty.

If that doesn't work, you're supposed to go in after it.

I'm not kidding. The doctor said that, if he doesn't loosen up with the prune juice, we're supposed to take his temperature with a rectal thermometer.

Excuse me while I puke.

Rectal thermometer? Didn't they go out with the Stone Age? Aren't they illegal yet? If they're not, will you sign my petition to ban them?

Yuck.

That's why I bought that thing you stick in his ear, so we wouldn't have to use that thing you stick in his rear.

Anyway, you're supposed to put the rectal thermometer in there and stand back. Apparently it's some sort of floodgate or something.

Well, I'll believe it when I see it.

Or when I see a picture of it.

Because the way the Princess Bride is talking about this Holy Crap we're going to have to name it and memorialize it when it finally takes its leave of our young son. This thing might need its own webpage. Maybe it could keep a blog or something.

I always hoped young Jack would grow up just like me.

And, look, he's already full of crap.

How could a dad be happier?

Six

"I did my best" is only an excuse

I did my best.

That's the long way to say: I failed.

And we've become a society too willing to accept "I did my best" as an honorable substitute for success.

But it's not.

And unless you're willing to believe that, you're going to be walked all over by people who are.

Because life isn't about doing your best; it is about succeeding. And failing to succeed can have extraordinary and horrendous consequences.

Now, don't think I'm a freak. I understand there are limitations, and that we all have them. I know that sometimes we can throw everything we are into a task, bending every effort and sparing no personal sacrifice, and still come up short.

Success can, honestly, be outside our abilities.

But not as often as we tell ourselves it is.

Because typically our best isn't. Typically "our best" is some standard of performance far beneath our true capacity. And the reason we sell ourselves short so often is because "I did my best" has become such an easy crutch.

We accept it in society because we accept the flawed premise upon which it is based. We think effort is more important than outcome.

And we are wrong.

It is not the earnestness of an effort which determines its worth; it is the consequence of that effort.

Years ago I was a sports reporter at a daily newspaper and would invariably be set upon by the angry parents of losing high school athletes. Didn't I know, they would shout, that the losing team worked just as hard as the winning team, that it had practiced just as long and its effort deserved just as much recognition in my stories.

They, of course, were wrong.

Because it didn't really matter how hardworking their children had been, it only mattered that they had lost.

They did their best, perhaps, but their best—as the final score showed—was not good enough.

And life is far harsher than the playing field.

You can do your best, but if you don't get the promotion, your paycheck isn't going to get any bigger. You can do your best, but if you don't control your weight, you're probably going to end up sick because of it.

Whether you "did your best" or not is irrelevant if you do not achieve what you need to achieve.

"I did my best" is not what you want to hear when the emergency department doctor walks up to you in the waiting room. And it's not what you want to hear from your investment counselor, or from the contractor who built your house.

"I did my best" is the first sign that something has gone wrong and that the person talking to you wants to avoid responsibility for it.

That's a harsh fact, but true.

An insidious consequence of our acceptance of "I did my best" as an excuse is that it takes away the fear and shame of failure. If we make failing easy we also make it more common. And that is not good. We might think we are being understanding when we console losers by telling them they did their best, but actually we are cutting them off at the knees.

We are paving the way for their next failure.

We are giving them an out which human nature says they will use.

Fear of failure, within rational bounds, is good.

When I was in high school, I ran cross-country. I was terrible at it. I am a poor runner. In our course there was a steep hill, maybe 300 yards long, behind our school.

In six years of cross-country I never ran all the way up that hill. I always stopped and walked. I couldn't do it. I did my best, but I couldn't do it.

A few years later, I went in the Army.

At Fort Knox there were two hills, steeper and longer, something like a mile long. If you dropped out of a run on those hills your life became miserable, the drill sergeants made sure of that. I was afraid of the consequences of stopping and walking.

So I never did.

"My best," it turned out, was far more than I had believed. For six years, I had been cheating myself and my team.

Because I was willing to accept "my best" as a substitute for success.

Granted, this can be carried to an extreme. We can set for ourselves and others impossible standards and destroy ourselves in pursuit of them. But in this day and age that is far less common that the opposite.

We tend to cop out far more often than we obsess.

We tend to expect far less from ourselves than our true capacities would dictate.

And we lead less fruitful lives as a consequence.

To grow you must stretch and to do that you must attempt the impossible and discover, like millions of those around you, that it wasn't impossible after all.

Don't set out today to do your best.

Set out to win.

You'll like the results better.

A girl on the radio

Saturday on the radio a woman called from Harrisburg. Some two thousand miles away on the banks of the Susquehanna.

A girl, actually, at least that's how she sounded. A wisp of a voice somewhat shy and high, calling a stranger in a studio in the mountains.

It had been a ragged half hour. Something about Colin Powell and what he said on MTV, about condoms and AIDS, and how abstinence education was best but that there needed to be a Plan B as well, for the ones who go astray.

And the conservatives had called in and they couldn't see that there was room in the world for both. And they were right but not completely and I went off on a jag. About the best way to teach chastity and virtue was not through fear, but through wonder and awe.

That it is not the fear of hell that controls conduct; it is the love of heaven. That people run best when they are running toward something, not away from something else. And I said that abstinence before marriage and fidelity after marriage brought a peace and happiness, and a sexual fulfillment, that no other way of life could.

I said that I didn't know this by experience, and that I was a failure in this regard, but that I knew it was true.

And then she called.

The girl from Pennsylvania.

The last caller of the day. Three hours of shouting and laughing and trifling matters. And then the girl. With two minutes left and the show almost done.

"But what," she began, "what if it's already gone?"

"What if you've already done something you shouldn't have?"

Asked of some jerk on the radio, somebody moonlighting for an extra $300, cursing the Saturday lost and wishing he'd been able to sleep in.

"What if you've already done something you shouldn't have?"

The fundamental question of our existence. Asked by a girl who was troubled and hurt. What if you've already done something you shouldn't have?

Actions can be like scars that bind and disfigure us, injuries from which there seems no prospect for recovery. A choice, a word, a deed, and life appears forever changed. Forever damaged. And we despair.

The promise of yesterday, and the innocence, look like they are lost. We look like we are lost. And the joy and the happiness seem reserved for others, and not ourselves, and nothing appears able to ever change that.

But that is wrong.

That's what I told that girl.

I told her that God is quick to forgive. That when we regret what we have done, and feel sorrow because of it, and abandon it, and move on different, asking God for forgiveness, he is quick to forgive.

To make us whole and new again.

That's what I told her on the radio.

And that she must forgive herself. I asked her when it was and she said she had been 17, four years ago, and I told her that it was time to let it go. She was a different person now, who had chosen a better way to live, and if she asked God to forgive her, and he did, then she must do the same.

And the two minutes were up and it was time for the out cue and the show was done and the headphones went dead.

And off somewhere in Pennsylvania was a young woman unsure.

Like most of the rest of us. Unable or unwilling to grasp the principle of repentance and allow it to work, for ourselves or for others. To let bygones be bygones and the new day truly new.

Rather, we hold ourselves and others to our worst days and our worst decisions. Defining ourselves and others by our most striking weaknesses and darkest hours.

Condemning ourselves in private and others in public. Neither seeking nor giving forgiveness. Forever barring the door to improvement and progress.

Which may be the worst thing of all.

Worse even than our original offense. Because the one can be overcome, and the other cannot.

And the one weighs like a heavy and wearying burden, its pain never quite leaving our consciousness. A dull ache that crescendos in the quiet when we look within ourselves.

But it's not supposed to be that way.

The way of forgiveness exists.

And I hope that girl found it. And I hope the rest of us do as well.

Recognize that you have done wrong, feel sorry for it, don't do it again, ask God for forgiveness.

And get on with life. Get on with being what you were meant to be. Have the burden of guilt and regret lifted from your shoulders.

I hope that girl found that. And I hope the rest of us do as well.

Optimism, gratitude and courage

There are three keys to life.

Optimism, gratitude and courage.

You can't live a day without them, and you shouldn't try. You should embrace them. Certainly when it's easy, but most importantly when it's not.

When it feels like you can't take another step, when it feels like life has torn you asunder, when it feels like you want to run away and hide. When it feels like you're beaten and dead.

Optimism, gratitude and courage.

On the brightest of days and the darkest of nights.

You must believe that good things will happen. You must expect a happy ending. You must look at life in such a way that its warts are less obvious and its beauties are more pronounced.

You must look up, not down, and see light, not darkness.

You must grasp for cheerfulness and resist the urge to complain. Think of how your words and thoughts can strengthen yourself and others. It is better to be silent than to be pessimistic, better to be unheard than to tear down. Better to spread cheer than gloom.

Optimism, gratitude and courage.

Be thankful for what you have, and know that if you can't find anything to be thankful for it is merely because you are failing to recognize your blessings. There is goodness all around, if we'll only look.

And each new day is a gift. So are health and love and the shining sun and singing bird. The ability to earn a living. A bed, a home, food on the table. The comforts and enjoyments of life, the promises and hopes of eternity.

The opportunities to learn and make friends and laugh. Gratitude is a perspective on life that grows and becomes richer. It appreciates the gems of life, no matter how deeply buried in the mud they may be.

Grateful people are usually satisfied, ungrateful people typically never are. Grateful people rejoice in what they have, ungrateful people mourn for what they don't.

Gratitude helps you appreciate the bleakest of conditions, and reminds you that at the worst of times you are still blessed and rich.

Optimism, gratitude and courage.

The fearful man is not truly free. The fearful man is not truly useful. The fearful man is not truly hopeful.

Because fear is a quicksand that slows and grips and strangles, leaving its victims unable to act, too timid to do what life requires.

Each new day demands courage, to lead out and make decisions, to risk and stretch. To get out of bed and see what comes. To run the chance of falling flat on your face.

To scream headlong into fate with all you're worth. To persist through the adversities and challenges, to push against the odds. To act and stand when others cannot.

Optimism, gratitude and courage.

You need those things. Sometimes you need them to be happy, other times you need them to survive.

I don't have any magic formula, or tips for how to do what, but I do know that if you remember those words and those traits, things go better. The bright days are brighter, the dark days are bearable. Ask yourself continually: How can I have more optimism, gratitude and courage.

And be aware that the difficulties and depressions you feel will be largely the result of a lack of one or more of those things.

I'm not saying this well. But I hope you understand. Because life is good. It is precious. It is a great blessing. Even on its worst days. And in its deepest valleys you must remember the view from its highest mountains. You must not forget that happiness is a matter of perspective, not circumstance.

The happiest people are the people with the best attitudes, not the best lives.

Misery can thrive in comfort and rejoicing can make a home in privation, and no matter what life gives you—or you give yourself—you will determine whether you weep or laugh, mourn or exult.

Optimism, gratitude and courage.

They are all part of faith. And they are what you need. They are what you cannot live without.

I know this by experience. Because I've been in difficulties a time or two. There are occasions when it seems that life has beaten me silly.

Just as it has done to everyone.

Just as it has probably done to you.

Just as it will probably do to all of us again.

But hear my certain testimony: Life is good. There is much to be grateful for. There is much to hope for and have faith in, and every reason to expect a happy ending. There is no reason to despair, no reason to throw in the towel, no reason to hang your head and cry.

But every reason to go forward.

Every reason to believe. Every reason to endure. Every reason to rejoice.

Life is good. God has blessed us.

Even on the worst of days.

Of deserts and mirages and the world of cyber dreams

In the dark they sit at the computer, typing to strangers far away, finding intimacy with a machine in a world of isolation.

A pretended intimacy, a wanted intimacy, an artificial treasure, nurtured and clucked over, like a hen with a china egg. It looks like something and it feels like something, but it's really not.

It's the Internet. Or an instant message or a chat room or an e-mail or a buddy list or some other means of making words appear on a screen to take the place of a life that will not be or which is not bearable.

And a peek turns into hours and then days and for many before long the world is no larger than the screen in front of their face. Families are ignored and work is neglected and it all goes soft and gray, like a dry alcoholism of obsession and fixation. And at 4 in the morning you sit in the chat room still, the last one, waiting five more minutes for you don't know what.

And at 5 you'll still be there.

It is a sickness, a pathology of pathos, a cutting kind of loneliness that manifests itself in the clickety-clack of a keyboard and the downloading of pictures, the sharing of secrets and dimensions and a completely illogical feeling of closeness.

It is strangers masquerading as friends and lovers. A couple of hours of electronically passed notes supplanting years of life in the real world. A turning from spouses and rejections and the creation in your mind of an idyll, a Christmas tree decorated with the ornaments of imagination, more beautiful and comely in fantasy than anyone or anything can be in reality.

It is inherent disappointment, a gossamer world of play acting and dressing up in Mommy's and Daddy's clothes.

And it all goes to ashes, and still you sit, answering the little message boxes that pop up, melded into a world of asl and lol and :) and brb and rofl and omg and imho.

A world where "How are you?" is followed by "What's your bra size?" Where everyone lies. Where everyone's jonesing for they don't know what and where the next fix has to be bigger and faster and followed hard on its heels by something better.

It's the mouse that roared.

And it is no respecter of persons.

Young and old, male and female, godly and godless. All the same creature, wrapped up in different robes. And people type desires they could never speak and form bonds they can never sustain.

All are predators and all are prey, and none recognizes either certainty.

And you wonder how this need manifested itself before the computer, or how this disease was expressed. Or how it was controlled and contained.

Because now it is neither.

And people marry and divorce and move across the country, all on the foundation of this shaky little world of pixels on a screen, glowing like the flame which draws the moth.

Fat women are beautiful and emaciated men are virile and people so broken as to be incapable of love find companionship, or the anesthesia of delusion, gobbled down like a box of Twinkies.

Until finally they are sick and sated and stumble away, beyond physical exhaustion, to collapse and finally stir and log on again.

And feel that all is perfectly well.

To be oblivious to the plague which afflicts them.

It's the opium den of our age. A place where life seeps away through a drain in the floor.

You see it in the hobby rooms and the singles sites and the regional chats and the places where people write about politics. It is the perfumed stench of decay. And some can dance through it and go on OK, and maybe take something or someone with them, but behind them they leave the others, the ones not so unlike themselves, caught up in it all, somehow unable to recognize that all it takes is a simple action.

The simple pressing of a button.

The realization that all are drowning in a two-foot ocean and need do no more than stand to save themselves. To shake it off and move on.

Because every knife cuts two ways, and the proportion of good and bad is always the same. The higher the high the lower the low.

And the Internet is the miracle of the age, the tree of life from which all want to eat. It is a medicine and a poison, and sometimes you just can't tell which is which until it is too late.

Too late to save yourself.

When it's actually so easy.

Click on Start. Click on Shut Down. Click on Shut Down The Computer?

Click on Yes.

And go out and live life.

Why can't we reproduce ourselves?

Get pregnant.

Do it for America.

In numbers out yesterday, word comes that the birth rate in the United States is the lowest it's ever been.

The birds do it and the bees do it, but Americans don't do it very well.

We're having fewer babies, and they're being born sicklier and earlier.

Which isn't good.

Because at the end of the day, you only get people one way. The old fashioned way. And our culture and its priorities have changed such that having babies and raising families—especially big families—are simply no longer as important as they used to be.

Demographers chalk this up to age. They say the Baby Boomers and their uteruses are getting too old to have children and so the wellspring of babies is drying up.

Which makes no sense whatsoever.

With normal birthrates, the Baby Boom would have produced plenty of breeders to take its place. But it didn't. And any impact of an aging population on the birth rate would seemingly be erased by the massive influx of Latinos in the United States.

The Latinos who come here are overwhelmingly young, and they value having large families. The odds are that, if you factored Latinos out of the American numbers, you'd see an even starker drop-off in our national birthrate.

Which is tragic.

It imperils our national security and identity, will change the nature and priorities of our society, and lead to a fundamental change in our collective culture.

And that's not the worst part.

The worst part is that we are shutting ourselves off from the great blessing of children. We are forgoing children, we are delaying children, we are limiting children. Our reproductive systems are being twisted from the fertility of their nature to the barrenness of our choice. We lie fallow and wonder why we die lonely.

There are various reasons for this.

One is the decline in religion, particularly Roman Catholicism. In an earlier era Americans believed that having children was a commandment from God, and Catholics specifically believed that the use of birth control was immoral. Religious families had lots of kids. Now there are fewer religious families. Therefore, there are fewer kids.

Another reason is the rise of feminism. The odd irony of feminism is that it is not feminine. In fact, it seems to oppose all things feminine, and urges the abandonment of what is wonderful about being a woman and the adoption of what is obnoxious about being a man. The feminist movement has ridiculed and demeaned motherhood, consigning it to "unfulfilled" women who presumably lack what it takes to go off and have a career.

Another reason is the love of money. We have become more concerned with how big our house is and what we drive or where we go on vacation than we have been about being moms and dads. We have delayed marriage until after college graduation and the purchase of a home and we "get on our feet." Then we delay having children until after we've "gotten to know one another." And by then it's been too late, or we have lost most of a decade of our reproductive lives.

Another reason is the demise of marriage. More than a third of all American births are to unmarried women, who not only provide weaker parenting but also become less socially desirable. Except for welfare recipients, it is very difficult for a single woman to support a child, much less multiple children. Consequently, her lifetime fertility is diminished, as is her likelihood of finding a spouse. In addition, high divorce rates produce middle-aged men who marry younger women and don't want children, effectively removing those women from the pool of likely parents.

Ironically, better-educated people—whose children would presumably have the best lives and the most to offer society—are the least likely to reproduce. The more money and education a couple has, the less likely it is to have children. Some successful segments of society—like Jews—don't even replace themselves.

High birth rates most commonly are found in families with the least money and the least education.

It's pretty sad, really. Those who think they have the most, really have the least. And those society thinks have the least, really have the most.

Because the best things in life aren't in your bank account; they are around your dinner table.

By suppressing our birthrate, we have chosen a direction contrary to nature and contrary to our own best interests. We have chosen comfort over joy and convenience over happiness.

Which is a national tragedy.

I am my children's friend

Actually, I am my children's friend.

And I'm proud of it.

It is a priceless thing to me, and I suppose it has some value to them as well.

I say this because I'm getting tired of people blurting out, "I'm not my children's friend, I'm their parent."

And then they launch into this bellicose tough-love sermon that sounds like warmed-over Dr. Laura.

About how they're not here to be pals; they're here to give guidance and lay down rules and provide structure. It's not about fun, they say; it's about discipline and respect.

I've heard it all, over and over again.

And I've thought about it.

And it's a bunch of crap.

It's the pendulum swinging too far from the common sense of moderation. It's a great slogan, but it's bad parenting.

Because our children should be our friends, and we should be theirs. And any artificial distance we place between them and us, in the name of parenting or anything else, is wrong.

And doomed to failure.

The first proof I would cite is the best. I would point upward.

To God, whom we call Heavenly Father. And who, throughout the scriptures, calls us "friend." We are his children, and he often calls us such, but he also freely and purposely calls us friends.

Does that diminish him? Does that make us his peers? Does that lessen his ability to give us structure and direction? Does it lessen his ability to discipline and punish us? Does it make him soft?

Of course not.

He is not a soft God, yet neither is he a shrill God. He is, in fact, our loving friend.

And he is, as parents, our best example.

We should be like him.

And we should know what a friend is, and what power a friend has.

A friend is my child's closest confidante. A friend will hear my child's dearest secrets and darkest fears.

Friends accept one another without question. They don't put on airs or lie to one another; they feel acceptance and safety in one another's presence.

Friends delight in one another's company; it is a comfortable and pleasant thing. They feel at ease and natural. They are themselves.

And I want that with my children.

I want to be among the people they consider inviting on a camping trip, or on a bike ride or to go to the movie. I want to be someone they can tell about their boyfriends and girlfriends, someone they can joke with, someone who they listen to their CDs with.

I want to be part of their lives.

Their real lives. The ones where they spend most of their time.

I am still their father, and I make the rules. I tell them when I'm disappointed and I tell them when I'm proud. We have guidelines and boundaries, and we respect them, and I enforce them.

And I am the older and hopefully wiser partner in the friendship. And I hope that that can be of use to them.

But I am not on a pedestal, and they are not beneath me. We are partners. We each have duties in life that are essentially the same, I merely took up mine a couple of decades sooner. I may have an earlier responsibility to be of service to them, but they through life will have an equal responsibility to be of service to me.

As time passes, our lives will become more and more alike. They will grow and take responsibility after having been small and dependent, and in time if I live long enough my power and ability will shrink until it is less than theirs. Over the average of our lives, we will be the same.

That is because we are brothers and sisters.

I am their father, but that is not all there is to our relationship.

If there is a common God who created us, who is our shared father, then we are also siblings. We have a shared obligation and parentage. We are on the same team.

And of course I am their friend.

I hope I am their best friend.

And any twisted sophistry that would take you as a parent away from saying the same thing is misguided and confused. It is based on an inequality that does not in fact exist. It presumes a superiority for mothers and fathers that is not spawned of love.

Because I am more than my children's father and friend. I am also their servant.

It is my job to humbly better their lives.

Christ, whose followers are called his sons and daughters, called his disciples "friends." Then he washed their feet.

I suspect that is the true spirit of parenting.

And I do not hear that spirit in the tired slogan, "I am not my children's friend."

Delaying family is usually unwise

When is it right to marry, and when, after that, is it right to have children?

Those are personal questions, and they have personal answers. Answers that are different for different people.

But there are rules of thumb, generalizations that hold true more often than society thinks. Our grandparents knew that, but modern America has largely forgotten.

Forgotten that the best things in life are actually the purpose of life, and that there is no wisdom in delaying what on our deathbed we will consider the jewels of our existence.

Marry early and have children early.

Be fruitful and multiply, create a home and a family, build a life that matters and has substance. Find purpose in something larger than yourself. Find purpose in love.

We live in an era when men and women are told to delay marriage until after they have gotten their educations, and established their careers, and had a chance to live. To buy a house perhaps, and see Europe and have some fun.

Delay, delay, delay. Thing after thing is held to be more important than marriage, and getting married is seen in a negative light, as something for later, not for now. Maybe a relic from another and less-evolved age, something for simpler people, the poor or naive.

And when people do decide to wed, increasingly they have engagements of a year or two in length. And sometimes they simply become engaged, without setting a date, and they step not closer to, but further from, the altar.

That's no good.

It's no good because life is not meant to be lived alone. Humans are not solitary creatures. We form, typically, lifelong pair bonds. We function best when we love and are loved.

So marriage is good. And delaying a good can only be bad. And it can solidify habits and tendencies of selfishness and singleness which will hamper the eventual marriage. During the formative and early years of adulthood, when nature intended us to be adapting to the new family that will be the structure of the balance of our lives, too many people draw within themselves and set out on solo lives.

And when people do marry, the custom of the day urges them to put off childbearing, to spend a year or two or five "getting to know one another" or to delay the arrival of babies until they can "afford them." These are both treacherous positions, seducing people into inactivity and procrastination, putting the insignificant in front of the significant.

Because two people spend a lifetime getting to know one another, and no one ever truly feels ready to have a child, and nobody can afford kids. And these excuses are a poor substitute for a babe in arms.

In fact, everything is a poor substitute for a babe in arms. Everything is a poor substitute for what is best and most precious about life.

Yet the poor substitute is increasingly society's choice. And where a generation ago many women were done having their children by 30, many now are just beginning. And they are discovering difficulties of fertility that were once rare, and they, having lost years of opportunity, have fewer children. And the children they do have are raised by people in middle age and beyond.

And the natural vigor of youth, the reproductive strength of the 20s, is spent not on family, but on self. Nature's plan is overturned, and it is only natural to wonder if that is for the best.

Marry early and have children early.

For many people, that is the right answer.

Certainly, it entails struggle, difficulty and challenge. It means more work and fewer of life's recreations. But good things come at a price, and the love and richness bought by the hard times linger like a treasure through life.

Life's seasons offer different rewards, but none are more sweet or precious than the years when children are young and at home. Their parents will call those the best days of their lives and they will similarly linger in the children's memory. Those times are life's best times. They are better than anything else this existence has to offer.

And yet there is a spirit abroad in the land that demeans and delays that stage of life, that shoos people away from marriage and curtails the birth of children. It is an evil spirit, and a selfish and miserable one. A custom and culture that cons people into fundamental error, that steals from them what ought to be their greatest joys.

Our lives have a purpose, whether you read Darwin or the Bible. And that purpose is to reproduce, to make more of our kind, to bring into the world little ones like us, not for our sakes, but for theirs. In this era we often lose sight of that. We see children as additions to our lives, new things to own, higher-order pets who must be adapted to our lifestyles and priorities.

But we have the cart before the horse.

They are not there for us, we are there for them. Our health and strength and breath are not for our enjoyment, but for their benefit. We are meant to serve, not to be served.

And marriage and parenthood are the pinnacles of service in this life. They are opportunities to give of ourselves, to love as God has loved.

And we are fools to delay them or pass them by.

Marry early and have children early.

Love and forgive, or lose

When I was young I prayed that the Lord would smite my enemies.

Now I pray that he will soften their hearts.

And that we will not be enemies at all. That they will forgive me. And I will not give them offense.

And that I will not take offense. That I will shrug off the attacks of life, intentional or inadvertent, and not waste a moment on bitterness and anger.

That is hard to do, because conflict is such an inviting intoxicant. We cling to it and treasure it up and in the absence of a better passion it grows and becomes a cancer. And some people come to a point in their lives where all they have is the bitterness and the bile.

I've known people like that, and been related to them, and either joined in or been the target. And I've seen those people driven away from their friends and loved ones and I've seen the putrid harvest of hate.

And they weren't bad people.

They just got hooked.

Hooked on being ticked off, sucked down by the allure of contention.

There may actually be an addiction. Some chemical thing, some adrenaline surge, or some transmitter in the brain which gets out of whack and there is an habituation to the quarrel and fight.

But even if there's not, it's hard to kick. Hard to have the humility to forgive. At least it has been for me.

When I was young I loved to argue. Actually, I loved to win. And I always did. To get in a discussion and attack people's ideas and tear them apart. About religion, politics, anything. I loved to Bible bash, as we called the arguments over scriptures, and I lived to debate. And each time I walked out with some kind of high, like a matador waving an ear for the cheering crowds, exultant at my dominance over this other person.

And I convinced myself I was doing good. That I was defending my religion from bigots, that I was standing up for true principles, that I was showing people the error of their ways.

When all I was doing was being a jerk. I was hurting feelings and embarrassing and pushing away.

It was wrong. I was wrong.

There is no joy in contention, or satisfaction or good. And I am grateful to have realized that, and to have thought long on the words of the New Testament where it says that we will be forgiven in proportion to our own tendency to forgive.

I have great need to be forgiven, but few opportunities to forgive. I've found that when I stopped looking for offense, there was far less of it. I've found that if I don't stick my toes in other people's paths, they tend not to get trod upon.

People are nicer than I had thought.

And when they are not, I have a better sense of why. There aren't many truly bad people in life, not many at all. But there are a lot of good people who will be occasionally—or frequently—big jerks. In recent years I've started to understand why.

And not hold it against them.

People usually go wrong because they are afraid. Because they are like me and sometimes they will feel threatened or out of their element or in some other way will be frightened. And somehow that gets twisted around and perverted and comes out wrong.

But that's OK, because I can understand fear and accept it.

And I can see myself in it.

And I can understand that we are all a bunch of fellow travelers, stumbling through life as best we can. Some know more, and do better, and others seem to be walking blind. But we are all struggling through, and it's the kind of race where it doesn't matter how fast you cross the line, just that you in fact cross the line. The kind of race where you cheer for the guy beside you. Where you run with him, not against him.

And that's what I want to do.

To wish him the best, not struggle against him. To lift him up, not push him down.

I am grateful for life, and its lessons.

It is not wisdom to gain advantage over your enemies. It is wisdom to realize you don't have any.

Come here, it's time we had a talk

I have a theory about sex.

I don't know whether it works or not, but I have a hunch it might.

You be the judge.

First, the problem: Many couples don't have sex. Twenty percent of married couples don't have sex. One-third of couples living together outside marriage long-term don't have sex.

At least not regularly. In both categories a new study says "don't have sex" means less than 10 times a year.

Which is no good.

Because I think sex serves several important natural functions. It is essential to the stability of a relationship, and to the emotional, mental and physical well-being of the man and woman involved.

I think that down deep, in our unconscious mind where instincts and psyche rule, having sex is welcomed and rewarded. It resets our being, and strengthens us. It is also a shellac which protects and strengthens a relationship, building that relationship little by little each time it is engaged in.

It is nature's way. It is a gift from God. It is about far more than pleasure and procreation.

And just as we are stronger when we have sex, we are weaker when we don't. I honestly believe that those who regularly have sex are more stable and sound, while those who do not become increasingly eccentric and imbalanced.

I also believe that marriages without sex twist and fray, that they grow cold and distant, and that they are not what they can or should be. I believe a sexless marriage produces individuals and a couple who do not function as they should, or as well as they should.

So what do you do about it?

You remember that humans are creatures of habit, and that we are wired to be constantly acquiring habits. That applies to everything in life. If we do something—good or bad—we are more prone to do that same something again. If we don't do something—good or bad—we are more likely not to do that same something again.

Translation: Tomorrow is going to look a lot like today, only more so.

Here are a couple of examples—prayer and exercise. Say you decide that you want to have a prayer life, that you want to talk to God every day. Fine. That's a great resolution.

But you are going to have to work hard to establish that habit. You will have to force yourself. You will have to set goals—when and where—and you are going to have to hold yourself accountable to meeting those goals. You will have to put up with the inconvenience of kneeling beside your bed when you want to be going to sleep, and you will have to pray even when you don't feel like it.

And over time it will become easier and more natural. You will find yourself wanting to pray more, and being reluctant to pray less. In time, it will become a habit, a comfortable and wonderful part of your life, and you wouldn't think of going to bed without saying your prayers first.

At that point, the beautiful wonders of prayer will begin to unfold for you. You will experience and feel things you never would have imagined.

The same thing is true of starting an exercise program.

And of building or rebuilding a sex life.

Every good thing takes work. And goal setting and responsibility. Nothing precious comes easy or free. We have to work and strive to develop good habits and desirable traits. And sex is no exception.

Foolishly, we forget that; we presume that this human endeavor is different from every other human endeavor. We wait to be "in the mood," and never quite understand that in life we make our own moods. We establish such elaborate mating rituals that having sex becomes perpetually encrusted with meaningless obstructions dressed up as "romance."

You don't have to have a hot tub, or a fancy dinner, or a sexy teddy, or a box of chocolates, or a roomful of candles, or soft music, or a bouquet of roses. All you need is a husband and a wife. Those other things can be pleasant, wonderful additions, but they are nothing more than parsley on the plate, meaningless garnish that ends up pushed away and ignored. Where we get in trouble is when we elevate them beyond a rational importance, and the romancing becomes the thing instead of the sex being the thing.

It's also best to lose the sexist notion that men and women have fundamentally different views on sex. That attitude—namely that men want physical and women want emotional—is itself an obstacle to sex and a healthy relationship. If you think about it, it makes the man a rapist and the woman a prostitute. He does it even though it's not what she wants and she does it to get his closeness or paycheck or to keep the family together.

The fact is that healthy men and women both fundamentally need sex. There is tremendous variation among individuals, but it is personality and experience based, not gender based.

In addition, ignore that nonsense about being too busy and not having time, and not wanting to wake the kids in the next room. All of that is an excuse. Few couples are honest enough to admit it, but it's the case. There is time for sex, you can do it without scandalizing the kids; you just have to want to.

Which gets to the plan.

You must establish the habit of having sex, and you must break the habit of not having sex.

So do it. Grab your spouse and do it.

Sit down first, talk it over, be brave enough to discuss it and open enough to make it happen. Decide to have sex at least three or four times a week, no less frequently than every other day. Check off boxes if you have to. Forgive one another for past misunderstandings and throw off the chains of embarrassment or fear. Be supportive of one another, no matter what, and let yourselves go.

Don't wrap yourself in cellophane, or parade around in feathers. Just go in the bedroom and get it done. It doesn't have to be fancy. We're not setting romantic records here; we're establishing a new habit.

If you need sex tips, there's only one that counts: Focus on pleasing your partner and everything else will take care of itself. If you please her, she's going to please you, and vice versa, forever and ever, amen.

Persist, and don't stop. Not after a week, not after a month, not after six months.

And in time it will become a habit. Your body, heart and mind will become accustomed to it, and comfortable with it, and the great benefits which flow from it—for every part of you and your relationship—will naturally happen. Eventually, you will find that what it brings you and your marriage will be beyond your happiest imaginings.

And I'm not just talking about sexual pleasure. That, honestly, may seem secondary to the love and well-being you feel. To want and be wanted, to belong to someone and with someone, to have the positive mental, emotional, spiritual, psychological and physical benefits of marital sex will do you overwhelming good.

And your love for your spouse will grow stronger by the day.

And your sex life will flower and fruit as it grows and strengthens and lifts you both. The natural processes of lovemaking will do their work and your sex life and marriage will be everything good that nature and God intended them to be.

After you make the effort to establish the habit, the miraculous blessings that flow from it will be more than you could have dreamed.

Because you will be doing what's right.

The institution of marriage is weakening in America. This is one of the reasons why. And this is how you fight it.

At least that's my theory.

You be the judge.

Guilt destroys happiness

Don't tell anybody, but I listened to Dr. Laura the other day.

I didn't actually tune in, but it was on when I went into the bathroom. Which is kind of scary. When you're standing there taking a leak, there's something troubling about listening to Dr. Laura.

Anyway, I was listening.

And it must have been pretty good because I dawdled over the hand washing to hear what she told this guy.

His deal was that he had poor self-esteem because he watched porn movies.

He was depressed and gloomy and didn't feel good about himself. He figured it was because he was watching pornography.

I didn't have time to hear all of Dr. Laura's answer, but I think she agreed. And I know I did. The guy was dead right. He felt miserable because he was doing something he believed to be wrong.

Unfortunately and ironically, though he knew the source of his discomfort and pain, he did nothing about it. He had the solution to his problem, but still he clung to his problem.

I'd make fun of him, but I don't think he's that unusual.

I think he's a lot like you.

I know he's a lot like me.

I think most of us create our own problems, yet most of us are slow to create our own solutions. And most of our difficulties arise from the fact we don't live up to our own expectations and values.

We compromise things that are important to us and are then surprised when we are not happy with ourselves.

It's called a conscience. It's called guilt.

And it can be a real kick in the pants.

And we fight it every way but the right way. We get counseling, we take medication, we get liquored up. We do everything but the right thing to make ourselves feel better.

But wickedness never was happiness, and despair comes from iniquity. And doing the wrong thing will never take you to the right place.

The happiest people are those with a clear set of values who live up to those values. The ones who have a code of conduct. Morals, they used to be called. Guiding principles that they are committed to and will not cheat on.

That's hard to do.

But maybe that's why it's so beneficial.

It is better to have the approval of your conscience than the praise of all the world.

Guilt, on the other hand, is a corrosive poison that burns through a life like acid. It leaves people without hope, optimism, enthusiasm and confidence. Sadly, we typically fight those emotions with everything but the right thing.

Counseling, money, medications, diets, New Age fads. Everything from aromatherapy to hospitalization. All to make us feel better.

When the only thing that will do that is a little internal housekeeping.

We simply need to put our house in order.

We need to live according to what we believe. And if we don't yet know what we believe, we need to learn. We need to decide.

And we need to commit to it.

Then we will feel better.

Like the porno guy. He watches it, it makes him feel guilty, he beats up on himself. Which leads to him watching more of it, which makes him feel guiltier, so that he beats up on himself some more.

And the cycle goes on.

And he's surprised that he feels bad.

He simply needs to stop. To get off the boat. To live a day or a week or a month without it, a day or a week or a month of living the way he knows he should.

And he will feel better.

Maybe not perfect, maybe not good enough. Not right away. But he will feel better.

Just like any of us.

You pick your own values. Just live by them. I'll strive for that. And you strive for that. And the pain of dissatisfaction and disappointment will be appeased. As we prove our integrity to ourselves, the opportunities for our growth and our happiness dramatically improve.

And we will simply feel better.

In a world where so many feel gloomy, discouraged and depressed, it is time to consider that possibly our problem is spiritual. That we need a pastor, not a psychiatrist. That pills and Dr. Phil only go so far.

At some point you've got to come clean with the person in the mirror. You've got to trust him to be true to you and what you hold sacred and important.

So it's not that big a mystery. If you want to feel better, do better. If you want to feel right, live right. Do the right thing.

And let it be more than lip service.

Because it's fairly common to know what to do, and fairly

uncommon to actually do it. Which explains why so many of us never quite have the joy this life was meant to give us.

A word about adultery

Adultery is the most selfish, destructive and hateful thing a person can do.

It's funny what you don't know going in.

Or what you choose to ignore.

And it's tragic that you don't realize until it's too late, until what's done is done, how utterly wasted a life can be. How hopeless hopeless can become. How the promise and joy of life can slip like water through guilty hands.

Hell is merely realizing what you've done.

Mostly to others, but ultimately to yourself.

Hell is the flash of memory, snippets and snapshots of a happy spouse, a newlywed or new mother, pleased and pledged, her future and hopes tied to you. Her whole life in all its stages gambled on you. The very nature, substance and quality of her life, through all its years, depending on a promise you have casually or repeatedly broken.

How you can take an hour or a decade of selfishness and condemn an innocent person to a lifetime of loneliness and disappointment?

How you can steal someone's dream and leave it tattered and stained, unrecognizable and unsalvageable? And not just any someone. The one person who has given you more than any other. The only one who truly understands you and cares about you, and who proved it by giving herself to you. By having faith in you and supporting you. By taking your name and taking your fate.

That's the one you destroy.

It's an emotional murder. The snuffing out of a life that should have been lived. Not the stopping of a heart, but the breaking of a heart. Taking the "happily" out of "happily ever after." It's an emotional murder.

And that's the hell.

For you because you deserve it, and for her because she doesn't.

Then there are the children.

Innocents whose lives are forever and unfairly changed. Who have a mommy and a daddy one day, but not the next. At least not in a real way. Not in the way they are supposed to. No Christmases and family reunions and weddings and graduations, no family nights around the dinner table or the TV. It's all just shattered and broken.

You'd kill someone who hurt your children a fraction of how badly you've hurt them, and yet you've done it, and they tell you it's OK but you know it's not and you've done it and you can't run away from it and Humpty Dumpty can't be put back together again.

And children cry.

When they are young, and decades later when they are old.

The family died, and Daddy did it.

That's the hell.

Realizing that.

Realizing that you did that to them. That you have returned hate for love, betrayal for trust, evil for good.

You have broken the only promise you really had to keep. And in the world of cause and effect they reap the harvest you have sown.

Adultery isn't something you do with another person; it is something you do to your family. To the hopes and lives of the only people who will ever really matter to you.

It is a blind and hateful selfishness, a universe out of kilter, an arrogance of priority and interest. You are all that matters, nothing else counts, and you have everything backwards.

And it seals you off until you are alone and they don't have you even if you are in their midst. Ultimately you rot so much that it collapses, the marriage and the family, and out you spin, not realizing a fraction of what you've done and who you've hurt and what you've lost.

But it comes eventually. In the dark of the night, in the realizations of the soul, in the honesty of humility.

And you can't think about what you've lost, because you're too ashamed of what you've taken. Ashamed and anguished and wrong.

And that is hell. The realization of what you've done. Of who you've hurt. Of the damage you've caused. Of the fact it'll never go away.

That is the lake of fire and brimstone.

You realize that life was a test.

And you failed.

You failed your family.

Adultery brings nothing but sorrow and pain. The likes of which words cannot communicate and imagination cannot conjure.

"Thou shalt not commit adultery" was not a restriction; it was a warning.

Which only fools fail to heed.

Something I learned while running

I've been running for 30 years.

Since the seventh-grade, on the first day of junior high cross-country, when Coach Duane Ball put us through some calisthenics and pointed out a course across the fields behind the school and told us to run.

An entire mile.

I almost died.

But I was too scrawny and uncoordinated to go out for any other sport, and that hasn't changed much in the years since, so I've stuck with running.

For 30 years.

And I learned something the other day.

You only notice the wind when it's against you.

Oh, I track the wind, especially on long or winding runs, and I calculate when it will help me and when it will hurt me.

But I only notice it when it's in my face. When it hurts me.

And the other day I wondered if life was the same way.

Because when you run, and there's wind, it's always either hurting you or helping you. It's pushing you forward or holding you back. It either makes your run easier, or it makes it harder.

I understand that in principle. But I only notice half of it in practice. I am only aware of the wind when it hurts me.

When it blows in my face and holds me back.

But when it helps me, when it pushes me along and makes my work easier, I don't notice. My mind goes elsewhere, daydreaming sometimes, or worrying about the heat or the steepness of the grade or how much farther I have to go.

And I am mindless of the fact I am being helped.

And consequently I am neither grateful for it nor am I encouraged by it.

That all occurred to me the other day.

And I've wondered about it since.

Because often in life I have a tendency to be the same way. To only notice the trials and the difficulties, and not the blessings and the helps.

To see the things that hurt me, but not the things that help me.

And consequently I am neither grateful for them nor am I encouraged by them.

And that's not a good way to be.

Because happiness in life is a matter of perspective, not circumstance. And most of us are apt to count our weaknesses, but not our strengths.

We are quick to see where we have it hard, but not where we have it easy. To note the opposition, but not the support.

To be pulled toward feeling sorry for ourselves, instead of developing a sense of gratitude.

And maybe that's because adversity slaps us across the face while encouragement whispers in our ear. A poke in the eye is discerned easier than a pat on the back.

So I've changed my approach to running.

I've made it a point to notice the wind. To recognize that when I don't hear the rushing as it blows past, it is because it is foursquare behind me. That as I run and the air feels becalmed, it is because it is at my back.

That when the wind seems most absent, it is really helping me the most.

I look to the grass and the leaves and the clouds, to see which way the wind is moving and how my meager journey correlates to that.

And I will try the same in life.

I will know that the wind is always blowing, that it is always pushing me one way or another, and I will try to track its course.

And while I won't ignore the fact that sometimes it does blow against me, I will not notice it out of proportion, or to the exclusion of the times it blows with me.

I will try to be more aware of the blessings in my life, and less aware of the trials.

I will try to be more grateful.

And I will recognize when things are going my way, and a force larger than myself is helping me along my way.

I've been running for 30 years.

But living longer than that.

But I guess some things take a while to learn.

Addictions are not diseases

It's not a disease. Alcoholism, drugs, smoking, sex addiction, molesting kids, beating your wife, shoplifting, telling lies. None of it's a disease. It's not. It's all behaviors.

Behaviors over which people have control.

And I'm sick and tired of this non-stop hand-wringing about people being powerless to control their addictions. If I hear another addle-brained apologist call any of those things a disease I'm going to explode.

A disease is something that comes to you as a process of nature and which creates in you symptoms which are automatic and uncontrollable. Drinking or drugging or any other noxious behavior does not fit that definition because you have to walk in the door of your own volition. It is not a process of nature. It is a matter of preference and decision. You begin it as a matter of personal choice.

And you continue it as a matter of personal choice.

If alcoholism is a disease, then drinking is uncontrollable. And yet it is not uncontrollable, it is completely controllable. All a person need do is choose to stop. Period. Granted, that's easier said than done, but it is a fact. The fundamental fact of everything the Oprah generation wants to call an addiction.

We are selfish whiners eager to find an excuse for our bad behavior. We are brats doing what we want and refusing to accept responsibility. And I can say this because I'm probably the greatest offender going.

But the bottom line is people do these things because they want to. And they don't stop because they don't want to.

And anyone who parrots the line about being "powerless over their addiction" is cementing into permanence misconduct which threatens to destroy their life and the lives of their loved ones.

It is ridiculous and dangerous to believe that you are powerless over an addiction or pattern of conduct. In fact, the individual involved is the only one with any power whatsoever to stop the damaging conduct. And the amazing thing about this powerlessness lie is that it seems to weaken the only hope a person has. It cuts the throat of the addicted person.

Instead of being pampered and coddled by lies about being the victim of a disease they are powerless to control, people with damaging behaviors need to get a cold dose of reality. And that reality is this: They are throwing their lives away, every day, and taking others down with them, out of selfishness and weakness. And the only hope they have of turning that around is by putting their foot down and doing what is right. By stopping. It's not brain surgery. It's pretty straight forward. Just stop.

And it can be done.

I know it can.

It can rip the guts out of you, and it can seem like an immovable burden. But the only people who have ever reformed themselves—from alcohol or drugs or other behavior—have done so by their own bootstraps. A massive industry has built up around "treating" these people, but that has almost exclusively been about money, just one more profit stream off the industry of addiction.

At the end of the day, some battles you fight alone. Not that support isn't important or useful, but when demons are wrestled with it's always one-on-one. And the man who comes out of it is the man whose will is strong enough to control himself.

I don't know why it's that way, but I know it is.

And I don't write this to attack drunks or addicts, or molesters or anybody else. Rather, I write it to help them. To point the way to recovery.

The road to wellness leads inward, and it is one which must be walked alone.

And it passes through regions where excuses are not accepted or believed. Regions completely unlike so much of the society's failed thinking about addiction.

There's a simple rule about bad habits:

Only you can start them, and only you can stop them.

The sad fact is, so few people choose to stop them.

So few people choose to stop themselves.

Whose fault is it when children stray?

When your kids go wrong, what are you supposed to think?

What are you supposed to feel?

And when your neighbor's kids go wrong, what conclusions should you draw?

It's a question in my life now because of the experience of a friend whose child has gone astray. A young person in the first steps of adulthood making terribly wrong decisions, potentially catastrophic decisions. And my friend is upset. He doesn't know what to think or feel.

Mostly he is afraid that he has failed. That he was a bad dad, that he and his wife were bad parents. That somehow he could have done something more or different to better equip his child for life, to better help his child avoid the pitfalls which have consumed him.

And I'm not sure what to tell him.

Because sometimes it is the parents' fault. Sometimes it is bad parenting.

And we see those times and we look down our noses on the parents involved. If we see kids who go wrong, we presume that their parents went wrong before them. We judge families as failures which produce children who stumble.

And I fear that is wrong.

Because increasingly in life, as I age and see more things, I come to believe that often the direction a child takes in early adulthood has very little to do with that child's upbringing. Great kids come out of terrible homes and terrible kids come out of great homes. The trend, of course, is to get good fruit off a good tree, but there are exceptions all over the place.

Like in the Bible.

Were Adam and Eve bad parents? Were they failures? Was there something in their home life that fundamentally corrupted their children? I mean, they did, after all, raise a murderer. Cain beat his own brother to death, to get gain and power. Does that mean he wasn't understood as a child, or raised appropriately?

The answer is probably no.

Adam and Eve were probably fine parents. One son, Abel, was pure and good, and yet the same parents and the same home produced the world's first murderer.

Why is that?

Probably because Cain, like all of us, was free to make choices. He decided the direction and course of his own life. He had a personality and an attitude and the challenge to control himself. He failed. His brother did not. That's more about them than it is about their parents.

And what about the Prodigal Son? The story told in the New Testament, where the guy has two sons, one good and the other bad. The bad one takes his share of the family loot and goes out and blows it on wine, women and song. He dissipates himself and his treasure and then comes begging back to dad.

Was the Prodigal Son's father bad? Did he raise his son poorly? Could he have done more? Should he have hung his head in shame? Should his neighbors have scorned him and thought less of him because his son was a wastrel?

I don't think so. That doesn't seem to be the point of the story. In fact, in the story, the father is analogous to God and the Prodigal Son is supposed to represent us. Do you think this story was told—by Jesus himself—to show that God was a bad dad?

Again, I don't think so.

And a last example. Didn't God make the devil? Isn't he his son? And yet, didn't he rebel, and go wrong?

Yes. He did. Just like my friend's son. Not because his father was not loving and skilled, but because he chose to.

The simple fact is we are all free. And so are our children. Free to choose right or wrong. To obey the rules of society or not. We reap the consequences of our choices, but they are, ultimately, our choices.

Not our parents'.

And the responsibility is also ours—not our parents'.

So I tell my friend not to feel guilty. And I tell his neighbors not to judge him. Because people are very complex creatures, and they do things for reasons which are sometimes beyond comprehension. Sometimes our children do things which are beyond comprehension. Things which break our hearts.

We must learn to endure those things without beating ourselves up.

It is our privilege and obligation to be the best parents we can. To give our children the love and guidance they need to lead happy and productive lives. We owe them that. But they don't have to follow it.

And they may stray. Maybe they'll come back and maybe they won't.

And their parents will worry over them and pray for them, and do what they can to get them back on the right path.

That is as it should be.

The guilt, however, is not. And neither is the condemnation and scorn.

Shoot the close ones first

Everything I need to know about life I learned in basic training.

Especially this.

Shoot the close ones first.

That's what the drill sergeant shouted. He stood behind me on the firing line, while I crouched forward in the foxhole, and brought the cleaning rod down hard against the top of my helmet.

Shoot the close ones first.

Then he called me Dick.

He called us all Dick.

I told the other privates that was his father's name. Or his little brother's name. Or his best friend's name.

Then we all started calling one another Dick.

Except this one guy, and his name was Peter, and we thought that was good enough.

So he whacked me on the helmet with that metal rod and it embarrassed me but the worst part was I knew he was right. And because he was right and I was wrong I didn't get to be the honor graduate.

I did everything else right, better than the others, and was a good troop. But if the close one gets you, you're dead. And in the Army business, that's a bad thing.

You don't shoot very much in the Army. Not as much as I

would have liked. Not as much as you probably ought to, given the nature of the business.

But it was in basic training and they had us on this rifle range, crouched down in these foxholes, with an M16. And stretched out in front of us was a particularly drab stretch of Kentucky.

At various distances in front of us, lying flat in the weeds, were several man-sized silhouettes, rigged to pop up randomly for different amounts of time. The closest ones were about 25 yards away and the farthest ones were 300 yards away. The farther a target was away, the longer it stayed up. The closer a target was, the shorter it stayed up.

If you shot a target down, you won. If it went down before you shot it, you lost.

And I was doing pretty good.

Pop, breathe, pull. Pop, breathe, pull. I had a rhythm. I was in the zone. I was feeling pretty good about myself.

And the first 300 yard target came up. I flipped my sight over to the long distance setting and got a bead on it. But my eye was watering in the Kentucky wind so I blinked to clear it and to my left close a 25-yard target stood up.

My eye was still watery so I blinked again and pulled and had a hit and swiveled slightly to the left and then it laid down.

All by itself.

And that's when he hit me.

Shoot the close ones first.

Then he called me our special name and threw down the cleaning rod in disgust and stormed off shouting profanities, angry that his platoon wouldn't have the honor graduate.

And I've never forgotten that.

Or what it means.

And to this day it is the way I do business.

There is only one target at a time, and it is the close one. One goal, one task, one responsibility.

Nothing else matters. Close it all out, don't give it a thought, simply do the job before you.

The way to do many things is to do one thing now. And when that is done, do another thing. And just keep going until you're done.

And if the nature of your workload is such that you are never done, then at least you will be able to keep up. To keep it all from suffocating you.

I bring this up because most people I know are buried. They are crushed sometimes by the burden of what they must do. Usually, they do well. People have great capacity for work.

But sometimes I can see it come apart on them.

They will have too many balls in the air, and they will lose track of them, and start dropping them. Invariably it all collapses on them, like a house of cards.

It is because they let the enormity and variety of their responsibilities overwhelm them. It is because they let things which are not truly important distract them from things which truly are.

When they should be worrying about the 25-yard silhouette, they're wasting time on the 300-yard objective.

I don't have that problem.

Oh, I fail. No doubt about that. But I can process tasks. Years of working on deadline has given me a good sense of what has to be done next.

And that is what I do.

Without giving anything else a thought.

I just completely throw myself into the next agenda item, and when it is done, it is done. I don't think about it again, I don't look back. And I don't look forward. I just do the next thing.

And when I fail, when I need to abandon a task. When I know I can't accomplish it, or I cannot do it right. My failure, like my work, is segregated. I missed this one. Oh well. Where's the next one?

Again, I'm not the best worker there ever was.

But I can carry my weight.

Because of what I learned in basic training.

Shoot the close ones first.

Seven

Good tidings of great joy

It was probably in a cave in the spring.

And it probably stunk.

The heavy odor of urine and ripe manure, the musky perspiration of draft animals and the steady hum of flies. But it was someplace, in out of the elements, and in that filth she bore her child.

Not at home, or with her family, but in her husband's ancestral village. A strenuous walk for a pregnant woman, come to be tallied and taxed, the only respite on the bony and swaying back of an ass.

And angels sang.

It's an ugly country, then and now. Barren and dry without natural beauty, adequate certainly, but not the best. Not compared to the beauty of this whole wide world, where waterfalls and flowers and grand canyons abound. Where the grace and glory of the Creator's touch is freely seen.

No, he wasn't born in a garden. He was born in Palestine. In Bethlehem of Judea. Where they kept their animals in caves, penned in against the night, a God in the gutter, a new baby born.

And an old promise kept.

To redeem and to justify, to deliver and delight. Born beneath all to reign over all. Suffering more than all to better comfort all.

A God and king ushered in with a mother's travails and laid in a manger.

And 30 years later he put down his carpenter's tools and set about the salvation of man. The blind saw, the deaf heard, the lame walked. The chained soul soared and the afflicted heart found peace. He forgave and loved as none had done before and he commanded us to do likewise, to be our brother's keeper, to give without thought of receiving, to nurse the sick and comfort the tormented. He unlocked the gates of prison and turned us sinners free.

And they plotted against him for it. They conspired and set traps and finally took him in the night.

But not before he knelt in Gethsemane and sweat red drops of blood. Not before the sacrificial process of atonement had begun. Not before the evil of the world rested on the only man who had not contributed to it. Without spot or blemish, led like a lamb to the slaughter.

Beaten and humiliated, spat upon and whipped, lifted by spikes through his flesh and left to hang in torturous agony.

It was probably on a hill in the spring.

And it probably stunk.

The putrid stench of flesh and blood and the sickening sense that mankind was killing its God. The same mother, come now to weep and mourn. The same baby, dying as he was born to do. Pain to pain, travail to travail, eternity to eternity.

And life to life. Life to all.

Victory over death, and victory over sin. The grand turning point of the eternities, the coming together of the plan, the reason this earth and these people were made. To be born and to die and to be born again. As themselves better and as themselves forever.

Like he was.

Like we are to be, if his birth is to mean anything to us.

On the subject of speech

There are two words I am going to use just once in this column. They are a name. A name and a title.

Jesus Christ.

I am only going to use them once because I'm trying to make a point. A point that seems for years to have been lost in this society.

And that is that those two words are not a curse or a profanity. They are not an expletive. They are not something to spit out of your mouth in a moment of anger, surprise or wonderment. They are a name, and a title denoting divinity, and should be used as such.

Or they should not be used.

This isn't Bible-thumping, this is simple courtesy. The respect one person pays another, or another's God.

They are tender words, wrapped for many people with love and purity. They are, for some, the center of a life's devotion. And their misuse is an act of desecration and cruelty. A stab at the heart of those who love the Son of God whose name they are.

And when you use them as an expletive, you commit an act that, for its thoughtlessness, debases you. It tears down something precious and sacred to others and within yourself. It displays a callousness that is offensive and brutal.

It is almost an act of religious bigotry.

Peoples the world over have reverenced the name of their deity. For thousands of years Jews did not utter the name of their God, and only wrote his name incompletely. That was to protect it, and to keep it from being profaned, from being cheapened or desecrated by uncouth usage. Muslims show respect for the name of Allah, and that of his prophet, Muhammed. And Christians similarly honor the name of the Savior, and his Messianic title.

This is natural. Just as it is natural to respect those customs, and to not inappropriately utter names or words sacred to others. It would be wrong to mock the name of the Hebrew God, or of Allah, or to use casually and profanely the name and title of the man Christians call Lord.

Those are words used by millions each day in prayer, as they ask favors of God and discuss with him the most important issues of their lives. They are words people will utter on their deathbeds, and as they stand above the deathbeds of loved ones. They are words we call out in times of crisis and joy, when we need love and comfort and some connection with the eternal.

They are words most Americans believe are tied directly to their salvation. A name they believe will give them victory over death, and reunite them in the next life with their loved ones from this life.

They are special words.

And to use them as a filthy cuss word, as a crutch in your conversation, is to track muddy footprints across a beautiful white carpet. To spit in the face of your mother. To throw dog feces across your dinner table.

So don't do it.

You control your speech. You decide what you will say. If you are going to use these two words, use them correctly. Use them reverently.

They are not cuss words. They are not for swearing.

They are for the best part of you, not the worst part of you.

They are meant to build up, not to tear down.

Use them right.

Why does God let us suffer?

As parents and spouses are beaten by the infirmities of age, as babies are born with life-cheating handicaps, as accidents leave us disabled or worse, what is the point?

Why does it happen?

How could a loving God let it happen?

Ironically, the truth may be that he lets it happen precisely because he does love us.

Let me explain.

The great challenge of mortality is that we can't see beyond the horizon. As we look forward or backward in time, we can only see so far, and only understand so much. Birth and death are impenetrable walls through which we cannot see. We don't know what existence we had before our birth, nor what existence we will have after our death.

We can learn by faith, but we cannot know by observation.

And that limits us and our understanding. It's as if someone were giving us directions to drive across the country and they merely said, "Turn left at Des Moines." Such a statement wouldn't make any sense because it is only a tiny part of a journey across the United States. With just a piece of the information—even though it is correct—we don't know why or how we got to Des Moines or where and how we go after.

Life is like that.

Our time on Earth is just a tiny piece of our eternal existence, and the things which happen here—without the context of what went before and what will come after—can seem to make no sense at all.

Like the suffering of the aged and the handicaps of the young. The things which seem to leave marginal lives and saddle loved ones with burdens of toil and care. From where we sit, they make no sense at all.

But life is not judged from where we sit.

It is judged from where God sits.

And the worst things for our lives can be the best things for our eternities. The trials for today can be the tutoring for tomorrow. And the lessons learned by the difficulties of this life can be the keys to happiness in the life to come.

Maybe people suffer because it teaches them something essential to their eternity. Maybe people suffer so that their families can learn the compassion and humility that come from caring for them. Maybe old people have Alzheimer's so their children can learn to love more purely. And maybe children have handicaps so their parents can learn the same thing.

Maybe on the other side of mortality's wall, when we can see more clearly the long journey through which we must pass, and its ultimate destination, the twists and turns of this life will make sense.

We cannot know that by observation, but we can believe in it through faith.

And we can have faith that the things which happen to us in this life are for our best good—even the bad things. Even the trials and torments. Even the disappointments and depressions.

Maybe we will discover that when we care for our handicapped child that it is really an act of service that goes both ways. Maybe that person agreed to accept limitation in mortality in order to prepare us for eternity. Maybe the decline of age is a last gift of instruction from a departing spouse or parent.

And maybe when we are reunited after this life, on the far side of the impenetrable wall, when we are perfect in mind and body, without disease or defect, maybe then, when we see why things happened and the good they did, tears of gratitude will replace our tears of sorrow.

That's what I believe.

And that's what God teaches.

We weren't sent here for recreation, we were sent here for instruction. There are joys in this life, but they are not the purpose of this life. They are mere samples of the joys that await us in the eternities, and it is those eternal joys that are the purpose of our existence.

And if acquiring them requires us, in this mortal sphere, to endure trial and hardship, then let trial and hardship come.

And let us not question why.

Let us have faith that God is in his heaven and that his hand is in our lives—on the good days and on the bad. And let us have faith that the pains of mortality serve a purpose in eternity.

The shortest verse in the Bible

It's the shortest verse in the Bible.

"Jesus wept."

I recited it Sunday after Sunday at the First Baptist Church of Canisteo. If you quoted a Bible verse in Sunday school you got a piece of candy. And on those weeks when you'd not quite gotten around to memorizing a new verse, the teacher was kind enough to accept an old one.

And we all chose the short one.

The one I've only lately come to understand. Or at least to think about.

"Jesus wept."

He had been teaching, out amongst the people, when word came from Mary and Martha—two women he loved—that their brother, Lazarus, was gravely ill. He said he would come and tend to Lazarus, to presumably heal him, as he had healed so many others.

But he delayed.

And his disciples wished that he wouldn't go at all. It was dangerous, they said. The people where Lazarus and his family lived—in Bethany of Judea—wanted to stone Jesus, and kill him.

But he was determined. And he tried to explain to his disciples what awaited them in Bethany. Not danger, but something they had not yet seen or understood. The absolute power of their master over life and death.

"Lazarus sleepeth," Jesus told them, "but I go, that I may awake him out of sleep."

There was confusion about his words, and the belief that if he was asleep then he was mending from his illness, so Jesus had to speak to them directly. He had to lay aside figurative language.

"Lazarus is dead," he said.

And as they journeyed they were met near Bethany by Martha, who mourned her brother, dead and buried now for four days. If you had only been here, she said to Jesus, my brother would still be alive.

He comforted her, and spoke to her of her faith, and her faith in him, and she went to get Mary, her sister. When Mary got to Jesus, she was broken hearted and mourning, and she, too, said that if only the Lord had come sooner he could have saved poor Lazarus.

Then Mary began to cry, and so did the friends who accompanied her.

And that's when he cried. The shortest verse in the Bible. "Jesus wept."

But why?

In moments, after being taken to the tomb, Jesus would raise Lazarus from the dead. Jesus knew that in a very short time this scene of mourning and grief would be one of miraculous reunion and joy. He knew, as he had known from the very first, how this would end. He knew that Mary was about to embrace her living brother. He knew that in moments her tears would be gone.

But they were not gone yet.

Her sorrow, though destined to be short-lived, was real. It was real then. And Mary's grief mattered to Jesus, and was moving to Jesus, and it brought him to tears.

Which ought to mean a great deal to us.

Because it shows the capacity of the Lord to understand our feelings, and to give them value and relevance, even when they are changeable and temporary. We often—naturally and appropriately— are dismissive of our pains, believing that, "this, too, shall pass." We endure hard times and sorrows by clinging to the belief that they will get better, and a brighter day will dawn. We ignore the pain of today in preference to looking forward to the relief of tomorrow.

In this instance, the Lord did not do that. He did not tell Mary and Martha to stop crying. He joined them. The knowledge that they would soon be freed from grief did not minimize his reaction to the impact or significance of that grief to them in that moment.

I believe that shows that the Lord stands by us each moment, and he understands and empathizes with our fears and sorrows, even when those fears and sorrows are unfounded. The Lord's perspective is different from ours, but he understands ours, and he understands the impact of ours on us.

Confusion often leads to pain. The Lord does not share our confusion, but he does share our pain. More correctly, he is pained that we are pained.

And that's why he wept.

Not because he mourned Lazarus. Not because he shared Mary's despair at the death of her brother. He wept because she wept. He wept not for his pain, but for hers. Because he understood her and her feelings better than anyone could. Because he understood her and her feelings better than she herself did.

Just as he understands us and our feelings better than we ourselves can.

"Jesus wept."

I memorized it 30 years ago, but have only lately come to understand it.

Judgmentalism can blind us to God's hand

There is a story in the Bible about a handicapped man who sat by a pool of water.

It was in Jerusalem and for almost 40 years he had been crippled, broken and weak in body, unable to do what others did.

And he sat beside that pool of water hoping for a miracle.

The story is that periodically an angel would come and stir the water up, splash it or something. And the first person to step into the fountain after it had been troubled would be healed of his infirmities.

And so the sick and handicapped gathered there, waiting for the stirring of the pool and the chance to bathe in its healing waters.

But this guy had a problem.

He was too slow.

And that's what he told Jesus.

One day, when the Savior was in town for a feast, he stood over the man and asked him if he wanted to be healed.

The man answered that he did, but he had no one to carry him to the waters. By the time he could crawl into the pool himself, others had already gotten there—the healing had been claimed.

So Jesus told him to get up.

He told him to get up, pick up his bedding, and walk.

And he was instantly healed, and able to do as he had been instructed. And on his way he went, carrying his bedding, presumably ecstatic at this miraculous gift of health.

Imagine it. Thirty-eight years of crippling handicap, and in an instant he was made whole. What a glorious thing to see.

And what an odd thing to ignore.

Because as he walked away with his bedding, he was accosted by others. Antagonistically, accusingly. It was the Sabbath, the holy day of rest, and it was against the Jewish law to do work. And that included carrying things around.

There was a rule, and this guy was breaking it, and everybody wanted to tell him about it.

They were seriously angry.

Somebody was going to get condemned over this.

It's amazing, if you think about it. These people—who well knew this man's history—saw the fruit of a miracle. A handicapped man walking about, completely whole. And yet they couldn't see the miracle because they were incensed by the violation.

They couldn't see the good because they were fixated on the bad. When they should have been rejoicing, they were busy judging.

Instead of asking how he came to be healed, or expressing amazement or shock, or sharing his joy, they saw a chance, an excuse, to criticize—and they took it.

They were so busy judging and condemning, they missed the grace of God.

I think a lot of us are that way.

We claim such a "right" to judge other people that we presume our entitlement is preeminent. If you have done something wrong, by our standards, then that wrong trumps everything else. It is the only consideration. It is all that matters.

What an impossible and unjust standard that is.

How poorly we ourselves would fare under such a standard.

How much good we are blinded to by our lust for seeing bad.

Too often this attitude of disqualification colors our perception of others. We judge people not by the good they do, but by the bad. Not by their strengths, but by their weaknesses. Their beauty is lost in our fixation on their warts.

The problem with that is, we all have warts.

None of us is perfect.

And while we all should constantly work to overcome our weaknesses and imperfections, it is usually wrong in the meantime to throw us away for being flawed.

In our relations with others, we ought to encourage the good more often than we condemn the bad. That is not an argument for permissiveness; it is merely a recognition of the reality of the human heart. You cannot chastise a man to glory, and you will get much further down the road of human progress by praising than by scolding.

Clearly, there are times to judge and condemn. Your desire to be positive must not be twisted into dishonesty. Bad things do need to be denounced, and people do occasionally need to have the riot act read to them.

But reproof must always be done in a spirit of love, with an eye toward change and improvement, not condemnation and rejection.

Because people are miracles, and they have the potential to be even more. And it would be a shame if our judgmentalism blinded us to that fact.

It would be a shame if our self-righteous desire to condemn our neighbor never allowed us to see him as God sees him—as a being as worthy and relevant and loved as we are.

If we can overcome our impulse to condemn the failings of others, who knows what miracles we will finally be able to see.

How about tolerance for all?

Some Muslims wear sacred clothing.

So do some Jews. The same for Native Americans and some Hindus and others.

Bits of cloth or string that are physical reminders of God and his bond with man. Sacred things, really. Prayer shawls or beads, head coverings or aprons, medicine bags. Things that are special to people, honorable and good things.

Things that should be respected.

One would not, for example, rip the yarmulke from a Jewish man's head and mockingly fling it like a Frisbee. Nor would you wear a yarmulke as a spoof or joke. Certainly not as an attack on Judaism. Not as a mockery of Jews and their faith.

Yet something like that happened this weekend.

In front of thousands of people in one of America's great cities. An act of religious desecration, bigotry and discrimination.

And the perpetrators boast of it to the press.

It was in Salt Lake City. And it was against Mormons.

And somehow that makes it acceptable.

Here's what happened.

Over the weekend, Mormons gathered for what they call "general conference." It is a twice-a-year meeting that draws tens of thousands to Salt Lake City and is broadcast around the world to an audience in the low millions. It is a worship service. It is sacred and special to them.

And each year it is protested.

So-called Christian evangelists stand on the sidewalk outside the Mormon meetings and shout rude condemnations of the religion to the thousands who pass in and out. It is an odd spectacle, unmatched in American society. To think that crude protesters would stand outside a mosque or synagogue, or a cathedral or church, and harass worshippers and denounce a religion is just beyond the pale.

It is an act of indefensible religious bigotry.

And yet it happens, and is often applauded and boasted of.

This column started with a mention of sacred clothing. Well, Mormons have sacred clothing, too. Like a variety of religious garments, it is worn against the skin. It is a type of underclothing. They don't talk about it. They don't show it to people. They keep it sacred. Like virtually all religious clothing, it is a specific reminder of promises made to God. Like virtually all religious clothing, it is precious and significant to the people who wear it.

Well, Sunday the evangelists had some.

Maybe six guys, Baptist ministers, mocking the Mormons as they came out of a meeting. Shouting rude things to people coming out of church.

And they had these sacred garments.

And one supposed minister of the gospel was wiping his backside with them, laughingly treating them like toilet paper as thousands who held them sacred walked by.

Can you see that being done to a prayer shawl in front of a synagogue, or a prayer rug in front of a mosque?

Wouldn't that sacrilege be publicly denounced by all decent people?

He also draped them around his neck, and pretended over and over to sneeze into them. And loudly blow his nose into them. While families and children walked past.

Stop for a moment.

Lay aside what you do or don't think about Mormons. But was that right? More to the point, was that Christian? Is that what Jesus would do? Is that what any decent person of any faith would do?

Absolutely not. It is wrong, bigoted and un-American. No matter who it's against.

It was an affront. It smelled like the bigotry of the Klan and the Third Reich. And yet the ministers boasted of it to reporters and posed for pictures and no one in the Utah or American religious, media or civil rights communities has condemned it.

And, oddly, two worshippers were taken away in handcuffs.

One man, dressed in his church clothes, walked past in the crowd, saw the insults and desecrations, and grabbed the piece of clothing. To protect it. He was charged with robbery and taken to jail.

Half an hour later another worshipper similarly grabbed a molested garment and attempted to take it away. He was unsuccessful and waiting police stepped in to take him into custody.

And that's the world we live in.

You are harangued for your beliefs and arrested for defending them.

And the bigotry of our society is illustrated by how selectively we practice tolerance.

The story of Cain and Abel

Why didn't God respect Cain's offering?

Did you ever wonder that? Way back in Sunday school, when they told you the Genesis stories over and over. Did you ever wonder why, when Cain and Abel made offerings to the Lord, that God accepted one and rejected the other?

Here's what the Bible says.

It says that Cain made an offering of the fruits of the ground. Stuff he'd grown on his farm. Vegetables and stuff, grains and fruit.

Then his brother Abel made an offering of the "firstlings of the flock." Abel kept sheep, and he took the best of his animals and sacrificed them to God.

Two brothers, worshipping, offering sacrifices.

But only one passed muster.

God respected and accepted Abel's sacrifice, but not Cain's.

One manner of worship pleased the Lord and had his approval, and one did not.

Did you ever wonder why?

It was because Cain did it his way, instead of God's way. There was a set way to offer sacrifices, it is all through the Old Testament. God told the people how he wanted it done, how he wanted them to worship him, what he wanted them to believe.

Sacrifices were to be animals.

And Cain didn't do it that way.

Cain did it his own way.

He sacrificed plants.

And God rejected it. Ultimately he rejected Cain. And Cain, undoubtedly growing in evil and alienation from good, became the first murderer, rising up and slaying his brother.

Not so much because of the difference between sheep and produce, but because of the pride and lack of humility, the sense that he would be in charge of his relationship with God, instead of letting the Lord be in charge.

It's an ancient lesson. If you're going to worship the Lord, you have to do it the Lord's way. And there is a Lord's way. There is a right way and a wrong way—as the sacrifices of Cain and Abel metaphorically and literally show.

Strait is the gate and narrow is the way that leads to life.

That is a lesson almost universally ignored in contemporary American Christianity. In fact, contemporary American Christianity has far more in common with Cain's sacrifice than Abel's. Certainly, it is done in the name of the Lord, but not in the spirit of the Lord, and not with his approval or acceptance.

Christianity is a religion which requires the bending of human will—through faith and free choice—to God's will. Yet, as practiced in our day and age, Christianity is a religion of consensus and popular opinion. Instead of molding our lifestyle to our faith, today we mold our faith to our lifestyle.

It used to be that consciousness of our sin prompted us to change our offending behavior. Now we merely change the prohibiting commandment. We live our lives as we wish, we create a dogma around our choices and we pretend it is the word of God, we pretend that it is pleasing to God.

"For the time will come when they will not endure sound doctrine; but after their own lusts shall they heap to themselves teachers.

"And they shall turn away their ears from the truth, and shall be turned unto fables."

And we mock the Abels of the world who faithfully obey the unchanging will of the Lord. And stoked by our envy and pride, we rise up and seek to slay the beliefs and institutions to which they righteously cling.

In a way, we are a nation of Cains, gods unto ourselves, consumed with the desire to do it our way. A desire, which the conduct of the biblical Cain shows us, is on the path of evil.

And so we ordain gay bishops. And perform gay weddings. We trivialize the Bible by calling it folklore, and we mock the Savior by deeming him merely a great teacher. And we forsake our religion by seeing it as just one of many, merely another path of a myriad, converging off in the distance somewhere at the feet of some undefined and amorphous deity whose exact characteristics we haven't yet decided upon.

It's religion by committee, where instead of seeking God's will, we worship our own will. We are modern idolaters kneeling piously in front of a mirror.

We reject the fundamental fact that truth is absolute, and instead bury our sin and foolishness in the morass of moral relativity and situational ethics. We have been offered a foundation of stone, but instead build our houses and our cathedrals on the shifting sands. And we skip blissfully along as they collapse into ruins all around us.

And we do all this while—just like Cain—self-righteously pretending that we are worshipping God.

The will of the Lord is not found in the opinion polls or the latest policies of cafeteria churches. It is found in his written and inspired word. It doesn't matter what the activist bishops and theologians think. It matters what God has declared.

The answer is in the Lord's Prayer, where Jesus told his followers to implore their Heavenly Father, "Thy will be done."

Not my will. Not your will. His will.

Abel understood that. Cain did not.

The great test of our lives will be whether or not we do.

When it seems the Lord isn't listening

I learned something in Sunday school, when I should have been paying attention.

It was a story I'd read many times before, and apparently never understood. Or maybe this time I was just supposed to understand it differently.

Because I've found the scriptures to be that way. It's not so much a matter of, "What does this mean?" But rather it is, "What does God intend this to mean to me today?" Because the message can sometimes be different for different people, and different for the same person at different times of his life.

At any rate, this is what a few verses of the Bible mean to me today.

"Have mercy on me, O Lord, thou son of David," a woman yelled through the crowd to Jesus. "My daughter is grievously vexed with a devil."

He was preaching with his disciples, kind of out of their home territory, where there were other tribes of people and not just Jews. And this woman yelled to him, pleading for his help, in anguish for her daughter.

And he ignored her.

He heard her. They all heard her. And he ignored her.

Which is just not how we picture Jesus. That's not the Jesus we expect, or the conduct we associate with him.

But he ignored her.

And his disciples came to him, arguing her case. "Send her away," they asked him, "for she crieth after us."

But he wouldn't do what they asked.

Instead, he told them, "I am not sent but unto the lost sheep of the house of Israel."

And she wasn't that. She was of a different tribe, a Canaanite, and he continued to ignore her.

So she asked him again. She approached him, and fell down before him, and begged, "Lord, help me."

Which is a pretty wrenching thing. She was pouring out her heart. She was pleading for assistance for her child.

But this time Jesus didn't ignore her.

He rebuffed her.

"It is not meet," he said, "to take the children's bread, and to cast it to the dogs."

Which must have hurt.

He was saying she had no right to his help or healing power. That she was unworthy by virtue of her race. That she was a dog.

Which must have hurt.

And I suppose she had tears in her eyes and in her voice as she answered boldly, "Truth, Lord.

"Yet the dogs eat of the crumbs which fall from their masters' table."

In my mind I imagine a moment of silence, and maybe the Savior's hands resting on the woman's shoulders as he looked lovingly into her eyes.

"O woman, great is thy faith," he said. "Be it unto thee even as thou wilt."

And her daughter was healed.

The miracle was done.

But why did Jesus do it that way?

The reason recorded, that this woman was not a Jew, isn't satisfactory. Before this happened, the Lord had already gladly complied with the request of a Roman centurion to heal his servant. Jesus had clearly already shown his love for all, regardless of heritage.

So, did the woman wear down his resolve? Did she get him to change his mind? Did she debate him into doing something he originally didn't want to do?

That hardly seems likely. That is not godly or divine. Our pleas do not change the Lord's mind, but they may, through the faith they demonstrate, merit for us blessings reserved until after the demonstration of that faith.

Which is the point.

The Lord knew from the woman's first word that he would heal her daughter. But first there had to be faith shown. But not to him. He knew what was in her heart. The person who had to be convinced of her faith was the lady herself.

She asked the Lord, and he ignored her.

Intermediaries beseeched the Lord, and nothing came.

She asked again, more personally and directly, and her petition was forcefully rejected.

And yet she believed in him and in his mission enough to ask again, in a spirit and tone of even greater humility.

And that was enough.

To show not him, but her, how much she believed.

I think it is often the same for us.

We take our troubles to the Lord and we feel that he ignores us. There is no answer to our question, no relief from our suffering, no direction for our journey.

And that is hard. It tries us.

And sometimes we fail. We respond incorrectly. We believe the Lord doesn't hear or care. And we withdraw. We stop pleading. In some small way, we lose our faith.

But the Canaanitish woman made no such mistake.

She persevered.

And it got worse. She was rejected. It must have felt like the Lord slapped her. Just as it feels for us when the things we pray over get worse instead of better, when it seems the heavens simply won't open in our behalf. When it feels like the Lord has spurned us and stopped caring about us.

But instead of sulking away, of taking the rebuke and retreating, she humbled herself completely, and chose faith over frustration. She didn't give up on the Lord, and he had never given up on her. He had merely taught her of her own faith, and of its preciousness and power.

And he had sent a message to us who, like that good woman of long ago, petition the Lord for blessings and answers which seem never to come.

Don't turn away when it seems your prayers are ignored. Don't turn away when it feels like the Lord has spurned you. Keep your faith, rely on your faith, build your faith.

And prove its strength to yourself.

When that is done, the heavens will open.

Faith is the first principle

The first principle of life is faith.

And the last principle of life is faith.

In fact, the only principle of life is faith.

You've just got to believe.

You've got to believe that there is a God in his heaven and that for reasons that make sense to him he allows things to happen as they do.

You've got to believe that there is a plan, and that you have a place in it. Rain or shine, pain or pleasure, sorrow or joy.

Not that everything that happens is good, or even for the best good. We have our freedom, and so does everyone else—the Mother Theresas and the Hitlers—and one person's choice can be exercised at another person's expense. And sometimes people choose evil. But God has to let them. Because if they couldn't choose evil, then they couldn't choose good, and there is no success where there is no possibility of failure.

So killers kill and rapists rape and robbers rob.

But God is still in charge.

And we still must have faith.

Because that's why we're here.

To have faith, and to prove ourselves by our fidelity to it.

But it's more than a test; it's also a solution.

In the darkest of our nights, during the most painful of our trials, when the disappointments and terrors of life seem poised to snuff us out, the only comfort is faith. The only answer is faith.

Because without it nothing makes sense.

There is no logical reason why one woman can bear a child and another cannot. There is no reason why two people fall in love and spend a lifetime together and two other people live lone and separate lives, forever bereft of the companionship they crave.

Nor is there an explanation for the handicaps of children or the suffering of the aged, the deaths of young parents or the privations of the poor.

None of it makes any sense at all.

Not from where we sit.

Not from the tiny box of mortality, where our view forward and back is obstructed by the veils of birth and death.

And sometimes we kick against that illogic, the seeming injustice, the abandonment and hopelessness. We curse God and despair of deliverance. And life becomes something bitter in our mouths.

Because we lose faith.

Because we do not cling to the faith that there is a God in heaven and that he loves us and wants the best for us. Because we abandon the only hope we have.

There is an old saying that that which does not kill us, strengthens us. But that is only part true. We can survive our trials and still be ground to powder. Our sufferings do not always strengthen us or teach us. They sometimes simply defeat us. Whether they do or not is determined by whether we face them alone or not, whether we face them with faith or not.

It all comes down to that.

You've got to have faith.

Those are easy words to say, and difficult words to live.

But God has his plan, and you are in it, and when life does you wrong, you must cling for strength and comfort to your belief that God is in charge and things will work out the way they should.

And someday we will understand.

Someday we will see.

And our tears of sorrow will be replaced by tears of gratitude. Our sufferings will appear as our deliverance. Those things which have most tortured us in this life may work to our best good in the next.

For we are eternal, and this little box of mortality is not all of our existence, it is not the destination of our journey. It is merely a way station on the road to forever, and the lessons we learn in these few short years will stay with us for all the eternities to come.

We came here to learn, and some of the lessons are hard.

And we may not discover in this life why we have to learn them. But we will, eventually.

And we must have faith in that.

We must have faith that there is a purpose, and that if we endure with faith in God that all eventually will be well.

And sometimes we must lean on that faith even in the face of oblivion, as the cyclone of difficulty or our own mortality picks us up and sweeps us away.

We must have faith in a God we have never seen, an eternity we cannot conceive, a salvation we will never deserve.

We must have faith.

That is why we're here.

It is the first principle of life.

A letter to a friend

Dear Friend,

I am so sorry about your son.

And I know that nothing I say can make a difference, or help you feel better. Your life has just changed, and become unrecognizable, and it will never be the same again.

You have awakened to every parent's nightmare.

You have lost a child.

And it hurts. Whether you have had him for hours or for decades. It hurts.

And I will pray for your comfort. I will pray for your peace.

And I will tell you what I believe.

And that is that it will all make sense. Not in this life, probably, or any time soon. But it will make sense. There is a God, and he is in charge, and he knows the tenderest feelings of our hearts. And he cares about those feelings.

Just as he cares about our families, and knows how much they mean to us.

He doesn't let things happen for no reason. He makes things happen for the best. He has a plan and someday we will see the reason of it.

But now we can only glimpse it through tears. And cling with faith to the belief that it does in fact exist. That he is watchful of us, and our loved ones, and that he will lead us through life in a way that is best.

Because he knows what it is like to lose a son.

And maybe only he can give you comfort, because only he can understand your loss.

There is something else I believe.

And that is that families are forever. That the love of parent for a child lasts beyond death because it has a purpose beyond death, that it is meant in the next life to do just what it does in this life—bind us together as families.

I believe that you will not only see your son again, but that in a better place you and he will associate again as father and son, with all the love and happiness that you enjoyed while he was here. I believe that association will last forever.

I believe that the great tasks of his life, his loves and obligations, will be taken up in the next life just as they were left off in this.

I believe that death loses, and that life wins.

In spite of what you feel today and in spite of the terrible shattering blow that any death is to a family. There will be a reunion.

I do not know why God took your son.

But sometimes I believe some people are taken young because they are too good for this world. They have a purity and a goodness, and are so beloved of God, that they are spared the challenges and evils of this life.

They come here to accomplish what they were sent to do, and then they are quickly gathered home.

Maybe it is to gain a body they can reclaim in the resurrection.

Maybe it is to become part of our families, that they may belong to us in the eternities. Maybe it is to find loves of their own, or to bring lives into the world.

And maybe it is to teach us.

By their presence, or maybe by their absence.

Maybe we are to learn by raising them, by standing with them through their struggles and joys. Maybe we are to learn by their loss.

Maybe their mission in life—gladly accepted because of their love—is to help us by teaching us or testing us, possibly by strengthening our faith so that we might eventually join them where they are.

It may well be that the great challenge your family faces today will strengthen some member of it for even greater challenges in the future.

We are the parents, but perhaps they are the teachers.

We don't know. But sometimes I wonder if when we finally understand we will see that they have actually performed for us an act of selfless service and sacrifice.

And there is a final point.

Your son missed out on so many of life's joys. But he also missed out on some of its sorrows. He was spared those.

He was, for example, spared the pain of standing at the side of your casket and seeing it lowered into the ground.

He was spared the loss of his beloved father and mother.

Instead, you will carry the pain of passing. It is a terrible and crushing thing. But you bare it for your son.

Because you're his dad.

And because you love him.

He was loved by many. Your goodness and his are well known to your friends and associates. He will be remembered, and he will be remembered fondly.

So God bless you, and may he give you comfort and peace.

With my love,

Your Friend

As we forgive those who trespass against us

Probably the cruelest thing I've ever done to anyone is make them angry at me.

And I've done plenty of cruel things.

They've mostly been accidental, the result of thoughtlessness and selfishness, but I've done them. And I've been able to observe the consequences of them.

I've been able to see the damage they cause. Rather, I've been able to see the damage I cause.

Thankfully, some of it has been fleeting. Thankfully, I have seen some of the hurt heal.

But not if there is anger.

I have seen people, offended by me or by others, become subject to the tyranny of anger. I have seen people consumed and destroyed not by the actions of another, but by the turmoil of their own festering emotions.

When Jesus commanded us to forgive, he wasn't trying to help the person we were angry at, he was trying to help us. He was trying to free us from a poison of our own making.

But too few of us heed his warning.

Too often we wrap ourselves in real or perceived grievances and allow them to define us and our behavior. Too often the easiest emotion in our heart is bitterness and anger, the passion of our life spilled in the gutter of conflict.

We carry the offenses against us like a cross, focusing on them and allowing them to grow ever more significant to us, until we are crushed beneath them.

And we are left bitter, shrill people, so cloaked in darkness that we can neither recognize nor find the light. The vacuum of our hearts is filled not by the tenderest of emotions and thoughts, but by the basest and harshest.

And it all begins so quietly.

So naturally.

Someone offends us. They do something to hurt our feelings or our interests, or at least we think they do. And that small germ of conflict grows within us like a blood poison, going septic and gangrenous.

Some stew over it, some plot revenge, some harbor ill will and bad feeling. All respond naturally. Many fall into a trap.

A trap which is sprung by ignoring the commandment to forgive.

A trap from which few escape.

Because once drunk in, the cup of bitterness is addicting and unsatisfying, requiring ever deeper draughts to quench whatever emotional thirst we think it satisfies.

Good people become angry people, and angry people become dark people, and dark people are not good people. They are people who have given themselves over to a personal evil, to a piece of the bile that powers all of human conflict and hardship.

But it is a weapon directed inward, and wounds we think to inflict on others are actually borne by us. The person for whom we hold anger or resentment or a grudge is invariably unaffected by our dark feelings.

Mostly, they are unaware of them. And even when aware, they ignore. We do not settle the score by being angry, we merely exacerbate our own wronging. Having been hurt by the other person, we set out unconsciously to hurt ourselves.

Ourselves and our loved ones.

Yes, our loved ones.

Our bitterness may not be directed at them, but it is unavoidably felt by them. Anger radiates like heat, and an angry person is less able to function properly in any relationship. The sweetest of human relations turns sour in the constant presence of anger.

And the grudge carried home from work, or the neighborhood or the church, puts down roots where they do not belong. They grow right through the heart of the family unit.

You cannot truly experience or share love if you give over even a portion of your heart to bitterness and anger.

As the harshness of your feelings in one area increases, your ability to share tender feelings in another area decreases.

I know this to be true.

So you must sweep it out of your heart.

You must not allow your opponent—real or not—to continue to harm you. You must forgive, and you must move on. You must not allow the offense of a moment to linger for days and years. You must not allow the actions of someone else to dampen or darken your feelings.

You must not allow your own obsession with anger or hurt feelings to weaken or even destroy you.

Anger must be chased away, and the offenses which give rise to it must be forgiven.

Not for the benefit of others, but for the salvation of ourselves.

Blind obedience isn't so blind after all

They taught us in school that blind obedience was bad.

And that made sense. I'm a Thoreau kind of guy, a go-my-own-way sort, and the notion of doing what someone else said, of following someone else's lead, just seemed alien.

It made no sense to me whatsoever.

I learned how to do it, I had to, life requires it, but I never meant it. It was a fake. Oh, sometimes I was agreeable, my judgement was the same as the direction I had received, but it was not true obedience. I was still doing my own will.

I did it if it made sense to me, and if it didn't, I didn't.

Which for a long time seemed like a good way to go. And in some areas of life, it still may be.

When I'm told to do something, my nature is to respond not "Yes" or "No," but "Why?" And then there will be a little debate, inside my mind or out, and the merits of the matter will be torn apart and contrasted. And my conduct will be determined by the outcome of the debate, by which side wins.

And, again, often I will agree with the wisdom of the order I've been given, and do it.

But sometimes I don't. And the issue is never obedience, it is always "what makes sense."

And I can see now that that is a dangerous practice, in part because it is dependent on my ability to make sense of things. An ability which, while it might be good, is not infallible. And relying upon it, with its inherent weaknesses and ignorances, will lead inevitably to failure and regret.

The other danger of my nature is that it denies me the benefits of obedience. It denies me the growth and strength which come from trusting something outside myself.

It prevents me from daring to be obedient, just for the sake of being obedient. Of doing what I'm told simply because I'm told.

We used to call that blind obedience.

I prefer to think of it as faithful obedience.

And I am learning to see it not as a weakness, but as a strength. That those who engage in it are not sheep, but disciples.

And that obedience is not a series of decisions, it is merely one decision followed through. Not, "Will I do this, this and this?" But rather, "Will I obey?"

And once that question is answered "Yes," the other questions are already taken care of.

That is what I am learning, and I hope it is what I am doing.

Not on the job, not in society, not with family and friends.

But in matters of faith and religion. In matters of God and commandments. I am learning to follow merely because I am led.

Not that reason and common sense don't bear out the direction one is given. They typically do. And that is nice. It is encouraging.

But it is not critical.

It is not necessary that what God says make sense. It only matters that God says it. Obedience teaches that, and keeps us in safe places. Requiring every direction we receive to pass the test of our understanding limits God to the realm of our understanding. In reality, he operates under no such limits. On the contrary, he typically operates far beyond our mortal ability to comprehend.

Which is where faith comes in. We have to believe, as a matter of faith, in his wisdom and love, and in the goodness of what he does and what happens in our lives.

The same principle applies to doing what he says.

We must have faith in him and in his word, and if we have chosen to accept him and his direction, then we must be obedient. Period. Not 80 percent obedient, or obedient in areas that make sense to us, or which are convenient to us, but completely obedient.

And that is faithful obedience.

And that is against my nature. It is alien to me. Or at least it has been. But sometimes in matters like this, the point is the bridling of who we are and the promise of who we can become.

At least that's how I see it.

So I choose to listen and obey. To learn God's will, as I understand

and believe it, and to make following that will my priority.

To serve him and not myself. To rely on his judgment, not my own.

Not because I'm holier-than-thou, but because I'm not. Because my way hasn't worked, and I hope not to be so stubborn that I can't recognize that.

Blind obedience is a sign of weakness. Faithful obedience is a sign of strength. I hope I am strong enough to turn away from my blind obedience to my own judgment, and take up instead a faithful obedience to God's.

And in our own ways, I hope we all are.

Whom say ye that I am?

There was a recent discovery in Israel of a fountain or bath which is supposedly mentioned in the Bible. Many people were excited by the find, and saw it as a confirmation of the truthfulness of the Bible, or of their own faith.

It was neither.

It was interesting, and worth studying, and may offer some archeological and sociological insights into the times of the Bible.

But it has nothing to do with faith.

In fact, no piece of evidence—or lack of evidence—can either support or refute faith. Unfortunately, few people realize that. Some people search for proof of spiritual things in the material world. That is foolish and doomed, because nothing material has any bearing on anything spiritual.

Spiritual truths can only be learned via spiritual means.

You can't prove that there is a God; you can't prove that there isn't a God. Science can't teach you about religion, neither can history, language, philosophy or archeology. And those who go looking in those disciplines for either faith or spiritual truths will ultimately fail. And those who take their faith into those disciplines, seeking to substantiate or promulgate it will likewise ultimately fail.

Because spiritual truths can only be learned via spiritual means.

At least that's what the Bible teaches.

Take the experience of Peter.

One day he and Jesus and other of the disciples were talking and Jesus asked Peter and the others, "Whom do men say that I the son of man am?"

Jesus was asking them who the people believed him to be. After the months and miracles of his ministry, what was the thinking of the people?

"Some say that thou art John the Baptist: some, Elias; and others, Jeremias, or one of the prophets."

The disciples answered that people thought Jesus was some dead prophet come back to life. They thought he was some mortal messenger from God, raised somehow from the dead, some great name from their nation's religious past.

"But whom say ye that I am?"

Jesus wanted to know who the disciples thought he was.

Peter was direct and certain.

"Thou art the Christ, the son of the living God."

Peter believed that Jesus was more than a prophet, that he was divine, that he was the Christ—his nation's prophesied savior and messiah.

That was Peter's faith. That was a significant piece of spiritual truth. It was, in fact, the spiritual point upon which the salvation of humankind hinges. In terms of spiritual truth, and a man's faith, this is as big as it gets.

And Jesus explains where it came from.

"Blessed art thou," Jesus said to Peter. "For flesh and blood hath not revealed it unto thee, but my Father which is in heaven."

What does that mean?

It means that Peter was a fortunate man, and that he learned that Jesus was the Christ not through "flesh and blood"—the testimony, evidences or observations of the body and mind—but by having it "revealed" to him by God.

Peter knew Jesus was the Christ because God had told him so. In the communion of spirit to spirit, the still, small voice of inspiration had given Peter faith that Jesus was the Christ. He had learned a spiritual truth by spiritual means.

The valuable and essential nature of that process is understood better when you think about who Peter was at that time and what experiences he had had. What were the "flesh and blood" evidences that were irrelevant to his faithful assertion that Jesus was the Christ?

Well, Peter had been with Jesus from the beginning of his ministry, and had seen and heard almost everything the Savior did.

For example, he saw Jesus give sight to the blind, and command the paralyzed to walk. He heard firsthand the sermons and parables.

He saw lepers healed at a word from Jesus' mouth. He saw Jesus pray over five loaves and two fishes and then divide them amongst 5,000 families.

He saw Jesus raise the dead. He saw Jesus rebuke the wind and the waves, which were stilled at his command.

He saw Jesus walk on water.

He saw firsthand with his own eyes the things Christians have marveled at for 2,000 years. He saw direct evidences—proof—that Jesus was miraculously different from any other man.

He saw things many people point to as proofs that Jesus was the Christ.

And yet, Jesus said that those things—"flesh and blood"—did not teach truth or give faith to Peter. Rather, the faith to testify that Jesus was the Christ was "revealed" to Peter from our "Father which is in heaven."

And just as it was revealed to him, it may be revealed to us. If we will seek it faithfully.

Not in a history book, or in an archeological dig or a scientist's test tube. Not even in the best of sermons or the deepest of theological arguments. There is no faith there, there is no proof of truth there.

Those come only as Jesus taught, through revelation from on high. From the individual witness to each of us that Jesus is the Christ.

So beware of arguments and proofs, whether they attack or defend your faith. They all are the unsure foundation which Jesus warned about, the one upon which we must not build. They all are the sophistry of men, and the wrong path can only take you to the wrong place.

It happened while they slept

It happened while they slept.

In the darkness of the second night, at peace in their homes. It happened while they slept.

In the borrowed tomb there happened first what will yet happen countless times. A victory over the absolute, a working of the impossible, a reflickering of life. And he who was pierced and hanged stirred irresistibly alive.

For since by man came death, by man came also the resurrection of the dead. For as in Adam all die, even so in Christ shall all be made alive.

And while they slept he did what he had been born to do. Half mortal, half god he succumbed like his mother and rose like his father.

And when they awoke and visited they found his burial clothes folded neatly, no longer needed, on the stone where he had lain. The tomb was empty, as they all one day shall be.

Why seek ye the living among the dead?

And little did they realize in the wonder of the moment that it was they who were different, they and their kin through all generations, still subject to death but no longer its slave.

As we are no longer its slave.

It happened while they slept.

In the loneliness of Gethsemane, when he bled from every pore. It happened while they slept.

The disciples on the path and the world on its course, not knowing or comprehending, while their ransom is paid. The great and mysterious atonement, universal and inscrutable, wherein one pays the penalty for all, and the innocent absolves the guilty. The unjust are freed by the just.

For God sent not his Son into the world to condemn the world: but that the world through him might be saved.

In a dusty land in the corner of nowhere in an era otherwise unremarkable, one night amidst the olives the sacrifice was made, and every moment of human life was given possibility and an escape from the burden of sin. It began with the pain and progressed through the humiliation and ended on the cross, the fulcrum upon which the universe turns.

For the wages of sin is death; but the gift of God is eternal life through Jesus Christ the Lord.

There are two deaths: one physical, and one spiritual. One is the loss of mortal life, the other is the loss of eternal life. We lay down our body, and we lay down the privilege of returning to God.

And both were subjugated a couple of thousand years ago by a humble messiah who walked the earth he created and spilt his blood into its dust, the dust from whence we are made and to which we must return.

It happened while they slept.

Life's short day was spent and their labor was undone. It happened while they slept.

The choices and attitudes and appetites of life run out like a race, each day passing into the next, faster and faster, and then it ends. It just ends. And the baggage of it all is a weight that drowns.

But if we walk in the light, as he is in the light, we have fellowship one with another, and the blood of Jesus Christ his Son cleanseth us from all sin.

But if we don't, it doesn't.

And for many of us, it doesn't. For me, particularly, it doesn't. Because it is one thing to be a hearer of the word and another to be a doer, and too many days end with wrong choices made and evil chosen over good. Sometimes small and sometimes large but mostly the free gift of salvation remains untouched where he left it.

In the rush to attend to life's minutia, we never get to its purpose, we delay the day of repentance until it is finally too late.

It happened while they slept.

The atonement, the resurrection, the working out of his plan. Then and now and until the end of time. They slept and he went on.

This is a faithful saying, and worthy of all acceptation, that Christ Jesus came into the world to save sinners; of whom I am chief.

But it is not an automatic salvation. Nor is it an easy one, gained by the muttering of words or the recitation of dogma. It is gained by faith and obedience, by taking Christ into your heart and into your actions, one meaningless without the other.

It is gained by repentance, by sorrow for sin and an abandoning of it, by turning aside the natural man and the natural world, by placing your hope in another, better way.

If ye love me, keep my commandments.

God laid a plan at the dawn of the eternities, a plan of redemption and exaltation, and he sent his son as the keystone of that plan, the part without which no other part could work. And today that plan marches on as it is intended, like it did in Gethsemane, and in the borrowed tomb.

The only question is, do we march with it?

Do we follow, or do we fall out? Do we pray, or do we prey? Do we know Christ, or do we not?

I am the way, the truth, and the life: no man cometh unto the Father, but by me.

Are we awake?

Or are we asleep?

Holy Week with Jesus

He had friends in Bethany, Mary and Elizabeth, and their brother, Lazarus. And he was pretty close to them.

And after staying with them for a couple of days he, on the first Sunday, decided to go down into Jerusalem, the giant city sprawling before them. The center of his religion and the capital of his nation, it was where he had come to die.

Walking into the city, as he came to the Mount of Olives, he stopped and sent two of his disciples ahead. He told them that at a certain place they would find a donkey tied. They retrieved it and he got on it and he rode it the rest of the way into Jerusalem, encountering as he travelled the most interesting display.

It was the people. The common people of Jerusalem. They took off their robes and spread them on the road before his donkey and stripped fronds from the city's palms, to wave at him as he passed. While they shouted their love for him, and adoration.

It was an entry fit for a king.

The king of the Jews.

We don't know what he did the rest of that day. But when it was spent, as evening fell, he and the apostles made the walk back to Bethany.

On Monday they came back. Back into the city and into its magnificent temple. A house of God, a holy of holies, the place man communed with the divine. A place that had been turned into something profane. Where business was done and animals sold for sacrifice and profit.

And he went wild.

He started turning tables over and chasing the vendors out. He chastized them, and said they had transformed a house of prayer into a den of thieves. He purged the temple and prepared it, and healed the blind and handicapped who came at first word he had returned.

And looking on, the chief priests, driven by jealousy and a threat to their power and riches, plotted to kill him.

The next day, Tuesday, he came back, from Bethany to the temple, for perhaps the greatest day of teaching the world had ever seen.

It began on the road into town, when he promised his followers that, if they had sufficient faith, they could move mountains and, "all things, whatsoever ye shall ask in prayer, believing, ye shall receive."

They challenged him and his authority as he entered the temple, but he rebutted them, and he told the story of two brothers—one who promised to do his father's bidding, and one who actually did it.

It was the first of a string of parables and stories he taught in the temple that day. Parables and stories that have become a part of our culture and faith.

Like the question about taxes, and the coin with Caesar's face. "Render to Caesar the things that are Caesar's," he said, "and to God the things that are God's." Then the seven brothers who married the same woman, one after another, and the question of whose wife she would be in the resurrection. His instruction about the "great commandment and the law," to love the Lord with all your heart and to love your neighbor as yourself. The widow's mite, and then a voice from heaven.

"Now is my soul troubled," he said in a speech that was half prayer and half sermon. "Father, save me from this hour."

He rebuffed the arguments of the Sadducees and he rebuffed the arguments of the Pharisees and then he attacked them both, calling them blind and foolish, greedy and self-important.

And then he left the temple and went to the Mount of Olives and gave a great prophecy of the last days, the end of the world, when there will be wars and desolations and the stars will fall from the skies and the sun will be darkened and the end will come.

Then he taught the parable of the 10 virgins and the parable of the talents and told of a day when the Lord would say to his followers in judgment, "I was an hungered and ye gave me meat: I was thirsty, and ye gave me drink; I was a stranger, and ye took me in."

While the chief priests and the scribes and the elders gathered at the palace of the high priest to plan his murder.

That night, back in Bethany, he ate dinner with a man named Simon, who had leprosy. Martha served them and a woman, probably Mary, poured expensive lotion on Jesus, and spread it on his head and feet. When asked about it, he said that it was in preparation for his burial.

After that, under cover of darkness, Judas Iscariot, one of the apostles, went to the chief priests and offered to betray Jesus.

Wednesday he stayed home.

At least that's the presumption. There's nothing in the Bible about it. But he was apparently in Bethany. Possibly he was saying private good-byes to family and friends. One last day of rest before the ordeal that would end and crown his mortal life.

The next day, Thursday, was the Passover. And he sent Peter and John into Jerusalem to prepare a a place for the disciples and their Lord to eat it. That evening he and the other apostles joined them.

It was the Last Supper, and the first communion. He knelt before each of his apostles and washed their feet as they sat, an example of service and love, and then he blessed the bread and wine, as a token of a new covenant, a promise between him and them. "In my Father's house are many mansions," he said. "I go to prepare a place for you."

Then he said, "If a man love me, he will keep my words," and he promised them that the Holy Ghost would come to them soon, to comfort them, and guide them.

By this time it was dark and late and Jesus and 11 of the apostles—Judas had already snuck out to summon those who would take the Lord—went to the Mount of Olives where he explained to them that he had to die, and why, and then he prayed for them in front of them.

"Neither pray I for these alone," he said, "but for them also which shall believe on me through their word. That they all may be in one; as thou, Father, art in me, and I in thee, that they also may be one in us."

Jesus and the apostles then went to the Garden of Gethsemane, where he left all but Peter, James and John and went further into the grove of olive trees where he had often gone with his disciples. There he knelt down in great anguish and fear, in such agony that he sweated drops of blood, and prayed, "O my Father, if it be possible, let this cup pass from me: nevertheless, not as I will, but as thou wilt."

And he began with those agonies to perform the atonement. The great reconciliation. The paying the price for the sins of billions of people. A wrenching horror of grief and guilt, borne by the only man not to have contributed to it.

While his waiting disciples fell asleep.

He stood over them when it was over, and off in the distance came Judas with a large group of armed men. They had come to take him to torture and death.

And that's probably where Thursday ended. In the darkness of treachery and the ravages of evil.

It was the pre-dawn hours of Friday when Jesus was dragged and thrown before Annas, where he was first beaten. Then he was taken to Caiaphas, the high priest, who had gathered with the chief priests and the elders and the Council and they shouted at him and mocked him and lied about him.

And they asked him a question.

"Art thou the Christ?"

"I am."

"Then the high priest rent his clothes, and saith, What need we any further witnesses? Ye have heard the blasphemy: what think ye? And they all condemned him to be guilty of death."

"Then did they spit in his face, and buffeted him; and others smote him with the palms of their hands."

"And the men who held Jesus mocked him, and smote him. And when they had blindfolded him, they struck him on the face."

It was daylight by then, an early spring morning. Good Friday. And they took him to Pilate, the Roman governor, who sent him to Herod, another government official, who laughed at him and ridiculed him and sent him back to Pilate.

Who wanted to turn him loose. He sensed what was happening, that the leaders of the Jews were trying to railroad him, and he found no fault in Jesus. Certainly nothing worthy of death. But a cry was raised by the chief priests, demanding that Jesus be crucified. Eventually, Pilate couldn't refuse. He eventually washed his hands of the matter and sent Jesus to be killed.

But first they whipped him. And they took a wreath of long sharp thorns and pressed it down on his head. And they spit in his face and in his wounds and beat him in the head with a stick.

And sent him walking to his death.

That was Friday about the middle of the day.

The crucifixion nails weren't like we think. They weren't thick spikes. They were long and thin and as sharp as the metallurgy of the day could make them. They weren't meant to crush the bones of the hands and feet, they were meant to go between them, to cut down on the chance of ripping through. The nails were meant to suspend.

It was a miserable death. The pain was excruciating. Usually it was dehydration and asphyxiation that killed, and sometimes it didn't come for days.

But they nailed him to the cross and raised him there and they did two other guys, one on each side of him, and the people stood around to mock his pain.

The soldiers rolled dice to see which of them would get his clothes. He looked down and spoke the first recorded words.

"Father, forgive them; for they know not what they do."

The words were labored and few.

"Today shalt thou be with me in paradise," spoken to a thief hanging beside him.

"Woman, behold thy son!" directing his own mother to John the Beloved. And then, to John, "Behold thy mother!"

Then three hours of darkness and a cry, "My God, my God, why hast thou forsaken me?"

"I thirst."

"It is finished."

"Father, into thy hands I commend my spirit."

And it was done. He slumped dead on the cross. It was probably about 3 o'clock in the afternoon. To make sure he was dead, a guard stabbed him in the belly with a spear. Blood and water gushed from his side.

Shortly thereafter, he was taken down and a man named Joseph of Arimathea asked Pilate's permission to lay him in his own tomb. Permission was granted and Jesus was wound in linen and rubbed with spices as the first step in burial preparation. Then he was put in the tomb and a stone was rolled in front of the door.

The next day was Saturday, the Jewish Sabbath. His followers and relatives stayed at home, probably in Bethany, in shock and grief. The chief priests placed an armed guard in front of the tomb, to make sure no one stole Jesus' body.

Early Sunday morning, before the sun came up, there was an earthquake, and an angel came from heaven—"His countenance was like lightning, and his raiment white as snow"—and rolled back the stone that sealed the tomb. Shortly thereafter, yet before the morning dawned, Mary came to the tomb and found it empty.

She ran to tell Peter and John, who in turn ran back to the tomb. Peter ducked into the tomb and saw it empty, except for the linens which had wrapped Jesus, and the cloth that had been around his head. The linens were in one pile and the cloth was in another. Peter and John were mystified, and walked back to where they had spent the night.

But Mary stayed there, outside the tomb, sobbing.

At some point she looked inside the tomb again, and saw there two angels. One sitting where the Savior's head had been and another where his feet had been. They asked her why she was crying and she answered, "Because they have taken away my Lord, and I know not where they have laid him."

Then she withdrew from the tomb and a man who she thought was the gardener asked, "Woman, why weepest thou?"

"Sir," she answered, "if thou have borne him hence, tell me where thou hast laid him, and I will take him away."

Then he called her by name. And she recognized him.

And she was the first witness to the resurrection. Because it wasn't the gardener who spoke her name. It was the Master.

He was alive.

That night, as the apostles ate their supper, Jesus appeared to them as well. They were "terrified and affrighted." But he calmed them, and spoke to them, and extended his hands to them, so that they could feel his resurrected body. Then he ate some fish and honeycomb with them.

"Peace be unto you," he told them.

He was alive.

He is alive.

And that was the last week of his life, and the first day of our salvation.

Eight

It's hard when your kid turns 9

It's hard when your kid turns 9.

And you stand for a day midway between the delivery room and the front door. The front door he will walk out as an adult someday, leaving pieces and memories of his childhood.

In a house that will be suddenly quiet.

And while you wonder how you're going to get the bike together you think about those things.

You wonder where it is all going. How half your chance to raise this kid is already gone and how everything you'd planned remains undone and distant and you realize that maybe the future isn't such a sure thing.

And it isn't such a long thing.

Like it was the day he was born. With tiny newborn fingernails and a pointy head from pushing too long and unfathomable expectations of what his life would bring. Back then the future stretched on forever.

There was some kind of warm Norman Rockwell print and it was always going to be there and it was always going to be the same and that was the future.

But life teaches you that time is fleeting and that a year can go and so can two and now nine years have passed and that fast again the game will be done.

When your kid turns 9 and you're wondering where to buy a Boy Scout knife you notice for the first time that it is slipping through your fingers. That it won't last forever. That your turn is half over.

That this kid has already logged half his childhood.

And you can't quite remember ever taking him fishing.

And though you bought him a little baseball cap when he was born, there have been, all these years later, very few times that you've actually thrown him a baseball, or helped him swing a bat or pitch a horseshoe.

Or lay down and camp under the stars.

And it takes a moment to remember the last time you made it home for dinner.

You break your back and you think you do it for him, but he probably doesn't care about your paycheck or how fast your career has moved or how much ground you still can cover if you really push yourself.

I have a son, you say, but he doesn't truly have me.

And when he lives this many years again he will be 18 and a man and those bony arms will be hard and strong and his grin will be surrounded by rude adolescent whiskers.

That's when they go to college. Or buy a bus ticket for California. Or make a deal with a recruiter. That's when they're not yours anymore.

And they go off and do things that you do and that seems a long time from here.

But it's only nine years.

And he's old enough to know that two times nine is 18, but he can't begin to know that two times this is a different world.

So you pick out a card and you resolve to maybe make the second nine better.

To do more and talk more and sit more. And try to remember the small enthusiasms of boyhood. To get more pleasure out of karate classes and BB guns and professional wrestling.

And to let this kid know what is truly important.

About values and character and morals, and how to work and save and excel. To be happy and independent and free. To read great books and think good thoughts and live by faith.

And be ready for 18.

And know that what you did yesterday isn't as important as what you do today and tomorrow. Like his dad is trying to learn.

That's all the stuff you think about, in the middle of a young man's childhood, when you ponder what was and what is and what still might be.

When your kid turns 9.

A father, a son and a dog

My son is 14 and just starting to grow, just starting to get lanky, only two inches shorter now than his mother, no longer the smallest kid in his class.

I sent him out ahead of me yesterday, on the five-mile trail at Rattlesnake Hill, sliding on the glaze snow on hand-me-down skis, so I could watch him move. To see the grace and stumble and the pure abandon when the trail fell away down a hill. To watch him move and to stay out of his way and to have an image to cherish when I'm old.

Cross-country skiing is an imprecise undertaking, an awkward equilibrium of pumping arms and thrusting feet and it all seems to go well until something happens in the balance and it changes in a moment and there is a stiffening or a leaning and you pitch over into the snow, legs twisted odd and wet snow crammed up into your face or your shirt or your socks.

Yet we took it up, after church and lunch, the rest of the family staying home, just him and me and Ike.

Ike, a black standard poodle, clipped rough by the high school agriculture class, bounding between us and darting into the woods, eager to smell it all and wet it all and be finally out of the house. Two of us stiff, working the skis, the third as free and as fast as the wind.

We parked where the plow stops and skied up the road past the blueberry meadow then over a hill and down it halfway to where the trail turns off into the woods. It was deep snow from the big blizzard, glazed by the sun and the wind and the thaw, and we followed the snowmobile tracks to keep from breaking through.

I don't know how it is for other men, but sometimes I am unsure of how to get along with my son. Unsure of how to be or what to say or what he thinks. Wondering if I'm getting through or if I need to get through or if he is doing fine on his own.

Not that there are any problems. No, not at all. He's doing great. A lot better than I did. So much smarter and so much more confident. So much more at ease with the world and his place in it. He runs where I walked and leaps where I balked.

Yet I wonder and so I try and sometimes on a Sunday I say, "Let's go to the woods." Hiking or fishing or shooting or stalking the big oaks for squirrels in fall. Berries in season and skiing when there's snow. The American stereotype: A father, a son and a dog. He either likes it or he tolerates it but either way he comes along most times I ask and though we don't always say much I think it does something.

At 14 he's wrestling with childhood and at 40 I'm wrestling with adulthood, each of us tripping and rising and tripping again and looking back at my own youth I wonder how it seems to him. How it seems the times I get angry or the times I get impatient or the times I disappoint.

How it seems to have me as a father.

I realize I can't know and probably he can't either. Not now, not maybe for years. Not maybe until it's too late to do anything different. Life is a gamble and its biggest risk is parenting. Mostly we try and mostly we fail, in some way, hopefully some small way, some way that won't scar.

So you plug away and sometimes on Sunday afternoons you go to the woods.

It was warm and we wore sweatshirts and baseball caps, sliding a mile one way, then cutting left down a gorge and a long fast glide and up a hill and between some ponds then hard skiing up through the spruce before level again in the open and the woods and the open again.

There was a raccoon dead by the trail and easy skiing across the frozen ponds and in the deep woods the exacting pattern of a snowshoe's track, all the while Ike running between us or stopping before us or peering curiously into a fox's hole.

The trail comes out of the woods through a series of three ponds, two on the right and one on the left, and then a short fire lane and a metal gate across it with a Stop sign in the middle. Then the road and the piece back to the beginning of the five-mile loop and then back where they don't plow going down eventually to the van.

It was almost past the third pond at the end when beyond my son's shoulder from behind a tree I saw something small and hunched, black and moving. A mink, maybe, but not a mink, it was too thick in the middle and in these woods that is only one thing and then I saw the white, a spot behind the head.

"Stop," I said softly to my son and then, "No!" I shouted as the dog took off at a sprint. "No. No. Bad Ike. Stop."

He is a curious dog, and friendly, and his tail wagged like he'd made a new friend. I called him and my son called him and he ignored us as he nosed the little black creature, waddling quickly across the trail. Two steps, three and four, Ike sniffing and following. Then a cartwheel back, like he'd been hit by lighting, writhing in the snow, getting up and falling, pushing his nose like a plow through the snow.

"Oh no," I said, "oh no."

"And we've got Mom's van," my son laughed. Ike trotted back to him and we stood nervously awaiting the smell. But it didn't come, not at first, and then it did. Not the smell of a dead skunk in the road, or of the scent caught sometimes on the wind. This was a gagging burnt rubber odor and we quickly skied away. Ike came with us, rolling as he went, making snow angels, trying to brush the scent from his muzzle.

We laughed like fools as we skied, wondering how we would explain this to his mother, and sniffed carefully as we drove home, trying to blow the smell out the vents in the back. And then a quick sprint upstairs to the bathtub and lather and a futile hope the smell would go away.

It was a fiasco, and it was a success.

The day was ruined, and the day was made.

Being a dad is an imprecise undertaking, an awkward equilibrium of cherished hopes and fumbled realities, and it all seems to go well until something happens in the balance.

And sometimes you fall, clumsy and unsure, tripped up by your own lack of ability. But if you're smart you get up and brush off and get back on the trail.

Sundays in the woods.

And if you're lucky one day there will be a skunk, so you remember it forever.

What my daughter taught me

I learned a couple of things this week.

My daughter taught me.

My oldest daughter. Aubrey. She is 13.

And she has had a very hard week.

It went wrong the other day after gym class, when she ran back to the locker room, to pick up her stuff.

Her stuff in the locker and the book bag beside it and as she picked it up it seemed different. Out of whack.

So she opened the book bag and inside were the tickets. The ones she had saved in her wallet. Scattered all around.

When she goes to a movie, she saves the ticket. She files it in her wallet and can go through them and the movies they represent and what she thought of it and who went with her.

And they were scattered around.

Because someone had been in her wallet, and in her book bag and digging around in it her CDs were gone. Twenty-four of them, all zipped up in a plastic carrier.

She almost cried as she told me.

Which is saying a lot, because Aubrey doesn't cry.

She sat at the dining room table with the stack of holders which had come with the CDs and said that they were her life. I thought it an interesting overstatement until she went through, holder after holder, recounting how long she had saved for each one or who had given it to her for what occasion and what songs she listened to on which CD when.

Her sad songs and her happy songs and her angry songs.

And they were all gone.

Stolen.

And at 40 years of age, watching the agony on her face, I understood why thievery was wrong. I understood it like I never had in my life. I had known intellectually that it was damaging and bad but she taught me emotionally and deeply how evil and selfish it was.

And for a day it weighed on my mind.

Until the next time she almost cried.

After school she had gone out with a friend, the day of the big rain, to a creek down the road from the house. It was running full and dirty but they were 13 and adventuresome and they made a mistake.

They went in swimming.

And it went well enough until the little waterfall and the decision to jump, one after another, off the top into its depths. Barely a trickle most of the year, fairly raging with runoff all muddy and brown.

And so, as seventh-graders will do, they lept as friends and went down through the water, which wasn't that deep, and kicked up for the air but it was strangely difficult.

The water was heavy with its load of silt and it buffeted them and spun them and it dragged at them in the swirl of undertow and when they breached the air the first time they were afraid and it quickly pulled them back down again.

After that it was a panic and a struggle and a reaching for one another, screaming when their heads broke the water and then, as she told it, the sad, heartbreaking realization as she clawed for breath that she was probably going to die.

Sheer panic and engulfing terror as she grabbed at anything and thrashed and it kept her down and she blacked out.

Just like her friend did.

Two kids in the undertow.

Unconscious and lost.

Dead

Or so it would seem.

But something happened.

They remember being in the water and feeling its pressure against them and pushing into their lungs and then they remember nothing. They were out. For who knows how long or how far.

But the water released them, and something bouyed them, and something brought them back.

He came to screaming her name and she came to on her back, her body rushing downstream, past a pile of flotsam which she reached out to and grabbed. And she lay there weak and dazed til he made his way to her and shouted that she had to get up.

And out of the water they crawled, their skin ashen and their lips gone black, the bruises and cuts on their limbs a strange purplish color.

They were weak and shaken and it hurt to breathe, but they were alive.

And maybe it was angels.

Or their parents' prayers or the God who walked on water freeing two of his children from its grasp.

And she told me with tears in her eyes and the quaking that comes from a meeting with death. Neither of them slept that night, petrified, and even now they shake their heads and sit wide-eyed, dumbfounded.

And when I saw that the CDs didn't matter so much. None of it seemed to matter so much. And that's the second thing she taught me.

Because they should have been dead, and it would have happened in a moment in the dark and we wouldn't have known and there would have been a search and the questions and the haunting hellacious terror too many parents know.

Until they turned up two weeks later at the Ford Street bridge.

But somebody saved them.

And it must have been God.

Aubrey taught me about him this week.

A Thanksgiving weekend at home

It was a good weekend. A long Thanksgiving weekend stored away on a couple of rolls of film and in a handful of stories that will be told and retold for years to come.

Like the Jenga tournament on Thursday after the plates had been cleared away.

Little blocks of wood stacked neatly into a tower and three teenagers, a fifth-grader and a couple of adults taking turns pulling one out and re-stacking it on top without knocking the whole thing over. Mom was out and Sophie was out and Hannah was out and it was Aubrey the 16-year-old and Lee the 18-year-old and the old man staring intently at a wobbly stack of sticks, each turn likely to send it crumbling and eliminate one more player.

The father and the son and the daughter and the father and the son and the daughter and as Aubrey walked around the table she was excited and anxious and her palms were sweating. And leaning in she nudged a piece and it slid and gently she pulled it from the listing tower, holding her breath as she then placed it back on top to the applause of her onlooking family.

She was so relieved that she cheered and jumped and turned and hit her leg against the table and collapsed on the ground with her hands over her head as the blocks scattered across the tabletop and she was eliminated.

High drama in the dining room.

Where a comfortable dinner was earlier served. An Amish smoked turkey and some stuffing and squash and Harvard beets. White potatoes and sweet potatoes and cranberry sauce in the shape of a can. The all-American meal on the all-American day. When the cooking wasn't such a burden and the cleanup went fairly well and we all clung to it like it was a dream.

A day begun in pajamas in the fireplace room with the parade on TV and a friendly game of "find the fat girl in the color guard." Herald Square was Main Street and all the family watched.

On Saturday Aubrey started in the first home basketball game of the season and Hannah, the 13-year-old, made her first appearance as a jayvee cheerleader. It was three hours in the gym with the townspeople and the popcorn, with last year's seniors back from college and everyone getting used to another season in the bleachers.

Just hours after we drove out into the blizzard, sliding in the snow and rolling through the whiteouts on the way to the Christmas tree farm. An early morning foray during the only gap in everyone's schedule. The same farm we go to every year, planted in the pastures of a second-cousin's old dairy operation, in the snow belt where the lake storms blow.

Wind howling between us, and the cold and flakes biting our faces, tromping through drifts in tennis shoes, looking for the right tree.

The one that's in the fireplace room now, with the accumulated decorations of 20 years.

Just off the kitchen where on Saturday night we had our family Fear Factor/Survivor game. The 10-year-old, Sophie, put it together, planning for a couple of weeks the stunts and challenges, crafting rules and rewards.

Push-up competitions and leg-lifts and the crouch and lean. You put your back against the wall and slide down until your thighs are parallel to the floor and you stay that way, two of you, until one of you quits and the other one wins.

Two teams of three apiece, blindfolded, racing to see who could drink glassesful of gross things carefully selected from supermarket shelves. An odd coconut beverage and a revolting malt drink from the Caribbean.

Then it was the drawing of numbers to see if you would eat pigs feet or octopus tentacles or kipper snacks in grapefruit Jell-O made with clam juice.

Some gagged and some kept it down.

And through it all points were kept, for the two teams, until—after the jigsaw puzzle competition—it was a tie. An evening of laughter and effort and it was a dead heat.

So Lee suggested a tiebreaker.

Him for his team against his mother for hers. A physical challenge. The 18-year-old man against the 40-year-old woman. He picked the crouch and lean. Backs against the wall, bodies lowered, thighs parallel to the ground.

Him versus her. One generation challenging another.

Earlier in the game—when it was cheerleader versus basketball player—the cheerleader won and she did so by holding out just over two and a half minutes.

So with the other four gathered around the mother and son leaned their backs against the wall and slid down and the clock started.

And with both of them in obvious discomfort it passed five minutes, with the time called out every 15 seconds. Until eight minutes had passed and then 10 and then 12 and finally 15.

And Lee was clearly in pain. Both of them were sweating and straining and it was getting out of hand.

Seventeen minutes and 20 and 22 and 25.

By then the three other kids had wandered off and the timekeeper suggested a draw at half an hour.

It was declined and the mother went into the "zone." She closed her eyes and softly began singing to herself, hymns from church, then the greatest hits of John Denver. And Lee hunched over with his elbows on his knees and closed his eyes, no sound but the steady, measured drawing of breath.

Thirty-five minutes, 38, 40 and 45. Counted off in 15-second intervals.

The occasional taunt. The turning and staring into the other's face, looking for signs of weakening. A gut match between two people who wouldn't quit. Him following her example of mind over matter, the cussed determination not to give up under any circumstances. Some lesson learned about self. Muscles knotting and cramping. Forty-seven and 50, 53 and 55.

The old man walked up and pushed them both over at one hour, three minutes and 30 seconds.

And eight hours later the mother and son embraced at the airport, trying not to cry, as one went back to college and the other went back home.

With one more Thanksgiving under their belts.

Christmas in America

We had something from the Easy Bake Oven for dessert, a little yellow cake with chocolate frosting and sprinkles, cut up into six triangles an inch long.

Christmas in America.

With the cat slinking beneath the 16-year-old's chair, gobbling a steady stream of ham chunks passed discretely from the table.

Christmas in America.

With scalloped potatoes and yams, cranberry sauce and prayers. For the poor and the beloved and the soldiers. Offered up by a 14-year-old with a new guitar.

Leaned up in a corner in the other room, it's lazy cord playing out across the carpet and into the jack on the front of a tiny amplifier. Where hours before and hours after she sits cross-legged mastering the new instrument and its vagaries. Rock riffs and Christmas carols and delicate tunes of her own creation.

A musical Christmas. With the guitar for one and a keyboard for another and a microphone for a third. With the fourth upstairs on the new computer moving songs through it to an MP3 player the size of a book of matches. A day of wonders and relaxation. A good Christmas. For the peace and the company and the gifts thoughtfully done. A keeper. One you talk about when you're old and scattered.

How the 11-year-old, with the big keyboard spread across the arms of a hundred-year-old chair, sat in pajamas before 9 playing Christmas carols while her 8-year-old sister sang dramatically into her Spice Girls microphone. A Kodak duet, burned in silver haloid on a piece of photographic film and recorded forever in the heart of a grateful parent.

Like the fashion show in the living room, with each new outfit modeled excitedly, tags and packing creases attesting to newness, hair messed and smiles bright, boxes and wrapping paper still scattered haphazardly, the family gushing over every shirt and pant, each one sitting next to an accumulated pile of opened presents.

The books and games, shoes and dolls, passed out one after another by a third-grader eagerly reading the tags, handing first one here and then another there, searching so that no one has two while another has none.

All the while collecting two or three for herself, sorting presents for others until it breaks down and she breaks down and she drops to the floor to rip back the paper and squeal.

Sort of like the cheers from upstairs as the computer went together and the plugs and cords found their home and the set-ups unrolled and there was the Internet, with no crashes, just technology and a little unblinking web cam sending greetings to grandparents and classmates.

Look at us. We got a new computer.

In a humble, grateful way. Shouted next to the tree and whispered with a hug passing in the hall.

Or reflectively in the evening, with the fire going, a succession of three pieces of wood, with youngsters and their parents watching it, like people always have, talking and laughing but watching, as it darkens and flames and burns bright and darkens again and crumbles to embers beneath the grate. And another chunk is added, aged and dry, to darken and flame and repeat.

While the ornaments of a couple decades hang evenly across the tree. A snowman family and embroidered dates and a few baby's-first-Christmases, gifts from others or crafted in the home, to spend most of the time in a box beneath the stairs and then to come out one month of the year like a link to the past.

And each one got a journal, a place to write the events and reflections of the day. This day and everyday. And maybe they will still be empty a year from now. Or maybe they won't. But either way under that tree will be what was under this tree. Journals for everyone.

The opportunity to record what we had for dessert.

Cooked up by a little girl opening paper packets and measuring water and watching intently through tiny holes to see her cake rise and darken, and then it is cut and passed around the table like a familial eucharist.

Take, eat, and do it in remembrance of our love.

While plates are scraped and stacked and the teasing and horseplay begin. Wrestling on the dining room floor, adults and children laughing and tickling and sweating.

Alive at Christmas.

Christmas in America.

Where the hearts are large and open and the optimism is real and rewarded. Where you find goodness and peace, undimmed by human tears. The land of the free and the home of the brave.

A land where such things are sacred.

Christmas dinner in America.

Where God smiles on us all.

Happy birthday, Lee

I met him 18 years ago in a dingy military hospital on a gray Illinois day. They wouldn't let me in and they probably botched the surgery anyway and I had slept in the row of chairs in the corridor, hunched over and resting on my thighs, while he came into the world.

He had the tiniest fingers, with odd gem nails that needed to be trimmed but which amazed me with their detail and fineness. He was put together right and seemed tired but fit and the only thing different was the shape of his head. Pushed long through a torturous labor it was more a cone than a point and it was days before it went down.

Now I can't see the top of his head.

And the toddler and boy he became have been lost in the passage of time and the imperative of growth.

My son is a man.

Registered for the draft, applied to college, ready to be on his own.

And I am still hunched over in the corridor, oblivious to the various miracles that have made him what he is, ignorant of the processes that have made him who he is.

But pleased nonetheless.

And grateful.

The whole thing wrapped up metaphorically in a footrace a few years back, in a blowing winter chill, of five miles through the city streets. I told him he had to run his own race and I couldn't hang back with him and when the gun went off he was on his own to the finish line.

We ran side-by-side for most of two miles until a group came past and we wanted to join it but I didn't have it and he did and for a while when I saw him through the crowd farther and farther ahead I yelled encouragement until finally he was lost over the horizon and he was on his own to the finish line.

That's kind of how it's been.

Mostly I yell encouragement as I glimpse him bounding farther and farther ahead. Sometimes they stand on your shoulders, but sometimes they climb much higher. He's been one of those much-higher kids.

He has done things I only dreamed of, and he hasn't even really started yet.

It was 18 years ago today and his mother was a poor bedraggled champion, worn by her labors and the rigors of incompetent and brutal medical care. Her face was swollen and her hair was mussed and as she cradled her baby she had an IV in her hand and a plastic bracelet on her wrist. This threshold is as much about her as it is about him, and about their relationship these many years. Sometimes sweet and sometimes stormy but always symbiotic, the one dependent on the other and vice versa.

She has known him all of his life and he has known her all of her adult life. And parting will be easier for him than for her. Nature will push him to adventure and achievement and nature will push her to tears.

And e-mails and phone calls will be poor substitutes for daily hugs and kisses, and the changes that come will be changes on his own, or at least changes away, the ones that finish the process of maturation and manhood.

We go where billions have gone before, and the passage breaks our hearts. Thrilled at what is and will be, and wistful for what has been, the palpable certainty of his childhood and nearness lost and irretrievable.

My son is a man.

And I have faith in the race he is running. I have faith that the new joys are as sure as the old, that tomorrow's sun will be as bright and warm, that the next 18 and 36 will be as sweet as the first.

And I am grateful to have been there. To have seen him grow and become. I feel like my life has had purpose and was worthwhile. I feel like it paid off.

I have a son, and he is a man.

A story about a friend of mine

I guess the thing I'll most be grateful for is what she taught us.

Little Rachel, our cat. The one who died yesterday.

Thirteen years and countless lessons. One more little story from Main Street America. Some kids and a cat and a precious bit of life.

We were out for a drive about the time our eighth-grader was born. Out for a drive because when you're young and short on money that's what you do for entertainment.

Out for a drive in the country with a 5-year-old and a 3-year-old and a sign on the side of the road that said, "Free Kittens." Free kittens in a box at a house with appliances on the lawn and the dark dirt of flea droppings in their ears.

And one spindly little gray one that somehow came home with us.

A quiet, retiring cat that wasn't much for snuggling and purring. More aloof, really. Fond in recent years of sitting and sleeping, in the sun on a cushion, her family nearby.

Which probably sounds pretty foolish.

But that's how it was. Two species and one family, us and her. Which made me glad God gave us animals. For the companionship, of course, and for the chance to learn.

I'm also grateful to little Rachel for all that she taught my children, and for the important role she played in making them better, more caring people.

She taught them, of course, responsibility. The changing of water and the replenishment of food, the never-ending battle to get the litter box emptied. They saw her needs as their own and pestered their shopping mother to get her special treats and toys.

And each Christmas they left her a stocking or a gift, some little ball or catnip trinket, something she would ignore as she swatted at bits of wrapping paper on the floor.

Responsibility, though, was the least of her lessons. Mostly she taught how to love, how to care and, yesterday, how to grieve.

Those are important things.

For children, and their parents.

We love instinctively, but we love well because we've learned how. You see it in your children. In the lugging around of a favorite doll the first lessons of loyalty and affection are learned, as the natural love of parents and self grows to include others. Then fortunate children have a pet, some animal that absorbs their awkwardness and ignorance and loves them and captures their fancy and growing affections.

Some creature that unnoticed takes possession of their heart, a possession that is only obvious when it is contested or lost.

Like when I would call her ugly.

It was true, of course. She was a homely cat, still spindly and gray and not particularly winsome. And when I would point that out it would unleash a firestorm, the angry rebuff of children who saw me as a traitor and an offender.

And I would smile, because I knew what it meant. She is ugly. And you love her. And that's just the way it is.

She had been vomiting for more than a year, when she ate rich foods or snapped up a table scrap. And when we asked the vet about something else, as she sat there on his table a dozen years old, he said she was doing well for an older cat. Which surprised and angered us.

She wasn't old; she wasn't halfway old. She was only 12 then, and cats live to be 18 or 20 or 24, don't they? What did he mean she was old?

But a week ago she looked it. She had stopped eating for a time and was emaciated and thin, bones showing through her fine coat. And two days ago the vet said maybe her kidneys were in trouble and yesterday he said maybe her kidneys were gone.

And then the call came to come and be with her at the end.

And she taught some more.

She taught how deeply roots can grow and how bad things can hurt. She made little girls cry, and not so little girls, and she left a college boy 2,000 miles from home a little bit more a man.

Her parting was a service and a sorrow.

And the house will be different now.

The family will be different now.

All we are is dust in the wind.

And across the country on any given day innumerable cats and dogs must die. Some neglected and abandoned and unmourned. Others pampered and preened and loved. And the passing of one more means nothing.

Except to us.

To those of us who lived a time with her.

I'd be ashamed of my tears, but I know I'm not the first to shed them.

Nor do I suspect I will be the last.

Godspeed, Elder Lonsberry

My son became a Mormon missionary yesterday.

We sat through a briefing in a crowded auditorium and then they said it was time to leave. The families were to go through one door and the new missionaries were to go through another.

We stood up, my son and I, and hugged each other. I kissed him on the cheek and shook his hand and he turned and walked away.

I will see him again in two years.

I have never been happier.

We both had smiles on our faces. Full, joyful, gleeful smiles. I whistled as I walked past the long line of crying parents headed back out to the parking lot.

It started when he was a little boy, I guess. I showed him pictures of when I had been a missionary, and as the years passed it was mentioned often and it became an expectation. When you turn 19 you will go on a mission.

And then as 19 approached he had to make a decision. He had to decide what he wanted. He had to decide if it was his dream or his parents' dream.

The hard part, as I look at it, is not what you go to, but what you leave behind. My son is a social guy, who is close to people and makes friends at the drop of a hat. He has a fun life, a very fun life. Things go his way. He's on top of the world. And saying goodbye to that is hard. It is difficult for a young man to lay aside the fun and frolic of life for two years of no dating and no movies and no Friday nights with his friends.

It's no fun knocking on doors and asking people if you can talk to them about Jesus. It's no fun missing Christmas and birthdays and the warmth and love of hearth and home.

But that's what Mormon missionaries do.

And I wondered if that is what my son wanted to do.

He never told us what he decided. He merely mentioned that he had begun the process. That he had gone to this interview and that interview and a doctor's appointment and that his paperwork was finalized and in.

And at Thanksgiving, home from college, a big envelope came from Salt Lake City. He was going to Mexico, it said, and was to report to the Missionary Training Center in Provo, Utah, on the third of March two thousand and four.

For a long time he didn't tell his friends. For most of a month it was a family secret. A private thing we didn't want to explain or be asked about.

But slowly it came out and the people in his life—who are overwhelmingly not Mormons—seemed curious and understanding and proud. It became a good thing in their minds. They were happy for him.

And Sunday night at the Rochester airport he sobbed with his mother and sisters. Tears down their faces as the finality of parting rang home. They had spoken in church the week before, each in turn, and the farewell had lasted for weeks. But Sunday night it was real and it was hard.

Tuesday he and I went looking for some bald eagles, out by the Great Salt Lake, in an old Jeep in four-wheel drive, bouncing through the mud and snow, laughing as the splashed water washed in waves across the windshield. Later we went to a Brazilian grill for his last supper before going in. Guys with foreign names kept coming to our table, each offering delicious meat they carved from huge skewers.

For desert to take home we got chocolate cake that was $7 a slice and worth twice the price.

His is still half eaten in the refrigerator at the motel.

Yesterday dawned kind of tense and distant, neither one of us really quite there. This was jumping off time. This was the brick wall and you're going 90 miles an hour. This was I've enjoyed the party but it's time to pay the bill. We got around and said a prayer and carried his suitcases to the Jeep.

Then we went to Denny's. His late-night place. His hanging-with-his-friends place. There wasn't much for us to say. He only ate half of his breakfast.

We got to Provo an hour early and drove past his apartment from school. Then we walked through the bookstore and stood for long minutes watching a ballroom dancing class.

On the way back to the Jeep we passed the college bowling alley and my son suggested we play a game of air hockey. It was 40 minutes before he was to report and I got change and he got the paddles and we tied at one game apiece before we put our suit jackets back on and left.

The training center is a big complex of buildings, and on Wednesdays when the new missionaries come old men, volunteers, stand out front in vests directing you where to go. You unload the missionary and his luggage and then the parents go to park and they get back together under a big canopy, where families of every type take pictures and clutch handkerchiefs.

For me, it happened when I walked through the door. It was as if someone had flipped a switch. A feeling of relief and then joy. Big full-face grinning joy. My son came in a different door and stood briefly in a line to get his nametag—a white lettering on black background thing that slides onto his pocket and which will for the next two years define him.

He carried it to me to pin on him.

He had the same smile on his face.

All the anxiety, all the sadness, all the uncertainty and sense of loss. For the two of us, it was gone. Wiped away. Replaced with a sense of rightness and gratitude. I don't know if we've ever been happier.

We took pictures and looked around and then went to the auditorium for the meeting. It was kind of a whir. Spiritual and sweet, but kind of in the way. He was champing at the bit and I could feel it. He didn't want to talk; he wanted to do. He was ready for this to begin. He had looked forward to it since he was a boy and he wanted to get after it. The time for goodbyes had passed. He wanted to get busy doing some good. He had gospel to preach and souls to save.

We both felt that whispered to us, in the happiness and gratitude in our hearts.

My son became a Mormon missionary yesterday.

We sat through a briefing in a crowded auditorium and then they said it was time to leave. The families were to go through one door and the new missionaries were to go through another.

My son did.

And he didn't look back.

Our trip to Mexico

The branch president stood to the middle of his calves in manure and mud, tromping it and breaking the clods with a hoe. It was sunny and hot and his was the last shack on the trail past where the pavement ended on the edge of the village.

They make bricks there and he has done it since he was 9, like his father before him and his father before him. The local soil and finely chopped straw and the manure of horses and cows. All mixed together by the bare feet of men and the circling hooves of horses.

There were eight of them, all related, on about two acres of land. Two in the mire and two in the shack and two on the pile and two on the wheelbarrows. While a dog suckled her pups under the truck.

This is where my son went on his mission.

He is 21 and last week he came home after two years. We went down to pick him up. His mother and me. On a voyage of discovery. A voyage to discover who our son had become and the people and places he had come to love.

The letter came two months before he turned 19. A large envelope from Salt Lake City unopened through the day until we all could be home to see what it said.

"Dear Elder Lonsberry—You are hereby called to serve as a missionary of The Church of Jesus Christ of Latter-day Saints. You are assigned to labor in the Mexico Guadalajara South Mission. It is anticipated that you will serve for a period of 24 months."

Then we drove up to the city to buy a tourist guide to Mexico, to look at pictures and read descriptions of that far and foreign place. But we learned nothing really. Nothing we could understand and comprehend.

And it wasn't much better with his letters. Words we couldn't pronounce and situations and cultures we couldn't imagine or conceive. For two long years we missed him and prayed for him and longed for him.

He was the tall, smiling white guy at the airport, as we came out of customs, standing in the crowd. His mother saw him first and they fell into one another's arms and for most of an hour they mostly just giggled and hugged. And then for a week we went where he'd been, a different city each day. Long drives over Mexican roads and long walks through big cities and dusty villages. Meeting people he'd taught and friends he'd made, people thanking us for sending our son.

Like the crippled fisherman from the city by the sea. A great spirit of a man who lost his legs to the bends and whose hands were scarred white from rocks and hooks and teeth. A man who fed us squid not two hours dead. A man who once cried as he told our son about the creatures he killed each day in the sea.

Like the woman who wept when we came to her door. Who said our son was also her own. Who served us lunch with near nothing on her plate. Who asked us to pray that her son would believe in God.

Like the grandmother selling flavored ice on the street. She asked him last year in passing to buy a cup of her wares. He did, and asked her if he could talk to her about Jesus. She was baptized on his 20th birthday. She knitted a hot pad for his mother and his mother gave her a Spanish Bible.

Like the Indian girl from the village in the mountains. She said the Spirit told her my son was coming back. A year after baptizing her, a year after leaving her people, she said the Spirit told her that Elder Lonsberry was coming the next day with his parents. The villagers laughed at her claim but she made them promise that if he came while she was at school that they would come get her.

And the next day we came.

And as we sat in the family's home an old woman spoke of her son who went to California and wasn't heard from again. She gave us his name in hopes we could find him and make sure he was OK. They got out his birth certificate to remember his age and date of birth.

They were humble people. They were gracious people. They were generous people. They called our son an angel. And the more you knew them the less different they seemed. The less relevant or foreign their surroundings seemed.

The branch president stood to the middle of his calves in manure and mud, tromping it and breaking the clods with a hoe. It was sunny and hot and his was the last shack on the trail past where the pavement ended on the edge of the village.

He ushered us inside to folding chairs that faced the perfectly made bed in an adobe building open on one side. A shotgun lay on the back of the bed and a raccoon skin was tacked high on the wall. It was less than 10 by 10 and home to eight, their bathroom out back in a shack and their kitchen outside on the fire.

They had two small bottles of apple juice, saved for their lunch, and they gave them to us.

A branch president is like a local pastor. A volunteer leader of a congregation, entrusted by the Lord with the oversight of that valley and its believers. And some few hours later those believers and that branch president would be a couple of miles out the other side of town, having traveled by foot, through a series of pastures and open ground, to a small stream dammed up by stones from its bed.

It was a lad's eighth birthday and they'd come for his baptism.

The branch president welcomed them, standing and sitting under the trees, and they sang a hymn and prayed. And the boy and his father stepped into the pool and a prayer was said. And the boy was buried in the water and raised to new life. Under the trees in the hot Mexican sun, while the angels above were silent notes taking.

He was gone two years, and we missed him so. He went to serve and he gave all that he had. And brought back more than he left.

A week ago his two years were done.

He has left Mexico. But it will never leave him.

About the Author

Bob Lonsberry is a radio talk show host who has also worked as a newspaper reporter and columnist. He is a decorated veteran of the United States Army and was a Mormon missionary on and around the Indian reservations of the American Southwest.

He grew up in Canisteo, New York, and lives in Mount Morris, New York, the birthplace of Francis Bellamy, the author of the Pledge of Allegiance.

He is married and is the father of six children.